*Psychological Bases for*
*Early Education*

# WILEY SERIES IN DEVELOPMENTAL PSYCHOLOGY AND ITS APPLICATIONS

*Series Editor*
**Professor Kevin Connolly**

**The Development of Movement Control and Co-ordination**
*J. A. Scott Kelso and Jane E. Clark*

**Psychobiology of the Human Newborn**
*edited by Peter Stratton*

**Morality in the Making: Thought, Action and the Social Context**
*edited by Helen Weinreich-Haste and Don Locke*

**The Psychology of Written Language: Developmental and Educational Perspectives**
*edited by Margaret Martlew*

**Children's Single-Word Speech**
*edited by Martyn Barrett*

**The Psychology of Gifted Children: Perspectives on Development and Education**
*edited by Joan Freeman*

**Teaching and Talking with Deaf Children**
*David Wood, Heather Wood, Amanda Griffiths and Ian Howard*

**Culture and the Development of Children's Action: A Cultural-historical Theory of Developmental Psychology**
*Jaan Valsiner*

**Psychological Bases for Early Education**
*edited by A. D. Pellegrini*

Further titles to follow

# Psychological Bases for Early Education

*Edited by*

**A. D. Pellegrini**
*The University of Georgia*

**JOHN WILEY & SONS**
Chichester · New York · Brisbane · Toronto · Singapore

**Library of Congress Cataloging-in-Publication Data**

Psychological bases for early education.

  (Wiley series in developmental psychology and its
applications)
   Bibliography: p.
   1. Child development.  2. Developmental psychology.
I. Pellegrini, Anthony D.  II. Series.
LB1115.P965  1987     370.15     87–18995
ISBN 0 471 91145 3

**British Library Cataloguing in Publication Data**

Psychological bases for early education.
  — (Wiley series in developmental
psychology and its applications).
  1. Educational psychology
I. Pellegrini, A.D.
  370.15     LB1051

  ISBN 0 471 91145 3

0000749

150.37
PEL

Typeset by Inforum Ltd, Portsmouth
Printed and bound in Great Britain by
Anchor Brendon Ltd, Colchester, Essex

# Contents

# List of Contributors

ROBBIE CASE, *Ontario Institute for Studies in Education, 252 Bloor Street West, Toronto, Ontario M5S IV6, Canada*

LYLE DAVIDSON, *Harvard Project Zero, Longfellow Hall, Cambridge, MA 02138, USA*

MARTHA DAVIS, *Harvard Project Zero, Longfellow Hall, Cambridge, MA 02138, USA*

DAVID HENRY FELDMAN, *Child Study Department, Tufts University, Medford, MA, USA*

HOWARD GARDNER, *Harvard Project Zero, Longfellow Hall, Cambridge, MA 02138, USA*

MATTHEW HODGES, *Harvard Project Zero, Longfellow Hall, Cambridge, MA 02138, USA*

JAMES E. JOHNSON, *Department of Early Education, Pennsylvania State University, 156 Chambers Building, University Park, PA 16802, USA*

ULLA C. MALKUS, *Harvard Project Zero, Longfellow Hall, Cambridge, MA 02138, USA*

ROY P. MARTIN, *Division of Educational Psychology, University of Georgia, Athens, Georgia 30602, USA*

MARGARET MARTLEW, *Department of Psychology, University of Sheffield, Sheffield, S10 2TN*

JOHN U. OGBU, *Department of Anthropology, University of California, Berkeley, CA 94720, USA*

A.D. PELLEGRINI, *Institute of Behavioral Research, Graduate Studies Research Center, University of Georgia, Athens, Georgia 30602, USA*

JANE C. PERLMUTTER, *Early Childhood Education, University of Georgia, Athens, Georgia 30602, USA*

LARRY SCRIPP, *Harvard Project Zero, Longfellow Hall, Cambridge, MA 02138, USA*

PETER K. SMITH, *Department of Psychology, University of Sheffield, Sheffield, S10 2TN*

ELIZABETH SULZBY, *School of Education, University of Michigan, Ann Arbor, Michigan 48104, USA*

JOSEPH WALTERS, *Harvard Project Zero, Longfellow Hall, Cambridge, MA 02138, USA*

DENNIS WOLF, *Harvard Project Zero, Longfellow Hall, Cambridge, MA 02138, USA*

# Foreword

The arms of my University carry the motto *Rerum Cognoscere Causas* from Virgil's *Georgics*, which translates into English as 'to discover the causes of things'. Initially the reference was to connections between basic scientific knowledge and the applied sciences of engineering and medicine but the principle applies equally to the social and human sciences and their links with practical affairs. If we are to improve and reshape our world we need knowledge and the understanding and power which knowledge affords. The education of the young, formal and informal, is fundamental to the continued existence and development of a society and its culture.

The way in which we set about educating the young is based upon our implicit theory of growth and development and on changing presuppositions about the perfectability of mankind. And these are set in a world which has changed profoundly and dramatically over the last 50 years and where one of the few certainties is that further great changes will come. As J.R. Oppenheimer the distinguished American physicist puts it, 'In an important sense this world of ours is a new world, in which the unit of knowledge, the nature of human communities, the order of society, the order of ideas, the very notions of society and culture have changed and will not return to what they have been in the past.' Such realization emphasizes the importance of knowledge and understanding as a guide for action, and this is nowhere more important than in the education of the young.

Over the last 50 years education as a whole, and more recently early education, has assumed a position of political importance in the developed countries, as it surely will in the less developed countries in due course. This emergence on the political stage is not without controversy and it has served to underline the enormous importance of a soundly based science of education. One element of this science of education is our knowledge and understanding of the growth and development of children and how this fits together with educational practice. As the editor has it in a simple but compelling sentence,

'After all in order to teach children we should know something about the ways in which they develop and learn.' The essays contained in this book are a significant step in linking psychological theory and knowledge with important issues in the practice of early education. Dr Pellegrini has recruited colleagues from the United States and Britain each of whom has made a significant contribution to some aspect of research on the development of young children and set them the task of discussing their work in relation to early education. There are many topics in developmental psychology beyond those treated in this book which have relevance to early education but those which Dr Pellegrini has chosen have a timeliness. In some cases the topic has been largely neglected, in others new and interesting ideas have recently emerged or there have been important additions to our knowledge. For the developmental psychologist these essays will surely illustrate the practical significance of their work, and for educators they should certainly dispel any lingering doubts about the value of theory and research in developmental psychology.

KEVIN CONNOLLY

# Preface

Most educators and psychologists would agree, in principle at least, that educational practice should be rooted in psychological theory and empirical research. After all, in order to teach children we should know something about the ways in which they develop and learn. This ideal state, however, is not often implemented. Educators often do not see the need for theory or research in their everyday teaching. They often choose strategies and materials that 'work', independent of the theoretical implications of the choice. Developmental psychologists, on the other hand, are often not interested in 'applied', or educational, questions; the obvious exception, of course, is the field of educational psychology.

This dichotomous situation is particularly obvious in many undergraduate and graduate teacher training programs. Students often take curriculum courses, e.g. in the teaching of reading, without understanding the process by which children learn to produce or comprehend language. It is not difficult to imagine a scenario wherein such course of study could lead to less than adequate educational practice. Educators may not realize that some of their practices may be contradictory, in a theoretical sense, to each other. It has been suggested by Kohlberg (Kohlberg and Mayer, 1972), and others (e.g. Pellegrini, 1987) that the apparent failure of certain educational programs is due to such theoretical and, resulting, practical inconsistencies. For example, many early education programs that are oriented to Piagetian and 'open-education' instruct their children in a theoretically consistent way (e.g. encouraging the divergent thinking and physical manipulation of materials). The evaluations of these programs, however, are theoretically inconsistent with the instructional techniques and the curriculum. That is, children are often assessed on language-oriented measures which call for convergent answering strategies. For this, and similar reasons, it is not surprising that many of these educational programs had less than optimal results.

In this volume an attempt is made to integrate the two fields of early education and developmental psychology. We do not claim that this is the first time that such an effort has been put forth. As noted above, the field of educational psychology is dedicated, in part, to such a marriage. Further, Head Start and Project Follow Through attempted to base their educational programs on state-of-the-art psychological research. In this volume, however, we are dedicated to addressing the needs of young children (birth through approximately 6-years-of-age) and their families.

An underlying theme of this volume is that children should be viewed as beings wherein social, emotional, and cognitive processes are integrated. The authors in this volume repeatedly make the point that cognitive and social processes are interdependent. As psychologists, such an orientation allows us to examine, for example, the ways in which social processes, such as parent–child interaction, mediate children's cognitive development. Further, this orientation also allows us to examine the impact of cognition on children's social interaction processes, e.g. making friends.

From an educator's point of view, such an integrated approach is also useful. The authors in this volume make the point that educators should teach and assess the many dimensions of children's behavior and 'intelligences'. Many authors explicitly outline ways in which we should teach and assess within these different dimensions.

Another theme of this volume is that systematic individual differences exist in children and these differences have both biological and cultural dimensions. Unlike the structural theory of Piaget, which suggested uniform socio-cognitive development, the authors in this volume suggest that socio-cognitive development has many systematic variations. The examination of such 'individual differences' has long been of interest to psychologists. Educators, too, are interested in this phenomenon. After all, we must be aware of such differences if we are to teach successfully and assess validly. Further, it is important for educators to realize that a child could be accelerated in one area but not in other areas.

The third theme of this volume is that children's behavior is embedded in and affected by different levels of context. The work of both Bronfenbrenner (1979), on the ecology of human development, and of Smith and Connolly (1980), on the ecology of the pre-school, have concisely illustrated the ways in which macro- and micro-levels of context affect children's behavior. This theme is certainly consistent with the second theme of the volume, individual differences. Macro-contextual variables, such as culture, have been long recognized as having potent effects on development. As such, the relations between context and behavior are of importance to psychologists. From an educational point of view, we must understand the demands of the contexts from which children come and the demands of the context of school in order to educate all segments of pluralistic societies. The chapters in this volume explicitly address these questions as well as addressing the ways in which we can optimally design early education learning environments.

The volume is organized into four sections. The first section, containing Chapter 1, outlines the relation between psychological theory and educational practice. In essence this chapter provides a tone for the remainder of the volume: good educational practice should be based on good psychological theory.

In Section 2 (Chapters 2, 3, 4 and 5) authors address the areas of cognition and literacy and early education. As noted in the Introduction to that section, the chapters raise new issues in both cognition and literacy. For example, the notions of different intelligences and different forms of literacy are addressed.

In Section 3 (Chapters 6, 7, and 8) the affective and social dimensions of early education are explored. As noted in the Introduction to that section, the interdependence between social and cognitive processes is stressed.

In the final section (Chapters 9 and 10) educational and developmental processes in context are discussed. The chapters examine the effects of macro-levels of context (e.g. community and school values) and micro-levels of context (e.g. play props and gender composition of groups) on children's behavior in schools.

In conclusion, this volume is intended explicitly to link psychological processes and early education. The discussions presented herein are of value to both basic and applied researchers. Hopefully, this effort will benefit both children and teachers by making schools more pleasant places in which to live and work.

## REFERENCES

Bronfenbrenner, U. (1979). *The ecology of human development.* Cambridge, MA: Harvard.

Kohlberg, L., and Mayer, R. (1972). Development as the aim of education. *Harvard Educational Review,* **42,** 449–496.

Pellegrini, A. (1987). *Applied child study: A developmental approach.* Hillsdale, N.J.: Erlbaum.

Smith, P., and Connolly, K. (1980). *The ecology of preschool behaviour.* London: Cambridge University Press.

CHAPTER 1

# Psychological Theory and Early Education

JAMES E. JOHNSON

## PRELUDE

Since the later part of the nineteenth century we have witnessed the evolution of the complementary relationship between the two sister disciplines of child psychology and early education. From their respective origins as academic disciplines in modern times, the pioneers of each field and their descendants have recognized and nurtured their special ties to each other.

The new science of psychology at the turn of the century in the United States was preoccupied with liberating itself from philosophy and in establishing itself as an independent academic discipline and as a viable economic institution. Identification with the educational establishment was indispensable. Psychological authorities who stand out during this time all affiliated themselves with education: Edward L. Thorndike at Columbia University, John Dewey at the University of Chicago, and G. Stanley Hall at Clark University. (Thorndike began the educational psychology tradition, Dewey was responsible for a participatory or social developmental psychology in relation to education, and Hall ushered in developmental psychology.) The first generations of doctoral graduates in each of these new strains of the infant science of psychology typically found employment in teacher's colleges and departments of education across the country or in joint chairs of psychology and pedagogy. An important trademark which remains to this day (perhaps especially for the cognitive developmental brand of developmental theory which derives from tradition of G. Stanley Hall) is the connecting of developmental theory to empirical

Acknowledgment: I express my deepest gratitude to Frank H. Hooper and Irving Sigel for their extremely useful and open remarks about an earlier draft of this chapter and for their invaluable support in general in my quest to understand psychology and early childhood education. However, neither should be held responsible for the contents of the final version of this chapter, nor assumed to agree with my interpretations.

research on the one hand, and to educational practice on the other hand (Siegel and White, 1982).

Teachers and other professionals concerned with young children at the turn of the century were eager to enrich their practice through exposure to the new science of the study of the child. For example, Hall's first issue of *Pedagogical Seminary,* published in 1891 and devoted to reporting research results from investigations of the child, enjoyed an unexpectedly wide circulation (ARPC, 1891). Educational meetings at the national level during this time were dominated by an interest in what came to be called the Child Study Movement (1892–1911). Soon leading educational reformers were clamoring that child study be made a basic part of the teacher's professional training (Hall, 1894). In short, just as researchers were strongly motivated by the practical implications of their work, professional educators looked to the products of these studies of the child with great anticipation. Thus the special partnership was formed. Their legacy persists.

In this chapter the relationship between psychology theory and early education is discussed. Selected theoretical approaches are seen to relate to specific models of early education with alternative approaches being influenced by various interpretations of classical or contemporary theories of psychological development—applications which derive from cognitive as well as humanistically or behavioristically oriented psychological theories. Societal trends and changes in psychological theorizing are seen as contributing towards developments in early education. Surveying them conveys a sense of the magnitude of the progress achieved in the century-old relationship between psychology and early education. As the role of psychological theory in early education is considered, teaching strategies and materials, evaluation and preparation issues, and types of theorizing in practice, are discussed. However, before addressing these issues some advantage will be served by first casting a wider net. What follows is a review of some selected background material related to the topics at hand.

## PSYCHOLOGY, PHILOSOPHY, PEDAGOGY

Strong consensus backed by considerable historical testimony exists in favor of the position that any productive partnership between psychology and early education is not due to any kind of explicit design or straightforward relationship between theory and practice. Indeed, any relationship approaching such an ideal would be viewed skeptically as happenchance at best and as hallucinatory at worst. Such sentiment prevails in recognition of the human frailty factor in the carrying out of even the best formulated plans. Moreover, macro-level 'umbrella forces' impinge upon the system of educational practice. The role of human values and belief systems must be considered as well the role of diverse components that intervene between theoretical rationales and early education programs (Johnson and Hooper, 1982; Peters, 1977).

These and other misgivings have remained strong. Other concerns have picked up steam, as attested to by the multiplicity of publications produced over the past three decades. Leading scholars have grappled with the prospects and difficulties of integrating psychological theory with early childhood curriculum and instruction. Many of their publications reflect the decades of the 1960s and the 1970s when various enthusiastic efforts were made to revive the importance of developmental theories to education and to society at large. Widely discussed were the implications, issues, and problems of translating developmental theory into early childhood educational practices (DeVries, 1974; Hunt, 1964; Katz, 1974; Kohlberg, 1968; Kohlberg and Mayer, 1972; Murray, 1979; Day & Parker, 1977; Peters, 1977; Peters and Klein, 1981; Shapiro and Biber, 1972; Sigel, 1972).

## 1960s

It is not surprising that a dramatic upsurge in the number of articles and books devoted to psychological theory and early childhood education appeared first in the 1960s and early '70s. Many prevailing societal trends can be traced back to the days of Camelot, the Great Society, Vietnam and Watergate. The phenomena of the single parent and the dual career family, for example, began in force then and have grown ever more common since—dramatically changing the demand and face of early childhood education. The considerable expansion and diversification of early childhood programming over the past 25 years has brought with it a great increase in print devoted to this topic. These trends have continued unabated throughout the 1970s and into the '80s.

The 1960s brought with them also a new interest in the developing child. Seminal theoretical works in general developmental psychology appearing at this time helped spark and justify the rapid growth of early childhood educational programs. Before this time it was widely held that the environment during early years helped form the child's character and personality. Bloom (1964) and Hunt (1961), among others, emphasized the importance of the environment to the development of intelligence. As a result, intelligence began to be viewed to a greater extent not as a fixed commodity determined by the genes at birth, but as something very malleable and modifiable through alterations of the environment. The dominant research interests in the 1960s soon turned to cognitive and language development, paling in significance the few concrete contributions from psychological research to early education which occurred before this decade, a decade which also ushered in a new variation of early education programming.

An initial purpose of compensatory early childhood educational programs, such as the federally sponsored Project Head Start, was to provide environmental enrichment to young economically disadvantaged children who were believed to be deprived of intellectual stimulation due to the impoverished nature of their early home environments. For professional educators and psychologists, the primary purpose of compensatory education was to foster individual change in preparation for successful formal schooling. The promotion of institutional change through family support and community action was an idea whose time had not yet come to full fruition. Concern with the young handicapped child with special needs was also growing at this time with programs and research centers coming into existence as a result of initiatives from the Kennedy Administration.

These early educational programs in the 1960s reflected major themes in developmental research and theory construction. Teaching materials and procedures often followed stage descriptions of the child's growth. A theme complementing a preoccupation with developmental stages and the criticality of early enrichment (as a keystone of compensatory education) was the principle of the optimal match. Developmentally relevant stimulation was said to be exposure to environmental events experienced as one notch above one's existing cognitive structure or level in terms of the demand features or difficulty level of the stimulation. The problem of the match for the educator was to find the appropriate mismatch between the child and the environment. Only an optimal discrepancy or a 'just noticeable difference' would be conducive to developmental change. Differences too pronounced would be incomprehensible and frustrating to the child, while differences that were not great enough would be boring or would fail to attract the child's attention. The problem of the match translated readily into the familiar dilemma of teaching children something too fast or too soon against too slow or too late (Duckworth, 1979).

The notion of the early years as a critical or as an optimal period for development, and the problem of the match, were twin concepts much in vogue in the 1960s and splendidly exemplified in the many experiments and demonstrations of infants' or pre-schoolers' prowess (or potential prowess) in diverse areas of perception, language, and cognition. Much of the early education and socialization practices both reflected and influenced this work in theory and research in developmental psychology, a discipline which itself was reeling from the discovery or rediscovery of Piaget. With Piaget, Bruner and others came a surge of interest in representation which formed a basis for a great deal of educational innovation in pre-school programming. The primary beneficiary, compensatory pre-school education, was not only upbeat but was also viewed by many as both a social action program and as field experiment for examining the impact of the environment on cognitive growth. Hunt (1964) commented on the activities of the time: 'Discoveries of effective innovations will contribute also to the general theory of intellectual development and become significant for the rearing and education of all children' (pp. 90–91).

The enthusiasm of the 1960s gave birth to various well-defined approaches to early education. Many now appear to have been somewhat simple-minded and naive if not ill-conceived. Benefitting from the value of hindsight, of course, three observations can be made. First, early education is not a panacea for society's woes through the 'fixing of the individual before it is too late' remedy. Much has already been written concerning the gross fallacies of the deprivation not difference argument (see Ogbu's chapter in this volume). Moreover, lessons have been driven home since the 1960s concerning just where intervention should be best attempted to break the poverty cycle. School improvement and community action, for example, are now familiar themes.

Second, on the theoretical side, the various model programs of early education founded in the 1960s are no longer popular in so far as they embrace a unitary model of the child as learner. Bruner (1986) recently commented on the past decades' ways of relating different theories to educational practice: 'There is no reason, save ideology and the exercise of political control, to opt for a single model of the learner' (p. 200). Gradually a theoretical pluralism has evolved. It is now common to apply contrasting concepts or interpretative schemes to phenomena of different behavioral domains. In short, banner carriers for the monotheoretically-based programs common in the 1960s are now an endangered species. Although many early education programs may still tend to subordinate secondary theoretical bases to a dominant one, overall there has been a definite movement away from establishing early education programs built on 'single theory' foundations. Moreover, having programs which attribute an inferior status to their clients as a matter of program policy is a thing of the past; there has been a steady rise in our awareness of cultural bias and in our acceptance of cultural differences and rejection of the notion of cultural deficits.

Third, major theoretical constructs of early experience and optimal match have proven vague and general and have raised many unanswered questions (Clarke-Stewart and Fein, 1983). In the context of psychology and early education, for example, how does one define 'experience,' 'early,' and 'match'? Is experience the available stimulation within the program or classroom? The effective stimulation? The perceived stimulation? How does one define each kind of experience? Does enrichment have to be of specified temporal duration? What is the match? How does one know if an effective match has occurred? Confounding factors abound in any definition and description of key experiential components of particular early education programs.

Some enduring and worthwhile general blueprints certainly emerged during the 1960s from the ferment of rich ideas spawned from the decade's revived interest in the development of the young child. However, many ideas were erroneous or have proven incomplete. Many well-intentioned aspirations of the decade have turned out to be less than realistic; still others seem downright paternalistic by today's standards.

**1970s and 1980s**

The 1960s saw a dramatic expansion of early education programs as part of the effort to win the war on poverty and to eliminate racial discrimination. These programs deliberately intended to stimulate the cognitive, physical and social development of economically deprived pre-school children in order to ameliorate apparent deficits in their functioning and thus reduce the gap between them and their middle-class counterparts. What crystallized during the 1970s was an understanding of the importance of the child's family and the family's support system for the attainment of these aims. The most effective early educational programs in general have been those that have involved parents in the education of their children (Lazar and Darlington, 1982).

The research supporting the importance of parent support of children's learning is one factor which has helped convince researchers, practitioners, and policy-makers of the error of looking at children and their families from a deficit point of view. Inherent strengths of families are indispensable ingredients in the recipe for success. Children cannot be seen merely as individuals. Such an outlook extracts them artificially from the context of their homes and cultures and risks damaging their self-esteem, particularly when program priorities and language and behavioral codes are at odds with those of the families served. Furthermore, insensitive communication can breed mutual contempt. Hostility often surfaces between families and educational programs when children are seen as needing to be rescued from their backgrounds in order to succeed in life. Positive feelings result when children and families are viewed as simply different from one another and respected as such. Human diversity can then be accepted and celebrated.

The value of parent education and involvement is seen in terms of the constructive outcomes that often result when parents are in a position to assist their children during their learning careers. The shift in recent years from compensatory pre-school education programs to family empowerment initiatives has meant a great deal to many children and their families in terms of improved health, nutrition, and cognitive enrichment. Improved educational mediation and communication within the family system, and in the home–school mesosystem, are two important factors responsible for the gains that have materialized during the 1970s and '80s.

The rise to dominance of the difference over the deficit model accompanied new psychological conceptualizing. Ecological (the 1970s) and then systemic (the 1980s) approaches emerged to account for individual and social processes occurring in early education, technology, and the media. This is evidenced, for example, in recent attempts to come to terms with the shifting emphasis to day care and nongovernmental human services forms of early education and away from the earlier unidimensional forms of publicly subsidized pre-school and parent education programs. The place of microcomputers in early education is another example where psychologists and educators are occupied with the conceptual and methodological problems related to the exposition of variable relationships pertaining to new phenomenon. Another complex trend for theory to deal with is the expansion and diversification of forms of early education. And what is more, for all of these developments, the stakes seem higher for theory to deliver guidance and understanding on, given the public's growing interest in mandatory schooling at an earlier age, among other germane topics such as the perpetuation, effects, and remedy of childhood stress (Elkind, 1981).

During the 1970s and '80s there has been a maturing of the models' approach to curriculum and program development in early education. Along with the growing variety of forms and delivery systems of early education, content variations derived from theoretical models have proliferated over the past two decades. Over the years many important observations have been made concerning the models' approach in particular and concerning the relationship between theory and practice in general.

The models' approach in early education originally assumed that practice should be derived from a particular developmental theory and supporting research. Models, or plans, for early education would be based on a framework such as cognitive-interactionist theory, behavior learning theory, or maturational theory of development (Evans, 1975). Corollaries of the models' approach are that absolutely pure derivations from a theory are not possible and that, in practice, often competing theories can be applied to different domains of the program. Furthermore, children are known to differ individually in how well they respond to practice based on particular models. Not all components in a theory are equally important in educational application. The importance of theory to practice has received much attention and is widely acknowledged in the field; interpretations as to how and to what extent theory is important vary considerably (DeVries, 1974), but it is generally agreed that program implementation is built from some theoretical base.

Systematic program implementation in early education based on theory requires answers to six key questions: What, when, how, who, where, and why (Evans, 1975). The answer to the last question, 'Why this set of experiences for young children?' suggests the conceptual or theoretical base of the program and reflects one's philosophical and psychological values. As program variations can be expected to be very great in the United States (given our commitment to democracy and belief in pluralism) the value of pre-school education for children and their families must be discussed in terms of various models and not just one model. However, it is only after answering the why question that working on the answers to the remaining questions posed by Evans makes sense (Sigel, 1972). Choice of a model in early education ultimately derives from one's world view which is deeply value-laden (Reese and Overton, 1970).

As suggested earlier, any kind of notion of a straight path from theory to practice has been dispelled as myth years ago (e.g. Kohlberg and Mayer, 1972; Shapiro and Biber, 1972). With the models' approach the same holds. In addition to logistical problems associated with the logos-praxis nexus, particularly those with sundry intermediary links such as seen in the connecting of theory to early education programs (Peters and Klein, 1981), there looms larger than life the role of values or personal belief systems in implementing educational programs (Johnson and Hooper, 1982).

> When psychologists like Dewey, Skinner, Neill, and Montessori actually engage in innovative education, they develop a theory which is not a mere statement of psychological principle, it is an ideology. This is not because of the dogmatic, nonscientific attitude they have as psychologists, but because prescription of educational practice cannot be derived from psychological theory or science alone. In addition to theoretical assumptions about how children learn or develop (the psychological theory component), educational ideologies include value assumptions about what is educationally good or worthwhile. (Kohlberg and Mayer, 1972, p. 463)

Convictions concerning what is educationally worthwhile or about the best way to teach something fall back upon one's overall world view and subsidiary theories about development and about other matters pertaining to education.

Qualifiers have been proposed regarding the models' approach to early education. For instance, Spodeck (1970) advocated that teachers view developmental theory not as a source of early childhood educational curriculum, but as a resource or a set of general guiding principles that may help in interpreting children's behaviors. DeVries (1974) and Hooper (1987), among others, have distinguished between narrow and broad definitions of theory in early educational practice. In its constrictive sense, theory is a formal system of axioms and postulates which comprise a deductive system that guides the choice of variables in research or practice. In its expansive, or general sense, a theory is a coherent perspective derived from a set of assumptions, attitudes, beliefs, philosophies, informal ideas or intuitions about children in general or about certain children in particular. Both narrow and broad theory affect educational practice. The practitioners' notions about the child, developmental change, intelligence, motivation, sex roles, ethnicity and culture, among other things, shape teaching, task structuring and child management. And, theories are often hidden. Although unconscious, these beliefs can still influence teachers' behaviors. Whether teachers consciously endorse any formal theory does not prevent their general informal theories from influencing their expectations and evaluations of children. In practice, teachers develop their own theories about growth and development, learning and instruction, and optimal teaching. This does not depend on a formal reading of Freud, Skinner, Erikson, or Piaget.

There are cases where formal theory is indispensable to practice. Investigators have found psychological theory integral to developing evaluative intervention projects comparing different pre-school curriculum models (see Day and Parker, 1977; Roopnarine and Johnson, 1987). Here teaching practice is based on or is at least strongly influenced by a particular theory of child development. For example, Weikart's (1981) cognitively-oriented program derives from Piaget, as does Sigel's Young Thinker Program (Copple, Sigel, and Saunders, 1979). In these cases the relation of theory with practice is straightforward relative to those areas deemed appropriate for theory to serve as a guide for accepting or rejecting action. For theory to be a major source for practice, however, requires special training for teachers in developmental theory, setting apart model programs from most others. Nevertheless, these model programs demonstrate that deriving rules of teaching from theory is possible, refuting those who would claim otherwise (Murray, 1979).

Murray (1979) analyzed the feasibility of programming teaching in early childhood education on the basis of various psychological theories. Murray raised the question of the extent formal theory informs practice by discussing the differences between teaching, teaching well, and teaching brilliantly. He concluded that theory is not very helpful in making these discriminations. Theories serve different but parallel purposes in research and in education. Research seeks to understand behavior in general, while education seeks to change behavior in the particular case.

In sum, the decades of the 1970s and 1980s have brought about important changes in how mainstream psychological theories and conceptual frameworks have been applied to early education. In part this has been a response to changes in society. Deficit notions about social classes and racial, ethnic, and subculture groups have lost their appeal in step with changing socio-political winds. A preoccupation with the individual has been surplanted by a concern for psychological and social processing in context, as illustrated by the growing popularity of ecological and systemic approaches in the social and behavior sciences (Bronfenbrenner, 1979; Campbell, 1984). Refinement of the models' approach to early education is part of the changing nature of the relationship between theory and practice.

## THEORY AND PRACTICE

The relevance of theory to early educational practices has never been in dispute. Although the nature of the relationship and the transformational rules connecting theory and practice have been subjected to much debate, no one has seriously questioned the value of theory as a guide for practice. Even a teacher who disavows the importance of formal theory for practice would admit that deciding what is working in practice depends on one's view of what accomplishment is, which in itself suggests the workings of some implicit view of development and achievement. Such implicit theories are formed on the basis of personal knowledge of children to go along with any formal knowledge and understanding of research-based theories a teacher possesses.

It is widely accepted in the field that practitioners should be aware of their implicit theories and conceptual biases behind practice. Teachers need to be aware of them in order to critically examine theory and research in the social and behavioral sciences. Theories can thereby serve a constructive role in practice. General orientations and specific theories of psychological developments are related to the models' approach in early education in particular, and to early education programs in general.

In recent years there has been an expansion of early childhood service alternatives available to families as well as growth in alternatives for early education curricula. Still, the theoretical underpinnings for them have remained fairly constant. Classical derivations from developmental theories, together with contemporary extrapolations, provide conceptual rationales for model applications. Selections of curriculum, instructional strategies and program priorities reveal the theoretical commitments of early education programmers.

The major strains of the models' approach in early education are based on distinct views of development: maturationist, learning, and interactionist (Kohlberg and Mayer, 1972; Peters, Neisworth and Yawkey, 1985; Shapiro and Biber, 1972; Weber, 1984).

**Maturationist view**

According to the maturationist view, the most important consideration in attempting to understand and nurture the development of the child is to realize fully the great extent to which it unfolds according to a maturational or biologically-based timetable. Pedagogy should be geared toward holding back instruction rather than risk hurting the child by premature teaching. Providing a generally ambient environment is really all that is necessary to assure normal growth since the child's development is under the primary control of inevitable natural processes. Kohlberg and Mayer (1972) have noted that 'What comes from within the child is the most important aspect of development; therefore, the pedagogical environment should be permissive enough to allow inner "goods" (abilities and social virtues) to unfold and the inner "bad" to come under the control' (p. 451).

Teachers need but to provide emotional support for the child to 'blossom.' This humanistic-romantic sentiment can be traced back to the philosophical writings of Rousseau. It frequently finds expression in teacher emphasis on social development, free play, make-believe, and creative activities. Premium is placed on self-expression and exploration within the warm and supportive environment of an early education program. The psychological theories of Freud, Erikson, Gesell, and Rogers are consistent with this orientation. The maturationist view in no small way continues to influence the practice and policy of progressive early education programs across the country today.

## Learning view

According to this orientation the most critical facet of development to keep in mind is the degree to which the external environment shapes its course. From the vantage point of the educator, special attention needs to be paid to the way the child interacts with the environment. Teaching should be done in a direct and efficient manner. Pre-academic skills, academic subject matter, moral knowledge, and the rules of culture are all important. Kohlberg and Mayer (1972) describe this view as one in which what is important in the development of the child is the child's learning of the cognitive and moral knowledge and rules of the culture; and, therefore, education's business is the teaching of such information and rules to the child through direct instruction.

This view can be traced back to the philosophical writings of John Locke and other British empiricists. Psychological theories of Thorndike, Watson, Skinner, and Bandura are based on this tradition. Principles of operant learning, reinforcement, observational learning, modeling and direct tuition are all relevant to defining teaching practice. The learning or cultural-training influence has found its way into almost all elementary schools. Many day care and pre-school programs, especially compensatory education programs and others serving special education populations, follow this position.

## Interactionist view

According to this perspective, the most important characteristic of development is its dynamic constructivistic quality. Knowledge of the external world is built; cognitive abilities develop through the child's active involvement with the surroundings. Processes internal to the child are most important; knowledge and development come from the dynamic relation between the child and the environment. A sharp distinction is drawn between development and learning with the latter subordinated to the former. Qualitative stages of development determine what the child can be expected to learn. This view is predicated on the belief that cognitive, social, and affective behavior and development need to be conceptualized holistically and that education should promote an integration of function.

The cognitive and affective structures which education should nourish are natural emergents from the interaction between the child and his environment under conditions where such interaction is allowed or fostered (Kohlberg, 1968). This view can be traced back to the philosophical writings of Kant. It is represented most predominantly in the theories of Piaget, Bruner, Vygotsky, and Werner. Interactionist or cognitive developmental theories have been becoming increasingly influential in US educational and early education programs (Weber, 1984).

## Recent developments

There have been important strides made in the psychology of cognition and learning which have affected psychological theorizing as applied to early educational practice. Various developments in psychological and educational theory construction which have occurred over the past decades as a result still owe considerable intellectual debt to the basic ideas indigenous to the three major views outlined above.

In the models' approach to early education, programs vary widely in allegiance to particular psychological theories. Programs that bear no model label seem to vary even more. Keeping abreast if not ahead of the increasing number, forms and contents of early education programs has certainly become a very demanding task. Theoretical rationales for programs have become more diverse and complex (Roopnarine and Johnson, 1987). There has been a trend away from monotheoretical orientations and toward theoretical pluralism (Hom and Robinson, 1977). There is considerable variation in the degree to which model designers hold theory to be important; and diverse programs exist which claim the same theory as the source of inspiration (Hooper, 1987).

The relevance of psychological theorizing to early childhood education is expressed in many specific ways. The next section discusses the importance of psychological theories for defining teaching roles and strategies including the selection and use of instructional materials. Distinctive patterns follow from the choice of a theoretical orientation. There follows a discussion of the significance of theory to evaluation and to teacher preparation in early education, concluding with a section on types of theories in practice.

## Teaching strategies and materials

Psychological theory and research continue to advance, creating new challenges for those interested in integrating and applying this knowledge to education. The past decade's advances in computer technology have brought about further possibilities. Teaching roles in early childhood education have become more demanding and more sophisticated as a result.

Traditionally teachers have used psychological theory as a general framework in planning and implementing instruction. Teaching strategies are determined to a considerable extent by one's views about learning and development even as these are also closely related to one's values and biases. Pet theories influence how teachers anticipate and explain children's behaviors. Learning diagnosis, management of behavior, and sequencing instructions are all based on them.

Theory-based model programs in early education vary in the degree to which particular teaching strategies and techniques as well as specific activities are bound to theory. For example, some programs, such as The School for Constructive Play (Forman and Kuschner, 1977) which is based on Piagetian constructivism, are heavily 'top-down' in their orientation. That is, teachers ask themselves what goals they need to accomplish tied to a relevant theoretical construct (e.g. transformations, representation) and then devise equipment and materials and procedures to achieve those ends. Other model programs are more 'bottom-up' in focus, justifying commonplace events in the classroom with loose reference to general theoretical notions. Regardless of orientation, there is evidence to suggest that staff morale and commitment to some framework are more important for program success than is the specific theoretical model or orientation adopted (Weikart, 1981).

Learning, interactional, and maturational views of development suggest different teacher roles and instructional materials. According to the learning position, teachers are the primary source of knowledge, resource managers, and agents for socializing the young in school settings. There is a preponderance of teacher-led activities in the classroom and an emphasis on convergent or product learning, skill acquisition, and external reinforcement. Instructional materials would include the use of structured kits, media, books and other written materials and playthings. When the theoretical commitment of the education program is to the cognitive-interactional or developmental position, on the other hand, then the teacher's role is defined as one of supporter, manager and guider of the child's learning and self-initiated activities. There are fewer teacher-led lessons and greater emphasis on divergent learning or processes in the classroom. Competence is more important than performance, intrinsic motivation is more important than extrinsic motivation, process is more important than content or product. Instructional and play materials that are open-ended are used extensively and there is a greater emphasis put on the significance of peer interactions.

In incorporating the new computer technology, learning theory would stress the use of the computer as a tutor, transmitting individualized and paced instruction and reinforcing skill or knowledge acquisition. Interactional and maturational views, in turn, would see computers as antithetical to program goals or might use them in a subordinate way, supporting activity in the three-dimensional concrete world. Computers would definitely take a back seat to peers and other materials. Cognitive-interactional theory and maturational theory would emphasis guided-discovery and play with computers in a social context. Game simulations, Logo-type activities, or using computers as a tool would be seen as well.

In sum, psychological theories are related to the modus operandi of early education. Teaching practices and materials vary in a systematic way in relation to them. Relative emphases are placed on direct instruction or enrichment, acceleration or facilitation of development.

**Evaluation**

Evaluation of the various components of the early education system relates to psychological theory in a number of ways. The evaluative roles of the teacher and the researcher vary and are affected by basic theoretical assumptions about development and learning.

For teachers, as one moves from the maturational and cognitive developmental perspectives and towards the learning perspective, evaluation takes on a different meaning: (a) there is less reliance on inferential observational skills to assess the effects of the program on children; (b) judgments about the children in relation to the program typically involve a narrower range of behaviors and attributes; (c) summative evaluation becomes more important to show achievement and readiness gains with formative evaluation less sophisticated. These changes in evaluation are traceable to one's theoretical assumptions about children and what is important in their development—for example, skill acquisition vs. cognitive abilities (Johnson, 1987).

Teachers in educational programs who follow the tenets of behaviorism and learning theory must possess basic observational skills in order to make judgments about individual rates of progress on the basis of children's classroom performance and test scores. Individual differences in performance on various criteria are noted with mastery of objectives being a major priority. On the other hand, cognitive-interactional and maturational teachers need to develop more sophisticated observational instruments to assess the child's overall personality and thought processes as expressed in the context of the social environment. Teachers, according to these theoretical perspectives, attempt to infer the contents of the child's mind from the child's overt social and verbal behavior and test performance. Furthermore, formative and informal assessments are as important as summative standardized test scores. Formative assessment suggests ways to improve classroom practices (see Malkus, Feldman and Gardner's chapter in this volume).

For researchers or program evaluators, assessment also takes on a different meaning depending on the theoretical perspective adopted. Learning theory and behavior modification is strongly associated with the classical experimental methods and the psychometric tradition of evaluation, while cognitive-interactionist theory is more aligned with descriptive-correlational methods and the clinical tradition of evaluation. The learning theorist is most interested in quantitative changes, in particular content domains; the cognitive-interactionist is most interested in qualitative changes which reflect stage transition phenomena (change of form). The learning theorist is more concerned about internal validity; the cognitive-interactionist is more concerned about external validity (Labouvie, 1975).

It is in the context of this polarization of structural/correlational and learning/experimental explanations of development that many controversies about program effectiveness are best understood (Johnson and Hooper, 1982). Claims and counter-claims about best educational practice often reflect different researchers' using different kinds of evaluation procedures reflecting opposing theoretical positions. For example, cognitive-interactionist theorists have claimed that conventional psychometric evaluations are philosophically and operationally inappropriate choices for genuine evaluation of programs built on the cognitive-interactionist model (Furth and Wachs, 1974; Kamii and DeVries, 1977). Instead, a holistic view of evaluation is advocated: 'What will the child get out of the program?'

In sum, evaluation is linked to psychological theories for both teachers and researchers. Distinctions between learning and development and competence and performance have remained especially important for those theorists, researchers, and practitioners who subscribe to the principles of cognitive-interactional theory. Whether further theory construction and research will lead to a reformulation of these long-standing divisions remains to be seen. Psychological theories continue to have an important influence on how teachers and program evaluators assess children and their environments.

## Teacher preparation

Another way that theory impacts early education is in the area of teacher preparation. Teacher training of either the pre-service or in-service variety is guided by psychological theory and usually involves familiarization with the models' program approach. Sometimes students become thoroughly indoctrinated with a certain theoretical model and its applications as part of their teacher preparation. Sometimes being atheoretical is encouraged.

However, perhaps more commonly, teacher preparation familiarizes students with alternative approaches to early childhood education without advocating a particular theoretical position. Ideally students are encouraged in early childhood teacher education programs to keep an open mind and remain noncommittal, at least for a while at first, avoiding what would be considered a premature personal closure of adopting or aligning oneself to a specific theoretical model. Implicit in this orientation is recognition that there are stages of development that the teachers themselves go through as their careers progress (Katz, 1972). The first lessons to be learned deal with translating theory into practice in a general way, setting short- and long-term program goals and priorities, and devising and evaluating curricular activities. Such broader concerns occupy new teachers' attention at first; later stages of teacher development may lead to embracing a formal theory in practice.

It is not only that basic survival matters more in the beginning for new teachers over theoretical banner-waving, but also that it takes time to acquire authentic ownership of a formal theory in practice. Theoretical commitment cannot and should not be imposed externally even if it is tried all too often in practice. Teachers can only begin genuinely to subscribe to a given theory by practicing it over time, allowing personal beliefs to evolve. Eventually experienced teachers become what can be called a personification or operationalization of a particular theory in practice, but only as their reading of strictures from theory changes too, as teachers accommodate theory in response to experiences with children. Otherwise, theory can become dogma, with theoretical constructs then often unfortunately finding a way of getting between the adult and the child, thereby clouding normal perception and communication.

In-service training is very important to reinforce and shape theoretically-based practice in early education. Intensive discussions with other professionals as well as relevant internship and workshop experience are important components influencing teacher development. Professional growth is respected by not imposing a given theory externally or pushing for a theoretical technique in the name of eclecticism (what may actually be a hidden theory belonging to someone else).

In short, psychological theory impacts teacher training as it does teaching practice and evaluation. Teachers construct their understanding of formal theory over time. Blending and integrating different theoretical ideas forming more pluralistic views for connecting theory to practice is a common outcome during the teacher's development. This matter is discussed in closing together with a final word about the need for more active collaboration between teacher and researchers to improve theory-based practice in early education.

## THEORIES IN PRACTICE

Psychological theories and research provide important bases for practice in early education but they are far from being the only influential factors. Societal and educational values, general intuitive understandings of children, pedagogy, and various practical constraints all have a place. Formal theories by themselves cannot provide specific prescriptions and proscriptions for practice.

There is considerable difference between *knowing about* children and *knowing how* best to teach and interact with them. Fein and Schwartz (1982) have labelled a 'theory of practice' that part which is needed to complement psychological and educational theories in showing the *how to* of program development. Whereas psychological theories suggest the overall goals, priorities, and the general orientation of a program, practical theories consist of bodies of knowledge which enable the practitioners to derive from psychological theories specific components that comprise an early education program. In that the teachers' theory of practice is based on personal experience and skill, they are active constructions. They help to translate psychological theories into curriculum outlines, specific objectives, and other practical program components, including various activities and formats and appropriate evaluation designs and related measurement systems (Peters, Neisworth, and Yawkey, 1985).

In sundry ways teachers are active in program implementation. Not only do they create theories of practice which evolve over time, but they also possess private intuitive understandings or implicit-belief structures ('theories') about child development and related phenomena. Direct experiences with children and one's history as a child are responsible in part for these informal theories. Teachers 'own' the knowledge that informs their private theories in a way in which they cannot 'own' knowledge gained from reading research studies or formal theory constructions in child development (although this knowledge is owned too, albeit with different significance). This difference in knowledge base is crucial and may underlie the skeptical attitude many teachers seem to have towards advice from so-called child development experts or from those who attempt to distill and transmit knowledge from their clinical work or research activities.

Teachers' informal theories are about children in general and are about specific children as well. These theories in a sense cover much more ground or at least ground of a different sort than that which is covered by the formal theories. Katz (1974) distinguished between *knowing about* the individual child and *knowing* the individual child.

> This distinction is a difficult one to illustrate. Teachers can relate a great deal about the children in their classes. They can talk about how many siblings a child has, whether his mother works, whether he has a father, etc. But that does not mean that the teachers know the child. This kind of knowing suggests qualities of immediacy and intimacy of the adult–child relationship; it suggests knowing or sensing something of what it feels like to be that child, knowing how that child constructs reality, understands his experiences. It suggests knowing and understanding his feelings, and knowing fairly reliably what he is attracted to and how he is likely to respond to given events or objects. Our chances of making good judgments about optimum experiences for the child increases as our knowledge of him increases. (Katz, 1974, pp. 32–33)

Teachers actively construct their general and specific theories about children and development, and change their constructions with experience. The teachers' constructions at these different levels interact together in some unknown way or are cogwheeled in some manner to determine practice.

Devising and implementing educational programs for young children requires a working knowledge of psychological theories. These have become incorporated in the models' approach with its insistence on having a conceptual rationale for curriculum and instruction. Theoretical understandings, however, are not static but change over time; they exist on various levels and map different phenomena. They operate as a composite in practice, and function to give guidance to curriculum building, deciding how to teach, and deciding the modifications needed to take into account individual differences. No matter how well thought out an approach or instructional plan might be, or how well it seems based on theory, teachers must constantly test their theory-based ideas in the real world. Teachers in this sense are as much like researchers as anyone else. Together with other early education professionals they are or should be active participants in 'experimental pedagogy' (Piaget, 1970).

Teachers are active participants in the translation of theory into practice in the way they assimilate new practical experiences into their understandings of different theoretical approaches to early education. Teachers are active in modifying their belief systems in response to their experiences. Practical experience often enables them to realize that a strict contrasting of approaches in early education is unwise. With increasing experience neophyte teachers come to realize that there is a constant interpenetration of various strategies and tactics which derive from alternative (and sometimes in principle incompatible) theoretical rationales. This experience often leads teachers to create additional gradations in the classification of theoretical model derivations of practical applications. Individual teaching characteristics, especially of experienced teachers, seem far wider and more subtle than what one would predict from knowledge of their particular program's rationale based on psychological theory or theories.

Recent advances in research and theory construction in diverse content areas, as indicated in other chapters of this text, further demonstrate the relevance of developmental psychology to early education. That these contributions eventually will materialize in improved teaching practice and programs for young children is more than an article of faith if the past is any indication. At the same time, further progress may only be achieved in the long-standing partnership between child psychology and early education if a serious bid is made for greater reciprocity and balance between the two disciplines. Mutual respect builds professionalism within each discipline. An earnest effort is needed to assimilate into existing psychological theories the plethora of educational phenomena as the practitioner experiences it. This will require raising to a new level of meaning the idea of communication and collaboration among teachers, educational psychologists, and other specialists in early education. The accommodations of psychological theories which could result from such corroboration will very likely yield over the long haul more refined and more inclusive conceptual rationales comprising the models' approach to early education programs, thereby improving the state of both practical application and psychological theorizing alike.

## SUMMARY

Psychological theories and educational programs in early childhood have a rich and unique history replete with various attempts to translate new psychological theories and research into practical applications for young children. In this chapter the allegiance that the discipline of psychology has had historically to philosophy was first acknowledged. The point was made that there is no such thing as a direct translation between psychological theory and practice; there exist social and philosophical values on the one hand, and practical complexities and human error on the other hand. Next, major issues and problems were discussed which have characterized the field from the years of the 1960s and 1970s to the present decade. Important trends as well as shifts in emphases were noted in relation to social changes and to changes in theory. For instance, both psychological conceptualizing and early educational programming have had to keep up with the proliferation of family types and child service programs, as well as with the changes in social values which have occurred pertaining to human diversity and acceptance in today's pluralistic society. Limitations of the ideas which prevailed earlier were discussed along with their improvements as witnessed, for example, by the waxing of contextualism, theoretical pluralism, and cultural relativity and the waning of individualistic, monotheoretical, and deficit notions.

In the second part of this chapter, theory and practice were discussed by first defining the major strains of the models' approach to early education programs (maturationist, learning, and interactionist). The significance of recent developments in the models' approach was noted, and there followed a discussion of the implications of theory for teaching practices, evaluation, and teacher preparation. Connections between theory and practice were seen in each area in line with different derivations from alternative conceptual bases or assumptions about child development. In conclusion, the concept of a 'theory of practice' was examined. A few nuances were made concerning the relation of psychological theory with educational programs. Here the bi-directional nature of this relationship was emphasized plus the need for new and continued cooperation to occur between professionals in each field. The result could be a maturing of the long-standing partnership between child psychology and early education and some reduction of what often seems to be a very big communication gap separating professionals in the two sister disciplines.

## REFERENCES

*Annual Report by the President of Clark University* (1891). Worchester, MA: Clark University, p. 8.

Bloom, B.S. (1964). *Stability and change in human characteristics.* New York: Wiley.

Bronfenbrenner, U. (1979). *The ecology of human development: Experiments by nature and design.* Cambridge, Mass: Harvard University Press.

Bruner, J. (1986). Models of the learner. *Educational Horizons,* **64,** 197–200.

Campbell, J. (1984). *Grammatical man: Information, entropy, language, and life.* New York: Simon and Schuster.

Clarke-Stewart, K.A., and Fein, G. (1983). Early childhood programs, *Handbook of child psychology.* New York: Wiley.

Copple, C., Sigel, I., and Saunders, R. (1979). *Educating the young thinker: Classroom strategies for cognitive growth.* New York: Von Nostrand.

Day, M.C., and Parker, R.K. (1977). *The preschool in action: Exploring early childhood programs* (2nd edn.). Boston: Allyn and Bacon, Inc.

DeVries, R. (1974). Theory in educational practice. In R.W. Colvin and E.M. Zaffers (eds), *Preschool education: A handbook for the training of early childhood educators.* New York: Springer.

Duckworth, E. (1979). Either we're too early and they can't learn it, or we're too late and they know it already: The dilemma of 'Applying Piaget.' *Harvard Educational Review,* **49,** 297–312.

Elkind, D. (1981). *The hurried child: Growing up too fast too soon.* Reading, MA: Addison-Wesley.

Evans, E. (1975). *Contemporary influences in early childhood education.* New York: H.H. Rinehart and Winston.

Fein, G.G., and Schwartz, P. (1982). Developmental theories and early education. In B. Spodeck (ed), *Handbook of early childhood education.* New York: Free Press.

Forman, C., and Kuschner, D. (1977). *The child's construction of knowledge: Piaget for teaching children.* Monterey, CA: Brooks/Cole.

Furth, H.C., and Wachs, H. (1974). *Thinking goes to school.* New York: Oxford University Press.

Hall, G. (1894). The new psychology as a basis of education. *Forum,* **17,** 710–720.

Hom, H.L., and Robinson, P.A. (1977). *Psychological processes in early education.* New York: Academic Press.

Hooper, F.H. (1987). Epilogue: Déjà vu in approaches to early childhood education. In J.L. Roopnarine and J.E. Johnson (eds), *Approaches to early childhood education.* Columbus, OH: Charles E. Merrill.

Hunt, J. McV. (1961). *Intelligence and experience.* New York: Ronald.

Hunt, J. McV. (1964). The implications of changing ideas on how children develop intellectually. *Children,* **11,** 83–91.

Johnson, J.E. (1987). Evaluation in early childhood education. In J.L. Roopnarine and J.E. Johnson (eds), *Approaches to early childhood education.* Columbus, OH: Charles E. Merrill.

Johnson, J.E., and Hooper, F.H. (1982). Piagetian structuralism and learning: Reflections on two decades of educational applications. *Contemporary Educational Psychology,* **7,** 217–237.

Kamii, C., and DeVries, R. (1977). Piaget for early education. In M.C. Day and R. Parker (eds), *The preschool in action* (2nd edn). Boston: Allyn and Bacon.

Katz, L. (1972). Developmental stages of preschool teachers. *The Elementary School Journal,* **72,** 50–54.

Katz, L.G. (1974). *Psychological development and education in early childhood.* Second Collection of Papers for Teachers. ERIC/ECE, Urbana, IL. Catalog #140.

Kohlberg, L. (1968). Early education: A cognitive-developmental view. *Child Development,* **39,** 1013–1062.

Kohlberg, L., and Mayer, R. (1972). Development as the aim of education. *Harvard Educational Review,* **42,** 449–496.

Labouvie, E.W. (1975). The dialectical nature of measurement activities in the behavioral sciences. *Human Development,* **18,** 396–403.

Lazar, I., and Darlington, R.B. (1982). Lasting effects of early education. *Monograph of the Society for Research in Child Development,* **47,** (2–3, Serial No. 195).

Murray, F.B. (1979). Educational implications of developmental theory. In H.J. Klausmeir *et al., Cognitive learning and development: Information processing and Piagetian perspectives.* Cambridge, MA: Ballinger, pp. 247–268.

Peters, D.L. (1977). Early childhood education: an overview and evaluation. In Hom, H. and Robinson, P. (eds), *Psychological processes in early education.* New York: Academic Press.

Peters, D.L., and Klein, E.L. (1981). The education of young children: Perspectives on possible futures. *Theory into Practice,* **20,** 141–147.

Peters, D.L., Neisworth, J.T., and Yawkey, T.D. (1985). *Early childhood education from theory to practice.* Monterey, CA: Brooks/Cole.

Piaget, J. (1970). *Science of education and psychology of the child.* New York: Orion.

Reese, H.W., and Overton, W.F. (1970). Models of development and theories of development. In E.R. Goulet and P.B. Battes (eds), *Life span developmental psychology.* New York: Academic Press, pp. 115–145.

Roopnarine, J.L., and Johnson, J.E. (eds), (1987). *Approaches to early childhood education.* Columbus, OH: Charles E. Merrill.

Shapiro, E., and Biber, B. (1972). The education of young children: A developmental-interaction approach. *Teachers College Record,* **74,** 55–79.

Siegel, A.W., and White, S.H. (1982). The Child Study Movement: Early growth and development of the symbolized child. *Advances in Child Development and Behavior,* **17,** 234–285.

Sigel, I.E. (1972). Developmental theory and preschool education: Issues, problems, and implications. *Seventy-first year book of the National Society for the Study of Education: Early Childhood Education:* Chicago, IL., pp. 13–31.

Smilansky, S. (1968). *The effects of sociodramatic play on disadvantaged preschool children.* New York: Wiley.

Spodeck, B. (1970). What are the sources of early childhood curriculum? *Young Children,* October, 48–58.

Weber, E. (1984). *Ideas influencing early childhood education: A theoretical analysis.* New York: Teachers College Press.

Weikart, D.P. (1981). Effects of different curricula in early childhood intervention. *Educational Evaluation in Policy Analysis,* **3,** No. 6, 25–35.

# Cognition, Literacy, and Early Education

The four chapters in this section represent a 'new look' at cognition and literacy. During the past few decades both educators and developmental psychologists have applied a Piagetian model to the study of young children. Such a structural theory, as is well known, suggests that socio-cognitive development is a relatively uniform phenomenon. That is, children's ability at a particular stage of development is thought to be uniform across all domains of knowledge (e.g. maths, science, language). Chapter 2, by Malkus, Feldman, and Gardner, challenges this structural assumption. The authors document the existence of different domains of intelligence and how children can be more or less adept in different domains. Further, these domains are affected by different aculturation processes. This discussion of the different domains of intelligence (music, athletics, dance, drama, interpersonal sensitivity, science, and language) should be of interest to both psychologists and educators. For psychologists, this examination provides an interesting discussion of the development of individual differences in children's intelligence. For educators, this chapter is also important. The notion that children have strengths and weaknesses in different subject areas should be a great help in attempting to write curricula and instructional strategies which are sensitive to such individual differences.

That different domains of intelligence exist does not mean, however, that we should not be concerned with the more traditional measures of intelligence. In Chapters 3, 4, and 5 we consider more traditional aspects of intelligence: language learning and literacy. The reasoning behind dedicating most of this section to language and literacy is relatively straightforward: Language is often considered to be the most important subject taught in many early education programs. Language skills are typically stressed in early education programs because of their relation to children's subsequent literacy. The language production and comprehension skills developed in pre-school are important factors in children's reading and writing development.

The two chapters on children's oral and written language development

(Sulzby's and Martlew's) both stress the connection between children's language proficiency and their emergent literacy. In these chapters both language and literacy are viewed as developmental processes, not as static states wherein a child is either competent (e.g. literate) or incompetent (e.g. illiterate). Sulzby and Martlew, like Malkus *et al.*, also stress the role of culture, in the form of adult–child interaction patterns, in these developmental processes. Each author illustrates ways in which adult–child interaction strategies are internalized by children to be later used as independent learning strategies. This stress on the role of culture, in the form of the adult–child interaction, in the development of language and literacy is relevant to educators and psychologists. Educators could use successful interaction strategies as a basis for instruction. Psychologists can examine the interaction process to determine the extent to which becoming literate is socially mediated.

Chapter 5, Beyond A, B and C, extends the traditional notion of literacy as being an alphabetical phenomenon. In this chapter Wolf and her colleagues examine children's literacy across a number of different media (i.e. writing, numbers, mapping, and music notation). Just as Malkus *et al.* suggested a number of different intelligences, so too do Wolf *et al.* suggest different forms of literacy. They outline the necessary knowledge and skill prerequisites for literacy in each medium. Generally, they suggest that becoming literate in each medium involves more than just mastering the code of each. Within each medium children must become aware of and understand specific domains, knowledge, dimensions, and tasks as well as reflection and editing skills. These skills and knowledge bases should provide educators with useful ideas for designing curriculum and instructional strategies.

To summarize, in this section we will be examining different dimensions of cognition and literacy. Each of the chapters suggests that both individual differences and cultural variation affect children's performance. As psychologists and educators, we should be aware of these differences in order to understand the way children learn and to design appropriate learning environments.

Psychological Bases for Early Education
Edited by A.D. Pellegrini
© 1988 John Wiley & Sons Ltd.

CHAPTER 2

# Dimensions of Mind in Early Childhood

ULLA C. MALKUS, DAVID HENRY FELDMAN AND HOWARD GARDNER

## INTRODUCTION: TWO APPROACHES TO ASSESSING CHILDREN

A typical pre-school classroom. The children are absorbed in a broad range of activities. We focus in to record Holly's behavior. As we enter, she is happily chanting a song about a bear to her friends. This is not surprising, for Holly tends to sing and dance given the slightest opportunity to do so. Holly also delights in drawing and creates the most imaginative creatures. One is less likely to note her presence at story-telling time, however. Neither does she deliver a rich verbal account of her day or play counting and sorting games. It seems that some classroom activities invite this child to return again and again, while a request to count the number of children present in the class leaves her quietly watching.

One can safely predict that many of this child's qualities would not have surfaced on a standardized psychological test, such as the Wechsler Pre-school and Primary Scale of Intelligence or McCarthy Scales of Children's Abilities. In the typical testing format, the examiner takes the child away from the classroom to an isolated room, where he or she probes the child's store of information in narrowly defined areas. Comprehension ability is tested by questions such as, 'Why do you need to take a bath?' (Sattler, 1982). The child is asked to repeat sentences given orally by the examiner and explain the meaning of 'boot,' 'book,' and 'annoy' (Sattler, 1982). The child may also be asked to complete a series of mazes, solve arithmetic problems, and copy different geometric and block designs. Some time later, the examiner reports

Work reported here was made possible by a grant from the Spencer Foundation. We are grateful to parents and teachers of the Eliot-Pearson Children's School, Tufts University, and to members of Project Spectrum staff: Laurie Erichson, Janet Stork, and Carey Wexler Sherman.

all the scores, typically in the form of a single number, the child's intelligence quotient.

While perhaps an adequate index of ability for some children, this result is likely to convey a skewed picture of Holly's abilities, since the main emphasis of traditional tests falls upon verbal and logical skills. Those are not Holly's chosen forms of expression. Though she often communicates with considerable success, she prefers to do so through dance and music, dimensions not traditionally considered 'cognitive' in Western culture. Thus, conventional intelligence measures produce a record of this child's skills which fails to reflect her full repertoire of abilities.

We may speak of two contrasting views of cognition. The usual approach, captured in psychometric form, considers intelligence to be a single overall property, which can be adequately assessed with a brief sampling of short-answer tasks. The other approach, innovative and still experimental, entails the assumption that individuals have distinctive intellectual profiles and that these can be most validly documented by the use of contextually rich instruments. In order to explain the long-term persistence of the first approach, as well as the reasons leading to the introduction of the second, it is necessary to review briefly the history of this conceptualization of cognition. We then introduce the alternative view of cognition, advocated here, a more pluralistic concept of intelligence (Feldman, 1980; Gardner, 1983). In the latter part of the chapter, we introduce the rationale and approach of Project Spectrum, a collaborative undertaking in which we are attempting to develop new means of assessing cognitive potentials and capture distinctive qualities in pre-school children.

## THE OFT-TOLD STORY OF INTELLIGENCE TESTING

A call for measurements of mental ability first arose around the turn of the century when there was a great expansion in public education. In 1904, the school authorities in Paris requested the assistance of an imaginative psychologist, Alfred Binet. Binet was asked to devise means to distinguish between children who were likely to thrive in school as opposed to those who might have difficulties (Wolf, 1973). Binet assumed that the difference between the two groups was one of general intellectual competence. Within this constraint, his approach was completely empirical. In collaboration with Théodore Simon, Binet compiled an assortment of age-appropriate tests, but retained only those items which correlated with future academic success. Their joint effort culminated in the first practical intelligence test. In spite of the limited theoretical framework for his exploration of thinking processes, Binet had achieved the results sought by the Minister of Public Education. Educators and psychologists on both sides of the Atlantic were extremely impressed by the Binet achievement and scurried to implement similar programs in their own spheres of influence.

Another line of investigation among theorists of intelligence carried Binet's notion of a unitary intelligence to an extreme. The British education psychologist, Charles Spearman (1927) aimed to discover whether different kinds of intellectual skills relate to each other in any systematic way. There may, for example, be children who excel on visual-spatial tasks, such as block design and maze tracing, while they fare poorly on verbally-demanding tasks. Spearman devised a statistical technique, which evolved into what we know as factor analysis, to explore correlations among a number of different test items. His analysis suggested a single dominant intelligence that was essential for the successful execution of all mental tasks. This was the 'substance' that one needed if one were to shine in nearly all school subjects and, ultimately, to qualify as a Cambridge don. There also appeared to be evidence for some other specific types of intelligence, such as those of being an author. But in Spearman's view, these more particular or specific skills were of limited importance.

Another school of factor analysis challenged Spearman's claims of a single dominant intelligence. L.L. Thurstone's (1938) statistical procedure yielded little support for a model based on general intelligence. Rather, by varying the types of tests to be compared, Thurstone found evidence favoring a multi-dimensional notion of the human mind. Ultimately, he postulated seven relatively independent 'vectors of mind': perceptual speed, numerical ability, word fluency, verbal comprehension, space visualization, associative memory, and reasoning.

Spearman and Thurstone epitomized two divergent views based upon the same kinds of test data. With the use of different factor analytical procedures, one authority nominated a monolithic model of intelligence, while the other favored a more differentiated interpretation. It is important to stress that this debate remains unresolved. As Stephen Jay Gould (1981) has indicated, either statistical manipulation is defensible and consistent with the data. Therefore, rival interpretations of intelligence based upon IQ-measures culminate in ambiguity rather than scientific resolution.

So far, we have featured one set of ideas about cognition which evolved in the context of standardized testing. In this setting, intelligence, whether unitary or pluralistic, was considered the pre-eminent entity. But another prominent contributor to the field of intelligence reflected an entirely different point of view. Although trained in Simon's laboratory, the Swiss psychologist Jean Piaget displayed little interest in intelligence as a single fixed commodity which could be rapidly assessed through psychometric instruments. Instead he viewed intelligence—or cognition, as he preferred to term it—as a natural developmental process which unfolded at its own pace in clearly defined stages. Piaget posited the existence at each developmental stage of rich mental structures or schemata, which themselves underwent reorganization at the transition to the next stage. While recognizing that individuals might differ in their rate of intellectual growth, Piaget was essentially uninterested in individual differences; his goal was to document the universal patterns of intellectual growth. Moreover Piaget was equally oblivious to the particular contents or domains where intellect was deployed. In these senses, at least, Piaget was faithful to the 'intelligence tradition' which has typically embraced a unitary and universalist view of cognition.

## A COMPETING VIEW OF INTELLECT

Recently, a number of developmental psychologists influenced by Piaget have once again proposed a more pluralistic view of cognition. In place of a belief in a single intelligence, or in extremely general cognitive structures, these investigators have presented the view that the mind is organized into relatively separate realms of functioning (Feldman, 1980; Gardner, 1983; Keil, 1984, 1986). Gardner, for example, has nominated seven different intelligences: linguistic, musical, logical-mathematical, spatial, bodily-kinesthetic, interpersonal, and intrapersonal. Evidence supporting this theoretical stance comes from a rich variety of sources, ranging from the study of *idiot savants* and autistic children to an examination of information on the evolution of cognition over the millenia. Gardner found particularly persuasive support for his multiple intelligences perspective in the neuropsychological literature. Thus, some forms of brain injury will destroy certain intellectual competences virtually in their entirety, while leaving other capacities essentially intact; moreover, a different brain lesion can yield precisely the opposite symptomatological picture.

From his research with child prodigies, David Henry Feldman has described a range of different domains in which talent manifests itself (Feldman, 1986). A child may express talent in a 'specific domain' such as chess or music, yet appear fairly ordinary across the traditional symbolic domains captured by classical Piagetian theory. While some fields of competence seem universal, the development of others hinges more on individual proclivities and cultural contingencies. For example, the skills of the fire dancer are only likely to emerge in the Indian social context. Hence, one must not underestimate the importance of the external forces necessary for potential to develop and flourish. Moreover, we have ample evidence that individuals differ in how quickly and how well they learn in different areas. Feldman's research with prodigies points to the accelerated, age-unrelated progress that a child may exhibit in one specific domain, for example music or chess. This kind of information about individual differences is necessarily lost in any model of intelligence which focuses on general performance or universal structures.

In light of this brief and necessarily targetted survey of earlier efforts in the field of intelligence, one fact becomes evident: the IQ-based view which stresses unitary aspects of intellect and ignores different content areas is being subjected to strong challenge. In spite of its intended generality, the end result is a paradoxically restricted notion confined to a few domains of cognition—in particular those problem-solving skills currently prized in most standard school settings.

While frequently challenged in its theoretical aspirations, the tradition of a unified intelligence and intelligence testing has remained dominant in practice. Indeed, Binet's research has had an influence far beyond the scope of its original intent as an aid to school streaming. IQ tests are still frequently treated as unquestioned methods for assaying a child's future prospects in life. If the child proves a master of language- and logic-laden tests, he or she will likely receive a wide range of opportunities. If, however, the child fares poorly on the standardized tests, yet exhibits another form of talent, be it interpersonal or artistic, his or her future remains bleak to the psychometric eye. This individual is likely to be labelled 'less smart' or even 'stupid.' Ultimately, that child may face a future life of very limited career choice.

## TIME FOR CHANGE

In light of recent scientific developments, the unitary, universalist view of the mind appears increasingly myopic and anachronistic. The time has come to try to capture a fuller range of individual potentials. Educationally-oriented psychologists and psychometricians need to incorporate neurobiological and other forms of evidence which point to the existence of discrete and relatively non-overlapping abilities.

For our part, we have joined with a number of others in using different symbol systems as a means for describing the core of human cognitive development (Feldman, 1980; Gardner, 1983; Olson, 1974; Salomon, 1979; Wolf and Gardner, in preparation). Recognizing that humans the world over have the capacities to express meanings through words, pictures, gestures, numbers, and other kinds of symbol systems, we describe cognitive development as the growing capacity to convey and appreciate meanings in the several symbol systems which happen to be featured in a given cultural setting.

This 'symbol systems approach' bears instructive relation to Piaget's developmental perspective (Piaget, 1965). In common with Piaget, we posit the existence of stage sequences, but argue for separate stages within each symbol domain, each having its own coherent structure. In contrast with Piaget, however, we assume no overall link between capacity or developmental stage in one domain of performance and capacities or stages in other domains. Indeed, individuals may exhibit striking performance in one or a limited number of domains, while appearing ordinary across other areas (Feldman, 1986). In charting the emergence and developmental sequence of abilities both within and across domains, we hope to gain a more comprehensive view of the coordination, or the lack thereof, among various mental operations.

Unlike earlier research into the nature of mental ability, our multi-dimensional model of cognition places significantly more emphasis upon the interactive aspects of the emergence of talent. Rather than conceiving of intelligence as a stable and contained characteristic, we try to take into account as well the external forces that shape and transform a natural potential. These environmental forces may be material, social, cultural or historic in character. It is our claim that a child will be drawn to materials which are of special interest—to materials which have inviting affordances for that particular child (Gibson, 1966). In the case which we introduced in the opening page of this essay, the availability of diverse materials afforded Holly the opportunity to create and solve problems in the visual arts. The materials may be interpreted as stimuli triggering the child's capacity to execute certain procedures within this particular domain (Gardner, 1983). Subsequently, such materials also permitted us to identify her strength in this area of activity.

In general, it is the synergistic effect of a number of external forces that facilitates the fruition of an individual talent. For instance, in addition to his native talent, it was the artistic expectations of the Italian Renaissance period and the faithful patronage of Lorenzo de Medici that furthered Botticelli's potential to emerge as a major artist. To take a contemporary example, the advent of computers brought to the fore the need for a new set of skills. These skills existed in earlier times but their linkage was now at a premium. In many cases, it is only the 'co-incidence' of a large set of independent factors which allows a particular talent to express itself under the particular conditions of a culture (Feldman, 1980, 1986).

To this point, we have delineated the major tenets of our theoretical approach to the study of intelligence. We have emphasized the need to recognize a range of cognitive dimensions rather than to limit an investigation of cognition to a purportedly stable, unitary measure of intelligence. Our perspective takes into account a child's biological makeup as well as the conditions of his cultural milieu. To start, some children may enter life with an exceptional sensitivity in one particular area. Because of the child's facile interaction with symbols specific to that domain, be they musical, linguistic or graphic, one can anticipate the emergence of unusual potential. This proclivity must be viewed in the context of the child's cultural milieu. One must take into consideration the variety of external forces that provide or fail to provide opportunities for the expression and practice of potential skills.

## APPLICATIONS OF THE THEORY

While our approach to intelligence merits attention and criticism on its own terms, it also suggests an approach to educational issues. In the pages that follow, we introduce Project Spectrum, an innovative attempt to measure the profile of 'intelligences' and working styles in pre-school children.

In turning to educational issues and introducing our own perspective on the assessment of mental capabilities, we should clarify one point: we are not proposing that standard psychometric measures be abolished overnight. We give credence to the 'general ability' measure as one form of assessment, but maintain that other kinds merit consideration as well. Indeed any attempt to consider the wide range of competences valued in one or more cultural settings will need to cast a far wider net, and to do so in ways appropriate to the particular competences at issue (see also Karnes, Schwedel, and Kemp, 1985).

While some skills emerge effectively when examined in the standard paper and pencil format, other domains lend themselves better to a less formal and more naturalistic measuring procedure. It is our goal to redirect the focus of assessment away from the 'snap judgment,' short-answer approach. Instead we wish to consider seriously the activities that are favored and the products that children create regularly over the school year.

Such naturalistic forms of data collection may prove more effective in various domains than traditional tests. For example, consider the visual arts. Children draw, paint, sculpt and fashion clay creatures all the time. Hence, their artistic competence can be reliably examined through the accumulation of a portfolio of their creations. Such an approach should yield a more representative and comprehensive view of a child's special skills than would any one-time, artificially imposed testing procedure.

Within the context of a more differentiated view of cognition and a concomitant desire for more appropriate modes of assessment, we have launched an exploratory study, Project Spectrum. This applied venture seeks to develop a number of ecologically valid monitoring procedures: we hope to identify a young child's preference for and competence in activities in several cognitive domains.

For a number of reasons, we have elected to focus on pre-schoolers. First of all, it is of scientific interest to determine whether individual differences can be reliably discerned early in life. Second, naturally occurring proclivities should be more visible at this age, since most young children have not yet encountered extensive training. This is also a time when parents and teachers can benefit from feedback about their children's cognitive competences, because educational interventions are maximally helpful during this period. The plasticity of the young mind permits significant improvements for those who lack in talent as well as an acceleration in pace for those who thrive (Gardner, 1983). Finally, the introduction of curricular and assessment innovations tends to be met with less resistance in the years before formal schooling begins.

The theory of 'multiple intelligences' provided the framework for directing our inquiry. Within this framework we have constructed categories appropriate to a pre-school classroom environment and pre-school children. Indeed, as we began observing the children at work and at play, we identified skills and competences which we have incorporated within the original set of intelligences. By and large, these competences can be viewed as subtypes or component skills within an enveloping intelligence. For example, under the rubric of interpersonal intelligence, we discerned the need for—and discovered the practicality of monitoring—a set of competences, including leader, mediator, and caretaker. Not all the competences fall neatly under a single intelligence: some bridge more than one (e.g. mechanical spans logical and spatial). In any case, our purpose was to use the theory of multiple intelligences as a point of departure for identifying the spectrum of competences of which pre-school children are capable. In sum, we have used our initial categories or 'intelligences' to cover the observed range of skills and to document discrete styles of working.

Faced with a large set of potentially observable capacities, we instituted another filtering procedure. Instead of examining all capacities on which children may differ, or embracing only Binet's emphasis of those skills prized in the schools, we have elected to focus on those skills and abilities which seem most relevant to the achievement of significant and satisfying adult roles in our society. Thus, instead of focusing on logical-mathematical skills in the abstract, we look for competences which may culminate in mechanical inventiveness; instead of searching for a vaguely defined social competence, we seek evidence of caretaking capacities. At present we have isolated many such categories of skills with apparent links to adult competences of consequence. We hope to select from these competences a representative list for incorporation in our research design and task development procedures.

Rather than relying upon traditional experimental laboratory procedures for assessment, our preferred method has been to work closely with students and teachers within an ordinary classroom context. Initially, we highlighted careful observation of the target children in an effort to capture the variations in skills that surface frequently over the course of days, weeks and months. These records helped us to identify the variety of ways in which children display their proclivities. We next sought to incorporate this information into tasks, activities and exercises. Whenever possible, we have used toys, games, and other ecologically valid materials which engage children and which allow us to observe in an unobtrusive way the children's relative sensitivities to different cognitive contents. Thus, instead of using long lists of unrelated questions as measures of a child's ability to comprehend, we have favored activities such as a classroom newspaper in which the children are asked to report on particular school events. By the same token, we have sought measures which can capture a range of skills. For example, in the social realm, we seek baseline evidence for what is typical sensitivity: 'if you are my friend I will invite you to my birthday party' as well as evidence for an unusual degree of sensitivity reflected in the statement: 'Eric is my friend, but I am not sure that he thinks of me as one of his friends.'

## NEW MEANS OF ASSESSMENT

Clearly, then, we seek to make the process of evaluation a more naturally occurring one by linking it integrally to the ongoing classroom activities. Children demonstrate their strengths and weaknesses over the course of every school day. They create elaborate tales, they sing and dance, and they argue their cases for how they want to spend their time more or less convincingly. It is into this framework of daily life that we aim to weave our measures of assessment. By providing the children with engaging materials and activities that relate closely to our categories of skills, we hope to maximize the chance that we can capture their abilities. For instance, a child's grasp of number concepts may be examined in the context of a game requiring counting and problem-solving skills. A bus game, originally designed by Joseph Walters, draws upon these competences. A colorful bus travels through a terrain containing a street with a number of bus stops. Passengers may be entering only or entering and exiting at each stop. It is the task of the 'conductor,' who is the child of course, to report the final tally of riders to the station. The game is easily adjusted to various levels of problem-solving skills. At the outset the child may be asked to increment while keeping track of only one variable, the adult passengers. Later, more items may be added. For instance, both adults and children may ride the bus or they may enter and exit at the various stops on route to the station. Hence, the very talented child may be challenged to perform a series of calculations drawing upon his or her skill to increment and reduce a number of variables.

In another realm, language skills may be trapped with the aid of a story-telling board, which gives children the opportunity to incorporate enticing figures into their stories. In this task the children are presented with a board containing interesting and ambiguous looking objects. The cast of characters ranges from clowns and kings to spider-looking figures. To create the scenery the children may choose from caves, arches, and transformable abodes. These materials may inspire children to deliver cohesive narratives and afford the teacher a detailed view of the kinds of linguistic skills that children rely on when asked to invent a story.

The open-ended design of such activities offers each child an opportunity to express himself in a preferred and comfortable fashion. They are also activities to which he may return again and again. Simultaneously, the teacher is provided with a setting in which to examine a child's evolving skills. By being linked to real world possibilities and containing challenges that actually make a difference to the child, this naturalistic form of assessment will provide a more meaningful view of the child's skills. It is also assumed that the net result points to a richer and more refined delineation of language competences than could be gained from any isolated testing procedure focusing, for example, on word definitions and single sentence responses.

We cannot here detail the procedures for task design in each category of competence, since they reflect the dimensions of that particular area. Yet it is timely to characterize the process in which we have repeatedly engaged. We begin by isolating the most representative and central abilities within a particular area of competence. To succeed as a dancer, for instance, requires a combination of talents: e.g. sensitivity to the rhythmic as well as the expressive element of the dance. These sensitivities may be explored in a movement sequence which is designed to be carried out during the school year. To start, the children may be asked to respond to pieces of music which differ markedly in rhythmic qualities. On a later occasion, the level of complexity may be increased and the children may be requested to interpret musical passages depicting more minute distinctions in tempo. Similarly, differences in expressive qualities may surface when children convey images through movement. Early on, the child may be asked to recreate the quivering or fluttering movement of a bird, while a more challenging task may speak to the difference in conveying the image of a snowflake and a balloon floating to the ground. Hence, to evaluate the potential of an individual to become a dancer or an athlete, it is necessary to take into account a range of both expressive and rhythmic skills.

Once a domain has been conceptualized into a subset of skills, the search for suitable materials begins. Primary emphasis is placed upon finding engaging materials whose affordances will invite the children to get involved, while evoking a range of performance styles and levels. Candidate materials are then reviewed by staff members and outside consultants before they are finally introduced into the classroom. Feedback from the children as well as the teachers often leads to useful revisions. Last, it is particularly important to verify whether the task is fulfilling its exact purpose. If, for example, the aforementioned task failed to capture the rhythmic and expressive sensitivities of the young dancer, then this assessment exercise did not accomplish its original intent.

Of course, how these accumulated data are interpreted is of the essence. To this end, we have embraced two different approaches. The first one takes the format of a checklist. This is a simple and straightforward procedure which any teacher can use. Such a method provides a rough approximation of the ways in which children differ from one another, and points to what may be each child's area of strength. The second approach more closely resembles standard experimental measures. In this instance we use structured tasks which can be administered in a one-on-one setting. This latter approach uses a more analytic scoring system, including traditional measures of reliability. This objective evaluation process can be used by teachers with extra time and interest, by schools which want to hire outside consultants, or by investigators who want to carry out their own research on, for example, the stability of distinctive differences among children over time.

In order to gain a better understanding of the ways in which children approach their work, it is also necessary to examine their degree of investment across a range of tasks. Although they have usually been absent from traditional measures of competences, the abilities to be planful, organized, or flexible are all factors of importance. Indeed, they may turn out to be powerful predictors of success. We propose to measure these and other 'working styles' on a number of tasks which span diverse domains, e.g. language, drawing, movement, and numbers. In this way we will be able to make a firm determinant of the child's major stylistic tendencies: at the same time we can ascertain whether these styles cut across materials or turn out to be content-specific.

## ASSESSMENT AND LEARNING: A SYMBIOTIC RELATION

Over the course of the task design period, it has gradually become evident that our work is not limited to the production of new assessment procedures. It appears, in fact, that we are having an impact on the pre-school curriculum. In creating ecologically valid means for assessment, we have also enriched the ordinary curriculum.

As an example, one of the materials we have designed for social abilities can be used for classroom exercises of various sorts throughout the year. This material is a model of the classroom depicting the play areas, teachers and children. The scaled-down classroom environment was originally created to explore a child's social analytical skills in a prescribed set of exercises. Topically, one may elicit a child's view of self or perceptions of friendships. It turns out, however, that the model evokes other forms of expression as well. For some children the materials elicit fantasy and story-telling activities. The children become the kings and queens of imaginative tales rather than restricting the use to real social themes. Similarly, we introduced a set of Montessori bells because we wanted to measure sensitivity to pitch and rhythm. Soon we found, however, that the bells had become a part of the regular classroom activity. The teachers were relying on them for exercises and the children returned to them to play their own tunes. Thus, it becomes evident that any effort to examine these many competences will inevitably color the classroom curriculum, since most classrooms sample only a subset of these capacities.

By linking our assessment closely to the regular events of the school year, we also hope to dissolve the traditionally observed boundary between learning and assessment. The children will be offered games and exercises which should expand their horizons and serve to interest and instruct over the course of time. With occasional scaffolding on the part of the teacher, the children may learn from these activities in expected as well as unanticipated ways. And while the child is learning, we are given an opportunity to look, in an unobtrusive way, at the ways in which the child approaches his work and in the process assess his potential.

Another consequence of our efforts may be a broadening of the scope of activities considered appropriate in the pre-school context. In recent years in the United States, the pre-school curriculum has placed great emphasis upon social and visual-artistic expression, at the expense of skills in other symbolic domains. The fostering of talents in music, mechanics, science, and the dance has often been skirted or purposely postponed for a later date. Yet, clear distinctions in the latter areas have already surfaced among the pre-school children in our sample. Our demonstration may have the effect of stimulating teachers and program directors to include such activities as part of their standard curricula. And this decision in turn will heighten the possibility that children can gain skills in these hitherto neglected areas.

This shift in emphasis might also impact upon the way in which the pre-school experience is viewed by elementary school teachers. There has been a struggle to find ways to translate typical pre-school activities into experiences relevant to the elementary school context. By weaving diverse forms of learning and assessment into the regular pre-school curriculum, we hope to lend a certain degree of credibility to the activities that take place in the pre-school classroom. Should our demonstrations of significant individual profiles be taken seriously by parents and teachers, it may be possible to incorporate a larger array of expressive symbolic materials into the standard curriculum in the primary grades.

## A MULTI-DIMENSIONAL PROFILE

Even as we treat assessment in a nontraditional way, we also have been experimenting with alternative means of conveying our findings to parents and teachers. At present, the results of standardized tests are generally presented without comment, and rarely, if ever, with concrete suggestions for 'follow-up' activities. Feedback on other activities is formal and nonsystematic. Having surveyed a wide range of competences and working styles, we believe it is appropriate to provide feedback on what we have found and to combine this feedback with suggestions about courses of action that might be followed.

We have designed our 'Spectrum Reports' to accomplish these goals. These reports describe in nontechnical language the particular profile of skills and abilities characteristic of a given child. The accent will fall on the positive, indicating the particular cognitive and stylistic strengths evinced by the child. We hope to suggest which lines of activities might be profitably followed up by the child and his family in the months and years ahead. Discussions of problem areas or areas where interest is lacking will also focus on constructive suggestions and courses of action.

A breadth of sources about each child will be distilled into the Spectrum Report. Not only do we expect to describe the proclivities that surface across a number of different dimensions, be they social, numeric, scientific, gestural or musical, but we also wish to highlight how these abilities exhibit themselves. Yet we recognize that these school-related achievements can only be fully appreciated if considered in the context of knowledge gained from parent surveys as well as the children's reflections upon their own skills. Parent observations might confirm or question our findings and also help us isolate which social and cultural forces influence a child's school performance. Hence, we intend to interview parents or have them fill out questionnaires which will provide information about their own perspectives.

In our communications to parents, we intend to distance ourselves from a strictly score-based report. We plan to offer a descriptive account of a child's emerging profile rather than an unmodified set of scores. Such a picture of the child will illustrate his or her relative level of achievement in a number of areas and compare this attainment to those of a local population. The Spectrum Report should also capture the flavor of a child's preferred engagement in an activity. There is something special about a child who transforms every opportunity into a story-telling event or the child who introduces her musical sensitivity into a number of different domains. By incorporating such qualitative information, we hope to provide a more complete view of a child's particular approach.

It is not sufficient to limit our Spectrum Report to the discussion of a child's unusual proclivities. Such budding potential can be nurtured with follow-up activities within or outside the school setting. Thus a section of the report will describe suitable after-school and community activities. The report will identify programs available for the budding naturalist, dramatist, or artistically inclined individual. In this sense, we are looking beyond school, both in terms of extra-curricular activities during childhood and in terms of the wide set of 'end-states' in society.

We hope that our pluralistic model of cognition will draw attention to dimensions of mind beyond those that predict how well a child will do in traditional school subjects. We anticipate that most children will exhibit irregular profiles of aptitudes, propensities, and interests, and that their educational well-being will be enhanced to the extent that these profiles are factored into their future educational course. Only if these more differentiated profiles have been considered by those charged with a child's education will it be possible to bring the most promising human potentials to full expression.

## REFERENCES

Feldman, D.H. (1980). *Beyond universals in cognitive development.* Norwood, N.J.: Ablex.

Feldman, D.H. (1986). *Nature's gambit.* New York: Basic Books.

Gardner, H. (1983). *Frames of mind: the theory of multiple intelligences.* New York: Basic Books.

Gibson, J.J. (1966). *The senses considered as perceptual systems.* Boston: Houghton Mifflin.

Gould, S.J. (1981). *The mismeasure of man.* New York: Norton.

Karnes, M.B., Schwedel, A.M., and Kemp, P.B. (1985). Preschool programming for the young gifted child. *Roeper Reveiw,* **7,** No. 4, 204–209.

Keil, F.C. (1984). Mechanics in cognitive development and the structure of knowledge. In R. Sternberg (ed), *Mechanics of cognitive development*. San Francisco: W.H. Freeman.

Keil, F.C. (1986). On the structure-dependent nature of stages in cognitive development..In Irish Levin (ed.), *Stage and structure*. Norwood, N.J.: Ablex.

Olson, D. (1974). *Media and symbols*. Chicago: University of Chicago Press.

Piaget, J. (1965). *The child's conception of the world*. Totowa, N.J.: Littlefield, Adams.

Salomon, G. (1979). *Interaction of media, cognition, and learning*. San Francisco: Jossey-Bass.

Sattler, J.M. (1982), *Assessment of children's intelligence and special abilities*. Boston: Allyn and Bacon, Inc.

Spearman, C. (1927). *The abilities of man*. New York: Macmillan.

Thurstone, L.L. (1938). *Primary mental abilities*. Chicago: University of Chicago Press.

Wolf, D.P., and Gardner, H. *The making of meanings*. (In preparation).

Wolf, T.H. (1973). *Alfred Binet*. Chicago: University of Chicago Press.

Psychological Bases for Early Education
Edited by A.D. Pellegrini
© 1988 John Wiley & Sons Ltd.

CHAPTER 3

# A Study of Children's Early Reading Development

ELIZABETH SULZBY

For decades parents have reported that their young children 'memorize books' and act as if they are reading. Researchers are currently turning attention to this phenomenon and are documenting how children learn to read from early interactions with their parents reading to them from storybooks such as *Three Billy Goats Gruff, Goodnight Moon,* or *Are You My Mother?*

This chapter reports results from a longitudinal study of storybook reading behavior of children aged 2 to 4, in a day care center setting in the USA. The study was conducted from the perspective of emergent literacy; in other words, we examined the reading and writing behaviors of young children with the assumption that they develop into conventional, or independent reading (Sulzby, 1985a; Teale and Sulzby, 1986). This study of children's storybook reading was a test of that assumption.

Typically in the past, research in reading only began after the child was reading conventionally. This conventionality barrier is currently being pushed backward to infancy by this study and other related research (Anderson, Teale, and Estrada, 1980; Clay, 1982; Cochran-Smith, 1982; Doake, 1981; Ferreiro and Teberosky, 1982; Harste, Woodward, and Burke, 1984; Martlew, 1983 and this volume; Ninio, 1980; Pellegrini, 1985; Snow, 1982; Snow and Ninio, 1986; Taylor, 1983; Sulzby, 1985a; Sulzby and Teale, 1987; Teale, 1985; for helpful reviews of this literature see Mason and Allen, 1986; Teale, 1981, 1984, in press; Teale and Sulzby, 1986). Research and theory from earlier social and developmental theorists such as Luria (1983) and Vygotsky (1978) are being rediscovered and Piaget's thinking is being used in new, direct ways to investigate literacy by researchers such as Papandropoulou (1978), Ferreiro (1978, 1986), and others. These researchers are asking the question, how do children learn to read (and write)? From theoretical frameworks that treat early reading and writing behaviors as legitimate parts of literacy.

In earlier approaches to reading development, not only did researchers wait until the child was reading conventionally to examine reading behavior directly, but they also treated reading as if it could only begin with so-called low level processes, such as word recognition and/or decoding. Comprehension was believed to be an even later development. Typical research designs would begin with a measurement of the children's 'readiness' in some manner 'before reading,' and then correlating the readiness measures with some subsequent measure of conventional reading, such as a word list or end-of-first-grade standardized test.

The research reported herein differs from earlier approaches in a number of related ways. First, the young child is not assumed to divide aspects of reading into so-called low- and high-level processes that coincide with adult processing models. Second, comprehension of written language is assumed to begin alongside other aspects of reading well before the child is reading conventionally from print. Third, reading (and writing) are assumed to develop within the child's growing distinctions between oral and written language—distinctions which are not tied firmly to the physical delivery modes of speech and print (see Sulzby, 1983, 1986, 1987, for expansions of these points).

The author's previous research (Sulzby, 1985a, 1986) indicates that early reading and writing behaviors develop into more and more mature forms that lead into the beginnings of what heretofore has been considered to be reading or 'beginning reading.' The term 'independent reading,' or, more recently, 'conventional reading,' is used to refer to the initial onset of reading from print. Conventional reading means that the child is now able to coordinate the flexible and consistent use of knowledges and strategies about three aspects of reading in order to render a text understandable. The three aspects of reading (Sulzby, 1985b) are comprehension (as shown by construction of probable meaning or use of memory to reconstruct text); word knowledge (as shown by treating the word as a bounded, stable, memorable unit of print); and letter-sound knowledge (as shown by flexible and developmentally appropriate use of letter–sound relationships). These aspects are learned from writing as well as reading activities and develop in different orders, but converge into a highly similar organization for conventional reading. After children first begin to read conventionally, they become more and more proficient, of course, but the current project was addressed at the period of development leading up to initial conventional reading.

## THE ROLE OF STORYBOOK READING

It has long been known that reading to children has a beneficial effect upon reading achievement (see Teale, 1984). More recently, researchers have begun to study what occurs in parent–child interaction with storybooks. Parents do not read conventionally to their infants; they interact with them in a special routine that includes features of both oral and written language (Heath, 1983; Ninio, 1983; Snow and Ninio, 1986; Teale and Sulzby, 1987). As Teale and Sulzby have recently documented, parents' readings to the same child change in nature as the child grows older and as the child grows more familiar with a given storybook. However, the speech modelled by the parent does not directly parallel the speech that the child begins to create for storybooks, although there are important relationships between parental and child speech.

A number of researchers (Clay, 1972, 1979; Doake, 1982; Goodman, 1980; Haussler, 1982; Holdaway, 1979; Rossman, 1979) extended research in parent–child interaction with storybooks to ask what young children do when asked to read a book alone. Following earlier exploratory studies, Sulzby (1983) asked a group of 24 kindergarteners to select and read a 'favorite storybook,' at the beginning and end of the 1980–81 school year. The resulting 'reading attempts' or 're-enactments' were classified according to a scheme that appeared to have developmental properties; by the use of this classification scheme, it was found that the children's emergent reading ability appeared to increase from the beginning to the end of their school year even though they were given no formal instruction in reading.

A methodological problem with the Sulzby (1983) study was the practice of allowing each child to select a different book and using only one book at each of the two sessions. The current study was designed to test the postulated developmental patterns of emergent storybook reading with group of younger children (ages 2 through 4), in a longitudinal study. Additionally, the issue of stability of emergent reading behaviour across books was tested by collecting two storybook re-enactments per child at any given session.

## METHOD

The overall design for this longitudinal study of storybook reading was case studies embedded within larger scale studies. Four separate studies over a year's interval included all of the children currently enrolled in a local day care center. From among those children, four children were interviewed monthly. Each study and the case studies are discussed separately.

### Subjects

A total of 32 children (14 boys and 18 girls) were included in the study over the year's time; however, at any one time the maximum enrollment was 25. The children's age at the time of individual enrollment ranged from 2 years 5 months to 4 years 11 months. At 5 years the policy was to move the children to a different classroom; however, the timing of that move was flexible. Four children became 5 during the year, including two case-study children and two who stayed in the classroom for a month longer. Data were collected from those children and were used in analyses when appropriate. Specific descriptions of subjects are reported with each analysis.

Parents were asked to allow their children to participate and each child was asked if he/she were willing to help the researchers learn more about how little boys and girls read. Additionally, parents were asked to send in books from home for the final study and were interviewed at the conclusion of the study.

According to the director of the day care center, the typical demographics of the center include two-thirds of the children coming from middle-income families and one-third from low-income families. At the time of this project, however, half of the students came from homes with 12 or fewer years of education and all but one of these was from a low-income home. About half of the children came from one-parent homes and about one-fourth were from black, Hispanic, oriental, Middle Eastern or East Indian families. The surrounding community was primarily middle-class with a high emphasis upon education and achievement. The day care center's philosophy appeared to emphasize children's social/emotional development. Academically-oriented activities were treated in a low-pressure, child-oriented manner rather than as formal instruction.

**Procedures**

The researchers began to visit the classroom in October 1981 so that the children and teachers would become accustomed to them. Late in October, a technical crew made three trial videotapes in the classroom and allowed the children to touch and see the camera.

Individual interviews were held seated at a table in an empty classroom across a hallway. Sessions began in late November for the four case-study children and in January 1982 for the entire class. When a researcher approached a child for an interview, she took time to talk a bit with the child. She then invited the child to select a stuffed animal from a large box the teachers had provided. For some sessions, children selected books from the classroom to bring with them as well; in others, the books were kept in the research room and the child selected the book after arriving.

The same general procedures were followed for all sessions. After the child had chosen a book, the examiner asked the child why he or she selected a given book and then asked the child to read the book to 'Snoopy and me' (using the name of whatever stuffed animal the child had chosen). If the child refused or said that he could not read, a structured set of encouragements was used:

Level one:      'Try.' 'Do your best.' 'Give it a try.'
Level two:      'Pretend.' 'Pretend-read it.'
Level three:    'I can help you.' 'What do you want me to do?'
Level four:     'I can help you.' 'Let's read it together.'

At any time the child began to read with the examiner's assistance, he or she was also encouraged to take over the reading independently. Sessions were videotaped and audiotaped and were subsequently transcribed first from audiotape and then expanded from videotape. The initial transcriptions were checked by a third researcher for completeness and accuracy and were continually checked during the analyses.

## Analyses

Preliminary analyses were conducted by viewing the videotapes and making a tentative placement of each child's performance on Sulzby's (1985a; see also 1982a) Classification Scheme for Emergent Reading of Favorite Storybooks (hereafter called 'the classification scheme'). Scores ranged from 0–11, assuming ordinal measurement. Any problems with quality of the tapes, application of procedures, and with the classification scheme description were discussed and, when necessary, the tapes were reviewed and transcripts rechecked.

Two research assistants independently scored data from two large-scale studies and the case studies from both videotape and transcripts. Since agreement was quite high between the two modes of scoring ($r = 0.99, 0.94, 0.96, 0.98$ for four sessions), transcript scoring was used for the remaining two large-scale studies. Final agreement for placing children at exactly the same score ranged from 82 to 96 percent for the first three studies, with 100 percent of the placements within one level of each other. The agreement for the fourth study was lower, probably reflecting the fact that raters had to judge the children's performance when the books varied by child: exact agreement was an average of 81 percent and agreement within one level was 88 percent.

## The studies

### Study I.

Study I was conducted in January 1982 with a total of 22 children (12 girls, 10 boys). One girl had just had her fifth birthday but was moving to a different school district so remained in the classroom. The remaining 21 children ranged in age from 2 years 10 months to 4 years 10 months (median 3 years 10 months). The children's teachers selected ten storybooks that the children had previously requested to be read repeatedly but that were not currently active. These books were reactivated for a two-week period. The teachers read the books at storytime, had them available during free time and the time structured for individual storybook reading, and kept records of how many times each book was requested. At the end of the two-week period the books were removed and the interview sessions were begun. All ten books were displayed on a table in the interview room and the children selected two favorites to 'read to Snoopy' and the examiner.

*Study II.*

Study II was conducted in May 1982. Twenty-six children were included, two of whom (a girl and a boy, each aged 5 years 1 month) had been moved to the next class. The remaining 24 included 11 boys and 13 girls (median age 4 years 1 month, range 2 years 8 months to 4 years 8 months). Ten books were selected, including a number that had been used in previous studies by other investigators. Teachers again read the books and kept records on the frequency of children's requests. The most frequently requested book was then used with all the children; they also selected one other as an individual favorite. The group favorite was read first and the individual favorite second.

*Study III.*

The procedures were identical to those of Study II, except that new books were used and half of the children read the group favorite first and half read it second. The study was conducted in August and 17 children were present, a large decrease due to summer vacations. The 15 in the regular classroom ranged in age from 2 years 10 months to 4 years 7 months, median 3 years 9 months. The two children who had moved to the older classroom were now both 5 years 3 months for a total of 7 boys and 10 girls.

*Study IV.*

For this study, in November 1982 the parents were asked to send two of the children's favorite storybooks from home. In the letter making this request, the term 'favorite storybook' was left vague, although the parents had been informed that the total project focused on storybooks that children particularly liked. The one specification was that the books had to have been favorites for at least two weeks prior to sending them to school. The book texts were either photocopied or copies of the same edition were purchased for use in data analysis. (Parents were later interviewed (Robinson, 1983) and their definitions of 'favorite books' were found to be consistent with our assumptions.) Parents' response to this request was enthusiastic. The total of 21 children (9 boys and 12 girls) included 3 children who were now in the older classroom. In addition to the boy and girl who were now 5 years and 7 months, a third boy had become 5 years 1 month. The remaining 17 ranged in age from 2 years 10 months to 4 years 10 months with a median age of 4 years 5 months.

*Case studies.*

Four children were selected for case study. Each child was seen monthly for eleven sessions over a year from November 1981 to November 1982 (data were not collected in the month of September due to staffing problems). The case-study children and their ages and income levels in November 1981 were Joleen, 4 years 7 months, low-income; Matt, 4 years 7 months, low-income; Nicki, 2 years 11 months, middle-income; and Timmy, 3 years 9 months, middle-income.

## FINDINGS

### Stability of storybook reading behaviors

The results of each study were analyzed to address the question of whether children perform the same way across storybooks or whether different story-books are more conducive to what is called 'emergent reading ability.' The results indicate that the behaviour is quite stable. For these analyses, the full number of children were used for each study—22, 26, 17, and 21, respectively. The Spearman correlation comparing storybook one to storybook two for Study I was 0.88; for Study II, 0.76; for Study III, 0.92; and for Study IV, 0.99 (all significant, $P = <0.001$). The data for Study II were analyzed in more detail to try to explain the lower (although significant) correlation. Examination of the data revealed 4 children who refused to attempt to read the first book independently but made a relatively high score on the second book (4, 5, 6, and 7). All other scores in which a refusal was paired with an attempt had ranged from 2 to 3. Study II's structure was also a problem, because all of the children read the group favorite as their second book. Removing the 4 children with suspiciously high second scores from the Study II data resulted in a correlation of 0.95. Hence, it can be concluded that children tend to perform consistently across storybooks, so long as those books are indeed familiar.

Further examination of children's scores across studies revealed that few children fluctuated so widely as did the 4 children removed from the Study II analysis above. Children tended to show a slowly increasing pattern overall with some children showing more variation than others.

### 'Refusals'

There are two types of refusals, those in which the child does not give a clear reason for refusing to attempt the book independently (scored zero) and those in which the child gives a clear statement that he or she cannot yet read based on specific grounds relating to print (level eight). Haussler (personal communication) also reports two levels of refusal but Rossman (1979) reports refusals 'occurring at every transitional point of children's reading of story-books' (p. 11). Haussler's and Rossman's sample sizes were 8 and 5 children respectively.

In the current study, a score of zero covered a number of kinds of responses.

No child completely refused to respond; the closest behavior that could be called not responding was that of a very young child who only nodded her head at points in the story and to the examiner's questions. Other children who were scored as refusing typically responded to the encouragements and echoed the examiner's reading, filled in pauses with sentence or phrase completion, interacted conversationally about the book, or paged through the book silently, carefully examining the pictures. One general finding was that refusals were found more often with younger children, more often in Studies I and II, and were typically given for both books. Refusals were, nonetheless, spread over children, with 15 children refusing at one time or another from the total of 32 involved in all studies.

This kind of pattern that Rossman (1979) reported was not clearly detected. In fact, only 5 children showed a score of zero close in time with a high score. These included the 4 children removed from the Study II analysis and one other child. Since there are so many more data that belie Rossman's claim, the explanation can probably be found in slightly differing scoring and methods of eliciting the reading attempts. Subsequent studies with low-income Anglo and Hispanic pre-school and kindergarten children (Sulzby and Teale, 1987) also undermine the claim for frequent refusals in this type of setting; however, in-home research supports the claim that children will frequently refuse to read for their parents and very familiar adults.

**Developmental patterns**

Children do increase in emergent reading behaviors over time and with increased age. Table 3.1 shows the percentage of re-enactments at different levels by age. Data from a previous study with kindergarteners are also included in order that the developmental patterns can be seen more clearly.

In Sulzby (1985a), results of which are included in Table 3.1, increased emergent reading ability was detected over a six-month interval. Now we turn to the day care data to see if a similar pattern can be detected across time with younger children. Only 8 children were present for all four studies; however, 16 were present for both Studies I and IV, conducted ten months apart. Children increased in emergent reading ability level over that period at a significant level, $t(15) = 3.58$, $p < 0.005$ (one-tailed).

Since those 16 children had varying numbers of sessions, however, those findings might contain effects of varying amounts of practice. Studies I and II were separated by almost four months and 15 children were present for both. The children's emergent reading ability also increased significantly during that brief period, $t(14) = 2.19$, $p < 0.025$ (one-tailed). This analysis still contained the 5 children who had been seen once previously (4 case-study children and a Hispanic girl tentatively considered for case study). The conservative test for increase by the remaining 10 children was also statistically significant, $t(9) = 2.63$, $p < 0.025$ (one-tailed).

Table 3.1 Percentage of children reading at increasing levels of sophistication by age.

| Categories of reading attempts | Two's[a] (n=8) % | Three's[a] (n=12) % | Age Four's[a] (n=4) % | Five's[b] November n=24) % | Five's[b] May (n=24) % |
|---|---|---|---|---|---|
| Governed by print | 0 | 17 | 25 | 21 | 42 |
| Written language-like stories | 13 | 17 | 33 | 25 | 30 |
| Oral language-like stories | 25 | 17 | 17 | 21 | 21 |
| Stories not formed | 13 | 17 | 8 | 17 | 0 |
| Refusals (low-level) and/or dependent reading | 50 | 33 | 17 | 17 | 8 |

[a] Data from the current study: counted here is only the first storybook attempt by each child on entry into study.
[b] Data from Sulzby (1983): reading attempts at the beginning and end of kindergarten by the same subjects.
[c] Percentages may not sum to 100 due to rounding.
Source: From E. Sulzby, 'Children's emergent reading of favorite storybooks: a developmental study,' *Reading Research Quarterly*, **20** (1985), 458–481. Copyright 1985 by the International Reading Association. Reprinted by permission.

Finally, we examined the raw scores of all children who were present for 3–4 sessions and for the case-study children (since the number of intervening studies might have had an effect, no statistical analysis was used). This examination revealed a pattern of primarily stable or increasing scores. Only one child, Scott, showed a drop of two or more levels for a given session.

## CLASSIFICATION SCHEME: CATEGORIES OF EMERGENT STORYBOOK READING

The preceding analyses indicate that the Classification Scheme for Emergent Reading of Favorite Storybooks (Sulzby, 1985a) was able to be applied reliably by trained judges to emergent readings by 2- to 4-year-olds; that it reflected stability of emergent reading behaviors by these children; and that it appeared to order children's progressive movement toward independent reading. A further question with young children was whether it would cover relevant behaviors sufficiently or whether new or slightly different categories or subcategories would emerge. In this section, the categories of the scheme will be examined in light of what we have learned about younger children's attempts to read storybooks.

Figure 3.1 displays the eleven subcategories of the scheme in a tree structure

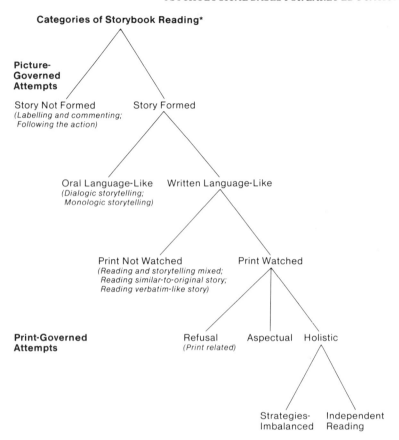

Figure 3.1   Tree structure of categories of classification scheme for emergent reading of favorite books. (From E. Sulzby, Children's emergent reading of favorite storybooks: a developmental study, *Reading Research Quarterly*, **20** (1985) 458–81. Copyright 1985 by the International Reading Association. Reprinted by permission)

that is successively branching, under five major categories. It should be noted that most studies of reading begin where this study ends, with 'independent' or conventional reading, the branch in the bottom-right corner.

### Attempts governed by pictures, stories not formed

We will begin with the least mature attempts, the lowest branch on the tree, and examine the subcategories in detail. The first two subcategories, (a) labelling and commenting and (b) following the action, were found rarely with kindergarten children, but were more prominent with the younger children. The primary characteristic of these attempts is that the child addresses speech to each page as a discrete unit, not weaving a story over the entire book. If one listened to the speech of the child alone, one would not be able to infer a story. The language is not tied together sufficiently for an audience to understand.

*Subcategory one, labelling and commenting.*

When a child reads or re-enacts a book through labelling and commenting, the child will turn to a page, point to a pictured object, and then either state a name for the object or comment upon its appearance or nature. In this study, it was observed that younger children who label and comment usually point or use large gestures toward the pictures, occasionally jabbing or slapping at the page. In this study, 2-year-old Nicki often stood up, gazed down her arm at the pictured object, named it, then turned dramatically to look full into the face of the examiner with glee or amazement.

The language used in these attempts is distinctive because it is markedly less mature than the child's normal usage. It appears to be a routine devised for book-reading, probably learned during parent-child interactions. Bruner (1978) and Ninio (1980; Ninio and Bruner, 1978) described interactions between mothers and children in which early reading is seen to be a structured dialogue. They describe this dialogue as a scaffolding in which the mother takes the child's slightest reaction as a interactional turn; the mother then builds upon the child's turn by responding and calling for another turn from the child. When the child begins to take part through linguistic devices that appear to be words or short phrases, the mother raises the expectations and indirectly demands more speech from the child.

For middle-class mother–child dyads in Israel, Ninio (1980) found that the speech seems to be tailored toward isolating the central feature in a picture, labelling it, and then adding relevant detail. The labelling and commenting subcategory of the emergent reading scheme appears to be the remnant of such previously-interactive behavior (see also Teale and Sulzby, 1987). Bruner (1978) gives an example of this kind of storybook interaction. The mother uses a vocative matched with a query; the child labels; and then the mother contributes the relevant comment.

| | |
|---|---|
| MOTHER: | 'Look.' |
| | 'What's that?' |
| CHILD: | 'Fishy.' |
| MOTHER: | 'Yes, and see him swimming.' |

Here is an example from Nicki (age 3 years 8 months) in which she uses commenting behavior with some full sentences. She remembers some information from the story she has heard read but she does not use it to weave a story. The example comes from *The Bear Detectives* (Berenstain and Berenstain, 1975).

*Example 1.*

CHILD:      There's the balloons man.
             (*Points to picture on title page.*)
             There's those missing pumpkin. Pumpkin.
             (*Pointing to pictures on pages two and three.*)
             That's the sun. (*Pointing to picture, page four.*)
             The tour and the bog. And that's Snuff. (*Pointing
               to picture of dog on page seven.*)
             Hmm. This is, this is book. (*Page 10.*)
             This is cow (*Page 12.*)

In her reading attempt Nicki uses both gesture and language ('there's,' 'that's,' 'this is,' or simply the label without article, 'cow') to point or indicate to the adult what she is attending to. She seems to have incorporated the adult's queries into her response.

Subsequent to the research reported here, in a project involving home observations of parent–child interaction in storybook reading, Teale (Teale and Sulzby, 1987) has observed children incorporating the parents' language into their own independent re-enactments at the 2-, 3-, and 4-year-old level. His work begins with the labelling and commenting level and moves through other parts of the storybook scheme.

Ninio (1980) argues that being able to identify a central focus before adding peripheral information is important in language/concept development. However, treating a picture as a static, present image for labelling and commenting does not carry the child beyond the present into the world of story in which past, present, and future are intricately intertwined. The next subcategory, following the action, seems to move the children toward such a change-oriented attitude toward books, even though a story is still not formed.


*Subcategory two, following the action.*

Children whose reading attempts could be classified at level two act as if the action in the picture is currently occurring. Again, they do not weave a story over the book but talk about each picture as a discrete unit. Their speech is again distinctive from their ordinary conversational speech. Speech is typically paired with pointing; the finger appears to trace action in the picture: 'Lookit, he's running. He's running. Gonna catch him. See.' The verbs used are typically present or present progressive tense; when verbs like 'gonna' are used they appear to characterize action solely in the picture being viewed.

The child's behavior toward the adult audience is similar to the labelling and commenting behavior. The child looks from the book to the adult and back. It seems that there may be more attempts to be certain that the adult is focusing attention to what the child is, often directed by words like, 'Lookit.' Younger children often stand up and gesture away from the picture into space. Similar to Vygotsky's (1978) description of very early drawing/writing, these children treat gesture, picture, and speech as intertwined. They may include 'sound effects' made by child verbally, 'Pow!' or 'Grrr,' or they may bang or rub across the page. Our case-study child Matt often picked the book up as if to make the characters perform an action, 'He's gonna get you!'

Following the action readings seem to contain the notions of past, present, and future in an embryonic way in relation to book reading. These readings are being done by children who understand and represent past, present, and future in their ordinary conversation but use a different kind of speech for storybook reading. Children occasionally include both labelling and commenting and following action language in the same re-enactment. When they move to following the action language, the notion of the picture/page as a bounded entity may begin to come into conflict with the language that begins to be part of a story woven over pages.

At age 2 years 10 months Patrick gave a following the action re-enactment to *A Pocket for Corduroy* (Freeman, 1978). He began making comments about his stuffed bear and the bear in the book, then he began to attend to the bear in the book alone, using progressive tenses (kissing, putting, 'going to hit').

*Example 2*

| | |
|---|---|
| CHILD: | The bear is in the cage (*Referring to the book.*) |
| | Look. (*Touching the stuffed bear.*) This one is not in a cage. |
| ADULT: | Um-hmm. |
| CHILD: | A red bow. (*Touches stuffed bear's bow and turns to page 30.*) |
| | Kissing him. See? (*About picture.*) |
| ADULT: | Is she? |
| CHILD: | She's putting him, putting him to bed. She's going to [make] his bed. (*Turns to page 10.*) |
| | Looky him. Look at him. |

Children at both of the 'story not formed' levels often read through the book by skipping pages, reading backward through the book, or varying orders, including recycling parts. It is intriguing that the children produce these behaviors with books that we know are familiar, including books identified by their parents as favorites. Nevertheless, in the data from the current study, levels one and two were concentrated in the 2-year-olds, practically disappearing with the 3- and 4-year-olds. (They did appear in a previous study (Sulzby, 1985) with kindergarteners at the beginning of the year, but in that study the children selected their own favorites without the books being reread to them in the classroom.)

As we move into the oral language-like attempts, the kinds of language used in levels one and two often appear sporadically embedded within higher attempts. Now, though, the child clearly weaves a story across the pages.


### Attempts governed by pictures, stories formed (oral language-like)

When children begin to treat the book as if it contains a whole story, they may either use language more like their typical oral conversational or narrative speech or they may attempt to use language that is like that found in books. The terms *oral language-like* and *written language-like* are used to indicate that the speech used by these children still seems to be a speech register used for storybook 'reading'.

Attempts that are oral language-like can be divided into two subcategories, dialogic storytelling or monologic storytelling. While both were found in this study and in previous work (Sulzby, 1985a) and both are expected theoretically, they appeared in unequal distributions with dialogic storytelling far more frequent than monologic. As will be explained in more detail later, children who are reared in a culture strongly affected by literacy may never give a complete oral monologue for a storybook but may move into the use of written language-like speech very quickly.


### *Subcategory three, dialogic storytelling.*

This level is a conglomerate category containing a number of characteristics more suited to oral than to written discourse. Sulzby and Otto (1982) previously called it by the awkward, but descriptive title 'Disconnected oral dramatic dialogue and/or interactive conversational comments.' It is basically dialogic, either as dialogue signalled orally within the text or as dialogue between the child and listener or a mix of these.

In subcategory three, the child may give dialogue for characters appearing in the pictures, but the dialogue will rarely have dialogue carriers or narrative ties connecting the dialogue. Instead, the child tends to depend on techniques appropriate to oral language like creating 'voices' for the characters. While this is an oral technique, again it may have been modelled for the child by the parent. A parent was recently witnessed 'reading' *Three Billy Goats Gruff* to her toddler with distinctive character voices for the four characters. While the story had dialogue carriers and narrative exposition, the voices were the salient features that the 21-month-old was later heard re-enacting. In the alternative form, children may interact conversationally with the adult listener, either looking at the adult or at the book.

The child's prosody is conversational and the wording tends to be highly contextualized, usually tied to the context of the pictures. Children may also insert unclearly signalled comments to the listener. Whereas in lower reading attempts, the child would tend to turn directly to the adult to address him or her, occasionally now the child may continue to look at the book and make a comment that is out of place as a piece of a supposedly autonomous story. The comments lack clear signals to differentiate them from other parts of the speech, signals which would be present in more advanced reading attempts.

In spite of all of these features, children's reading attempts at this level do show some awareness of audience needs. An odd mixture of present, present progressive, and past tense verb forms may add to the impression that the re-enactment is disjointed, yet the child creates some indication of past and future and overall conveys a story-like sequence.

Nicki (3 years 6 months) showed a number of these behaviors in reading *Are You My Mother?* (Eastman, 1967). This book was chosen as the favorite by the children in Study II and is used for many examples that follow. The book appears to have special significance for many children and has been used in other storybook reading discussions (see Holdaway, 1979). In the book a baby bird is hatched just after his mother goes to get worms for him to eat; the remainder of the book describes the baby bird's search for and final finding of his mother. In the beginning of Nicki's re-enactment, she used the exact words of one page of text but in the tone of conversational exchange. On the next pages, she seems to continue the sentence but connections are missing. During this sequence she is turning to face the adult, giving another signal that her speech is conversational. Finally, her statement on page 7, 'They're going to get a worm,' is bound to the context of the story but is not decontextualized for the listener.

*Example 3*

| Page | Text | CHILD |
|------|------|-------|
| 3 | A MOTHER BIRD SAT ON HER EGG | |
| 4 | THE EGG JUMPED. | /n/ the egg jumped (*Points to picture and looks at adult*) |
| 5 | 'OH OH!' SAID THE MOTHER BIRD. 'MY BABY WILL BE HERE! HE WILL WANT TO EAT.' | |
| 6 | 'I MUST GET SOMETHING FOR MY BABY BIRD TO EAT!' 'I WILL BE BACK!' | And flied away. (*Looks at adult, then points to picture.*) |
| 7 | SO AWAY SHE WENT. | They're going to get a worm. (*Spoken looking directly at adult, who replied, 'Oh, really?'*) |

Typically, Nicki's contextually-bound speech resulted in her using pronouns inappropriately for written language. As the baby bird went to a kitten, a hen, and a dog to ask if each were his missing mother whom he had never seen, Nicki called each one 'he.' (Gender confusions are common with pronouns at this age.) This usage is appropriate to oral language, of course, and to the fact that the adult can see the pictures. Finally, when the baby bird comes to a cow, Nicki identifies the creature, 'And she's a cow!' Her emphasis on 'cow' seemed to be 'labelling' behavior rather than decontextualization in a written language sense.

Nicki's gestures were large, sweeping across pages or indicating her meaning. She described the baby bird's ride in a steam shovel as, 'then he went up, up, up,' with gestures for each 'up'. When she thought the bird would fall, she gave a sweeping motion with, 'Then he, he, almost, he's falling down,' with speech reminiscent of the action-governed category.

*Subcategory four, monologic storytelling.*

The more advanced level of oral language-like reading attempt is a complete story, delivered in storytelling intonation (in contrast with reading intonation). The story is context-dependent, assuming that both the child 'reader' and the adult can see the pictures in the book. Syntax and specific phrases sound like a told story; however, the story is basically monologic in nature. The stories contain many of the surface features of oral informal speech, like conjoining sentences with *and* or *and then*, seemingly fragmented ideas, and personal involvement with the audience (Chafe, 1982).

This category has few examples from US English monolingual children who have been read to, perhaps because children who live in a highly literate society quickly learn the relevant features of written language. Such children might be prone to recite an oral monologue in a storytelling setting but not in a reading setting.

The examples which we do have are difficult to understand from the printed transcript without numerous written explanations of what can be heard and seen on the videotape. With the younger children, in particular, immature speech patterns often give a more disjointed appearance when transcribed than when the reading attempt was face-to-face.

The clearest example in my US English-speaking data comes from the kindergarten study discussed earlier (Sulzby, 1985a). Don re-enacts *Henry Explores the Mountains* by Taylor (1975). The protagonist was never introduced by name in the child's speech. The first part of the re-enactment is given here.

*Example 4(a)*

CHILD:       This is his house and he is going to sleep. He was reading a
             book. And he was going to bed and then after he was reading

the book he saw pictures of the mountains up here. Here (*pause*) there's some pictures, here, and then he thought he was going exploring the mountains, he's going to, oh yeah, about the mountains and he thought I'm going to explore the mountains tomorrow. . . .

Don continued all the way through the book, giving a very full story, understandable to the adult listener. When he finished, he gave an orally-appropriate comment, 'And then it's finished,' rather than the kind of formal conclusion, 'The End,' intoned by children giving written language-like reenactments.

In the current study, Paul (3 years 10 months) gave a level four re-enactment of *Are You My Mother?* At the beginning of the book, he started speaking while looking at the front cover, 'Man. He sees his mother.'

At the conclusion of the book a friendly steam shovel, called a Snort, puts the baby bird back in its nest where the mother bird has returned with a worm. The conclusion recapitulates the animals with the baby bird naming all the animals the mother bird is not. Paul concludes with an oral language rhetorical question, 'Know what?' which serves the interpersonal function of contact with the adult audience.

*Example 4(b)*
CHILD:    Know what? The, the Snort put the baby right back in the, in the tree.
Know what he said? You're not a kitten or a hen or a, or-r cow, or a (*pause*) car (*pause*) and you're not, you're not a Snort and you are my MO-ther!

While level four, monologic storytelling, was not found frequently in this study, we have found it more frequently in our studies of Spanish-English storyreading (Sulzby and Teale, 1987). The conclusion is that the fourth subcategory exists and that it would be found more prominently in cultures with a strong storytelling tradition and/or little exposure to literacy. It would be helpful to have research in which we elicit both told and read stories from the same children within and across cultures that differ in how oral and written language are related.

**Attempts governed by pictures, stories formed (written language-like)**

As we move into instances in which children use written language characteristics in attempting to read storybooks, the data seem to fall into three categories. The first subcategory is a transition between oral and written language. The other two come very close to being a restatement of the actual text, differing in how close they are to being verbatim or showing an attempt to retrieve the verbatim text.

*Subcategory five, reading and storytelling mixed.*

In this type of re-enactment, the child inserts sections that sound like written language, either in intonation or in wording or both, into parts that continue to sound like oral language. The story created may depart from the actual story but it shows a clear sense of audience and contains major portions that are decontextualized. Jodi's (3 years 2 months) re-enactment of *Are You My Mother?* begins with an unsmooth shift between the language of the book (capitalized) and her own wording that includes oral intonation and some interactive speech.

> *Example 5*
> CHILD:     Where's my mother?
>            It's gonna go way up there and go up to there.
>            THE EGG JUMPED and jumped.
>            He cracked out.
>            MY BABY BIRD WILL BE HERE anytime so he cracked out.
>            (*Looking at adult.*) Eggs don't jump, do they?

More typically, children do not quote sections of the book but they recreate them, using similar patterns. Later in the book, Jodi used this more typical behavior. On pages 14–16, she used character voices without the dialogue carriers and represented the action of falling with cries, forms appropriate to oral language. In contrast, for pages 30–31 she recreated the list of animals almost verbatim. She turned the section on pages 31–35 into something even more written language-like than the actual text, self-correcting 'he said to the cow,' a written language form, to 'baby bird said to the cow.' But then she omitted dialogue carriers in the cow's response.

Dialogue carriers are important ways of making written language clear. In *Are You My Mother?* the dialogue carriers often come after the dialogue, a characteristic that Chafe (1982) found to be more typical of written than oral language. Jodi moved the dialogue carriers in front of the dialogue but she made it more specific than the text, changing *he* to *baby bird*. Children giving written language-like reading attempts often insert these complex devices into text over-abundantly.

For children at level five, the mixture of oral and written language characteristics often results in their re-enactments seeming to be somewhat disorganized. In the next sections, we see how children re-enact stories when they use language almost totally suited to written language.

*Subcategory six, reading similar-to-original story*

When the child reads a similar-to-original story, the wording and the intonation are written language-like but they depart from the specific story a bit. The child often creates patterns that are like those in the book or in similar books. Children often insert a 'pattern of three' or other repetitive patterns into stories that lend themselves to such manipulations. More typically, the child may simply come close to the actual story, without showing the effort to retrieve the verbatim story (discussed in level seven). In the following example, Megan (3 years 8 months) recreates a section about the steam shovel which is never referred to by anything but *Snort*. Notice such created book-like language as, 'and the shovel came to a stop.'

*Example 6*

| Page | Text | CHILD |
|---|---|---|
| 44 | JUST THEN, THE BABY BIRD SAW A BIG THING. THIS MUST BE HIS MOTHER. 'THERE SHE IS!' HE SAID 'THERE IS MY MOTHER!' | Now he came to a shovel. 'Here I am, mother! Here I am, mother.' (*Turns to page 46.*) |
| 46 | HE RAN RIGHT UP TO IT. 'MOTHER, MOTHER! HERE I AM, MOTHER!' HE SAID TO THE BIG THING. | 'What is the shovel gonna do to to me?' said the baby bird. (*Turns to page 48.*) |
| 48 | BUT THE BIG THING JUST SAID, 'SNORT.' 'OH, YOU ARE NOT MY MOTHER,' SAID THE BABY BIRD. 'YOU ARE A SNORT. I HAVE TO GET OUT OF HERE!' | 'Help, help! Get me out of here!' said the baby bird. (*Direct quotations could be inferred easily from her intonation. Turns to page 50.*) |
| 50 | BUT THE BABY BIRD COULD NOT GET AWAY. THE SNORT WENT UP. | And the shovel went up and up and up. (*Flips page then turns back.*) And the shovel came to a stop. |

*Subcategory seven, reading verbatim-like story.*

Children have often been described as 'memorizing', or 'just memorizing' a book as if that behavior is rote and inconsequential. In this highest level before the child is attempting to read from print, the child shows an awareness and partial memory for stretches of the text that is not rote, but is highly effortful and conceptual. At this level the child shows self-correction behaviors that indicate that he/she is trying to retrieve the actual story rather than simply lacking fluency or using local monitoring of speech. He/she typically uses overgeneralized patterns from written language, such as inserting overly-specified dialogue carriers before and after a quotation. 'The baby bird said to the dog, "Are you my mother?" said the baby bird to the dog.'

Brian (4 years 8 months) seemed to have a hard time getting started on *Are You My Mother?* because he wanted to get the text just right. His intonation was reading-like and he sounded as if he were asking the adult to help him read print although he was looking at the pictures. (Note also that he comes close to a refusal to read based on print awareness, subcategory nine, the next higher level.) The text page was, 'A MOTHER BIRD SAT ON HER EGG.'

*Example 7(a)*

| | |
|---|---|
| CHILD: | Um, the mother egg was sitting on her—(*pause*) |
| | 'kay, I want you to help me. (*Looks up, rubs chin.*) |
| ADULT: | You're doing fine. |
| CHILD: | I just want you to help me. |
| ADULT: | Okay. |
| CHILD: | (*Turns back to book.*) A mother—bird was sitting on her egg. |
| ADULT: | Um-hm. |
| CHILD: | (*Looks at adult.*) C'mon, help me to— |
| ADULT: | You did fine. |
| CHILD: | 'kay, I want you to help me. |
| | How come you're not? |

Brian dealt with his frustration well and completed the book. As he came to details that he did not remember immediately, he paused as if to retrieve the forgotten word or phrase. As in the example given earlier, Brian specified the speaker/hearer relationship even more than the text did.

*Example 7(b)*

| | |
|---|---|
| CHILD: | 'Are you my mother?' said (*pause*) um, said the bird to the (*pause*) hen. |

Because he is trying so hard to retrieve the story as he thinks it should be, his ending sounds quite disfluent, in contrast to the speech he used between the beginning and the end.

*Example 7(c)*

| | |
|---|---|
| CHILD: | Do you know who I am? (*Brief pause.*) |
| | Yes, I know who you are. (*Pause, scratches head.*) |
| | You're not a cow, you're not a bird— |
| | I mean—you're not a—a—not a kitten, |
| | you're not a—um—hen, you're not a—um—dog, |
| | you're not a—um— (*indecipherable*) |
| | and you're my mother. |

Martin (4 years 8 months) deals with the ending rather successfully but self-corrects to be sure to include the boat which he had already included. Starting a series again in the middle is quite difficult, yet Martin does it with grace and self-corrects his initial use of a contraction, 'you're' to the more formal 'you are' for the crucial ending, 'You are my mother.' He also adds the formal words for 'The end,' which are not part of this book.

*Example* 7(d)

| Page | Text | CHILD |
|------|------|-------|
| 60b | 'DO YOU KNOW WHO I AM?' SHE SAID TO HER BABY. | Do you know who I am? And he said (*Turns to page 62.*) |
| 62 | 'YES, I KNOW WHO YOU ARE,' SAID THE BABY BIRD 'YOU ARE NOT A KITTEN. 'YOU ARE NOT A HEN. 'YOU ARE NOT A DOG. | You are not a kitten. (*Pause.*) You are not a kitten. You are not a hen. You're not a dog. |
| 62 | 'YOU ARE NOT A COW. 'YOU ARE NOT A BOAT, OR A PLANE, OR A SNORT!' 'YOU ARE A BIRD AND YOU ARE MY MOTHER.' | You're not a cow. You're not a boat. you're not—uh—I think I I skipped the boat. (*Looks briefly back at prior page.*) You're not a boat. You're not a cow. You're not a cow. You're not a boat. You're not a snort. And you are a bird, and you're— you are my mother. The end. |

Children who give verbatim-like re-enactments often pay some attention to print but not the kind of attention that children do in higher levels. They act as if the pictures are read but if there is print in the picture, they may read the print or comment on it. Joleen read *Sammy,* shown on a picture of a chalkboard in a classroom in *Sammy, the Seal* (Hoff, 1957). She read, after initially confusing them, the words *cat* and *dog* on blocks in a picture, but ignored the text not in pictures.

Another important way in which they attend to print, however, has to do with the central concept of this subcategory, the attempt to retrieve a text in verbatim fashion. They may seem to forget a section, stop, and ask the adult to read it to them. Now they indicate that it is the text print that is read but will return to looking at the picture when they restate what the adult read.

*Comparison across reading attempts governed by pictures.*

The written language-like subcategories regularly increase across ages 2, 3, and

4, while the lower subcategories decrease. In both level six and level seven, the child's speech is worded like written language, is reading-like in intonation, and is primarily decontextualized so that it can be understood without looking at the pictures. In contrast to the 'stories not formed' levels (one and two) in which the child uses speech that is less mature than his or her ordinary usage, in these two written language-like categories, the child's speech sounds more complex and more formal than ordinary conversation or storytelling. These are the final two categories in which the child is acting as if the pictures are read. In the four categories that follow, the child is attending to print as the source of what is read.

**Attempts governed by print**

If we consider the data presented here to describe reading development, the child makes tremendous conceptual changes about reading from the levels of unexplained refusals and/or dependent re-enactment (scored zero), through storybook routines that do not weave a story over the book, through oral and written language attempts to read from the picture. In the subcategories called 'Governed by print,' the child makes even more conceptual changes before reaching the highest point, conventional or independent reading. Most examinations of reading only begin at the final point of this analysis; now we are examining levels that directly precede conventional reading. It should be noted that none of the attempts at these levels was shown by 2-year-olds and they appeared only scantily with the 3-year-olds.

*Subcategory eight, refusing to read based upon print awareness.*

Refusals to read based upon print awareness may be detected either by the child's explanation, a behavior more typical to 5-year-olds, or by the child's sudden refusal after high-level picture-governed re-enactments with accompanying behavior during assisted reading that reveals a fairly well-developed awareness of print. The latter behavior was more typical for the 3- and 4-year-old children in the current study.

5-year-olds will explain why they cannot read: 'I don't know the words,' 'I can't read yet—I need you to help me sound-out the words,' 'I can't really read—I was just pretending,' (paired with a refusal), or 'I can't read but I can tell it to you.'

Two of the children in this study gave repeated high-level refusals. Brian refused at both 4 years 3 months and 4 years 8 months. Each time he said he could not read and asked the examiner to help him. When she asked what she could do, he indicated the print. At 4 years 3 months, he said, 'Help me read. This—numbers of these,' indicating the print. (Using the term *numbers* for *letters* or *words* is not unusual with young children.) He was even more specific at 4 years 8 months. After telling the examiner, 'Oh, just help me read it,' he told her where to start, 'Um, this is where we should start.' At that, he turned to the title page and ran his finger across the title: 'Can you—try to help me read it?' His subsequent dependent re-enactment showed a high level of knowledge of the text and his second storybook for that session was the level seven re-enactment discussed earlier (Examples 7a, 7b, 7c).

Rani refused for both Study I and IV and gave high-level re-enactments for the one study she was present for in between. Her dependent re-enactments subsequent to the refusals were also high-level. She was quite adamant that she could not read and gave a verbal explanation in Study IV when she was 4 years 8 months.

*Example 8*

| | |
|---|---|
| ADULT: | Read this one to me and Pinky. |
| CHILD: | I don't know this story. |
| ADULT: | Well, I don't either. [Not true; deviation from procedures] |
| CHILD: | Yes, you do. |
| ADULT: | I have never read it. |
| CHILD: | Well, you can read it. |
| ADULT: | What would I do? |
| CHILD: | Read this part. (*Points to print on page 4.*) |
| ADULT: | What's that? |
| CHILD: | It's the words. |

While Rani gave a verbal and gestural explanation that it is the print that is read, what she meant by not knowing the story was not probed directly. Evidently, 'knowing' the story was tied to print as well because she gave a verbatim-like re-enactment of the story after refusing to attempt to read it. Her other independent attempts were verbatim-like (level 9) and aspectual with an emphasis on memory for text.

*Subcategory nine, reading aspectually.*

Before children become independent readers but after they are attending to print, they often start to focus upon one or two aspects about print to the exclusion of other aspects. The major aspects are words, letter-sound relationships, and comprehension but they appear in rudimentary forms before independent reading. Comprehension, for instance, is displayed in storybook reading as memory for, or re-creation of, text. The child may have only a little knowledge of the aspect focused on at a given time. The child may focus on combinations either serially or in parallel. In some cases, the child may focus on a few known words; in others, upon sounding letters out to nonsense words; in others, upon the remembered text with an indication that the speech comes from the print. The key feature is that in all cases the child attempts to use print.

In aspectual attempts, the child seems to be practicing parts of the repertoire that will be put back together in conventional reading. From previous research with kindergarteners Sulzby (1981, 1982a) described the parts of the reading aspectually category as being variant across children and not sequenced developmentally. The current data raise some questions about this claim but do not constitute sufficient evidence to answer them firmly.

Kindergartners furnish examples of children focusing on words or sounding-out in isolation from evidence of comprehension. All of the examples from the day care children come from five girls, three of whom clearly focused on memory for text. A fourth shows evidence of memory for text and the belief that every word can and should be identified, or a focus 'word as a stable unit' (Sulzby, 1982a). The fifth, Joleen, gave as her highest re-enactment a recitation of *Jack and the Beanstalk* in which she used the print only sporadically but clearly in an attempt to confirm the speech she was using. Some of the children gave refusals similar to the level eight refusal. In contrast with level eight children, though, they then began to interact with the adult and to 'read,' clearly treating the print as what is read. Thus our judgments placing children into level nine are based on a richer reading of the context than was necessary with the kindergartners.

Four of the five day care children had scores in other sessions that were consistent with a level eight performance. At 4 years, Kathy gave two level nine performances and by Study II she was clearly reading independently. All six of her subsequent storybooks were read independently, through Study IV. Her focus was on memory for text, as were the attempts of Karen (4 years 5 months) and Rani at 4 years 7 months. Both Kathy and Karen recited the story while looking at the print and only occasionally pointed directly to it. Rani, on the other hand, gave a delightful performance, reciting words intended for the text and then pointing to the print, dragging her finger across it from the bottom line to the top line, sometimes going right to left.

When Joleen (5 years 6 months) attempted to read *Jack and the Beanstalk,* she pointed to the print occasionally, as if she were reading from it, in a manner similar to Rani's unmatched pointing. The storybook had a number of pages on which the print was spread out

graphically
over the page
like this.

She made up text that fitted the story quite well without actually tracking the print, particularly embellishing the repetitive elements. When Jack went to the beanstalk, Joleen said, '. . . he climbed, and he climbed, and he climbed, and he climbed, and he climbed, and he climbed.' For the last three *climbings*, she pointed to the left-hand text page three times with diagonal slant across the print. Then she came to a page on which the text ends with the giant coming

THUMP

THUMP

THUMP.

Joleen continued her rendition.

*Example 9(a)*

CHILD:    So he came to a brick road and Jack—(*pause*)
and it went on and on and on.
So Jack walked and walked. (*Pause.*)
That says walked and walked. (*To adult while
pointing to the 'thump, thump, thump' display.*)
But it has no /t/ at the end,
it has a /p/.

Betsy (3 years 8 months) appeared to be investigating the roots of the idea that words are stable units and are written down through a stable representation. Her notions are very rudimentary but they may be important because she also tied them to labelling behavior, asking first what things in the pictures were called and then incorporating them into her speech while looking at the print of *A Pocket for Corduroy* (Freeman, 1978).

*Example 9(b)*

CHILD:    Corduroy came to a box of snow. (*Turns to pages 20–21*).
Then he tipped over—(*looks at page 21, points to text
beginning*) I don't know what this word is.

ADULT:    Oh (*pause, child looks expectant but doesn't speak*)
what (*pause, with same child behavior*) fun (*child smiles,
turns page, and says, 'What else?'*)

Betsy continued to 'read' parts and ask the adult for help by pointing to text and saying, 'I don't know what it says there.' These requests for aid did not give her pieces of text that fitted into her own re-creation of the text but she did not seem to notice. At one point she pointed at a section that the adult had just read for her as, 'for Senorita.' Then she pointed to the 'senorita' part and asked the adult what it said.

But what do these examples mean? Similar examples have been interpreted as revealing children's cognitive confusion (Downing, 1979) about reading and written language. Rather these examples show the child's growth in a manner that looks like a confusion or regression. Before, the child was less specifically aware of the role of print; now, she knows a few more things about print and is working on figuring out more. These aspectual attempts can be treated as exploration of how print works and as a time of practice in which the reading process is temporarily dissected for closer examination.

Children who have built a fairly extensive knowledge of the wording of written language and the prosody used by readers now are integrating knowledge about a few words that they know conventionally, or a few letter–sound relationships that they are learning either conventionally or through invention, with their ability to predict the contents of a storybook.

The current data prompt a question about whether the comprehension-based aspectual focus precedes focusing on words and/or letter–sound relationships. Both theoretically and empirically, a case can be made that all three aspects are developing from infancy and require high-level conceptualization from the child. However, this position is not a typical one for reading researchers until recently (see, for example, Ferreiro and Teberosky, 1982).

In spite of the question about when each aspect begins and the level of reasoning required to develop each, there may nevertheless be a point after the child begins to attend to print in reading attempts in which comprehension focus precedes the other two aspects. The present data base from kindergartners and the day care children is not sufficient to answer the question but it does present evidence that what I am calling 'aspectual' attempts do not appear early in development; instead, they appear after children can give a story with features of written language while gazing at the pictures.

The next two levels are closely related, both being called 'holistic,' to indicate that the child seems to be combining the relevant aspects of reading from print. The coordination of the aspects appears tenuous with level ten, still reflecting the aspectual tendency but less drastically, and in level eleven the aspects are fully coordinated into conventional, or independent reading.

*Subcategory ten, reading with strategies imbalanced.*

The strategy-dependent reader has coordinated the aspects of reading but not sufficiently for easy and independent reading. The child is dependent on strategies in a manner that lacks flexibility. As with aspectual reading, this level may take many forms: tending to omit unknown words excessively and to substitute other 'known words' from his or her reading repertoire; sounding-out excessively, often leaving 'nonsense' words uncorrected; or over-depending upon the predicted or remembered text rather than the written text. In all of these variations, the child will show only sporadic control over the neglected elements.

Kindergarteners who have been placed at this level appear to be quite different from children who are reading independently. However, there were no instances of strategy-dependent reading with the younger children in the current study. The example given below is from a kindergartener, Tanya, who varies from a few stretches of reading in which she seems to be in coordinated control to stretches in which she depends excessively on the adult to tell her 'what it says' or upon letter–sound cues that she uses with nonsense words (a longer excerpt appears in Sulzby, 1985a). She is reading *No Roses for Harry* (Zion, 1958).

*Example 10*

| *Child's Speech* | *Book Text* |
|---|---|
| The next day when Harry went downtown with the children, he wore, wear hi, his new sweater. When purple? (*Adult: People.*) people saw it, ₁they liked? (*Adult: They laughed.*) laughed. When dogs saw it, they braked. Harry met? (*Adult: Made.*) made up his mend then and there to lo-lost Grandma's present. | The next day when Harry went downtown with the children, he wore his new sweater. When people saw it, they laughed. When dogs saw it they barked. Harry made up his mind then and there to lose Grandma's present. |

Reading at this level also appears to be quite effortful. Tanya completed the entire book, an impressive feat. She read some pages quite fluently, sounding as if she were reading independently and others with the faltering behavior seen in Example 17. She is using all three strategies in this selection but shows her 'strategy-dependence' in the miscues.

If we accept the claim that aspectual attempts and strategy-dependent attempts precede and are different from conventional, or independent reading, there are implications for research and instruction. Many children called 'low readers' would not be called independent or conventional readers even in first, second, third grades. Longitudinal research has reported individual differences in children's focus during initial acquisition that may reflect these pre-independent levels (Amarel, 1977, 1981; Lesgold, Resnick, Roth, and Hammond, 1981). Harste and Burke (1977) reported an effect of teacher's model (skills or word-focus, decoding or letter–sound focus, and whole language or comprehension-focus) upon the child's strategies in oral reading; this effect may be bi-directional, an interaction between the child's developmental level and the teacher's focus. Classroom process research (Collins, 1981; Green, 1977; McDermott, 1976) has documented that teachers treat low readers differently from high readers, putting a focus more upon reading as a non-integrated rather than integrated process. The current study with 2-, 3-, and 4-year-olds documents that at least the aspectual focus can be found in younger children who are not receiving formal instruction, making the argument stronger that these patterns are developmental.

*Subcategory eleven, reading independently.*

Independent reading is what people think of as conventional 'reading.' The child is reading the print independently of an adult, using comprehension, letter–sound knowledge, and known words in a coordinated fashion to recreate the text. The child may not read 'word perfectly,' but will make high-level miscues showing all aspects of independent reading. The independent reader will make self-corrections that show evidence of a wide and strategic use of knowledge about reading. The independent reader can be described as being both less text-bound and yet more accurate in reproducing both the wording and the intended meaning of the author. The child is in charge.

Some kindergarteners in my research (Sulzby, 1981, 1985a, 1985b) have come to school reading and some have begun to read prior to formal instruction. In the current study of day care children, only two children began to read independently during the study; neither was reading at the beginning of the study. Kathy, an Anglo girl, began to read conventionally just before 4 years 4 months and Martin, a Hispanic boy, began just before 5 years 1 month. Unfortunately, we did not witness the transition for either child, in Kathy's case due to the interval between Study I and Study II, and in Martin's case due to his absence between Study II and IV.

Independent reading was not displayed dramatically by either Kathy or Martin. Both children read orally in low and rapid voices and the examiner had to watch closely to be certain they were using the print. Two casual experiments were conducted that relate to emergent reading.

Kathy had demonstrated in Study I that she could recite storybooks almost verbatim. During Study IV in which she brought two books from home, I asked her to play a game with me in which I would show her the pictures and she was to tell me what the text was. This was an attempt to see whether she was still using a verbatim-like memory for the text or was using more cues from the print. Her attempts were qualitatively inferior to her performance to Study I and she asked to re-examine the print on each page, seeming to pick up more verbatim language each time. She did seem to have a notion that she should render the language of the book when she retold it as well as when she read the pages.

This little experiment indicated that she was not just relying on 'memorizing' this favorite book from home. However, there is need for caution. In following kindergarteners into first grade (Sulzby, 1983) we found that children could recite with amazing accuracy storybooks like *Where the Wild Things Are* (Sendak, 1963) and often their basal reader stories. These children were being asked to retell the stories and they acted as if retelling meant giving a verbatim recitation. At times, children would stop, look off in space, and resay what they thought the story contained at that point. They displayed a clear attempt to retrieve the text as a stable, memorable entity.

We have given insufficient attention to the character and importance of children's 'memorizing' or use of memory for text. First, it is clear that children do not just memorize as a rote technique but they learn the text 'by heart' as some kind of conceptual entity. They seem to retrieve the text by various strategies which indicate that they are integrating parts of the comprehension process. Second, we have a small but intriguing start on understanding how children learn the text in the first place (Snow and Ninio, 1986, Sulzby and Teale, 1987; Taylor, 1986; Teale 1986; Teale and Sulzby, 1987). Clearly, repeated readings in home storybook readings (or bedtime reading) are important, along with children attempting to re-enact stretches of text. School readings also appear important (Feitelson, Kita, and Goldstein, 1986; McCormick and Mason, 1986; Teale, Martinez, and Glass, 1987). Memorable stories with rhythmic, repetitive, or emotionally salient features are important (however, 'pattern books' without a story line do not appear to allow the developmental behaviors to be displayed; see Sulzby and Teale, 1987). Also, when children ask an adult for aid such as rereading a section they often try to restate it to their own satisfaction.

Another important question is how children use memory for storybook texts after they are attending to print, during the aspectual and strategy-dependent periods, and how this use of memory changes as they begin to read independently. Presumably at the lower levels, memory works to allow the child to continue 'reading' with understanding while slowing down the process to decipher or to recognize the marks on the page. It is probably 'normal' for some children to abandon temporarily comprehension strategies in the aspectual level but 'not normal' to fail to return to them. We clearly need to examine memory for text and other roots of reading comprehension in more depth and Kathy's case offers a beginning.

Kathy's parents demonstrated an attitude often found in children of 'precocious readers'; they were concerned and somewhat apologetic about her reading. Unfortunately, many parents have been advised 'not to teach' their children to read before first grade and they are afraid that they will be seen as 'pushing' their children if the children do learn to read. Kathy's parents had never heard of the work of Durkin (1966) or Clark (1976), tracking the in-school progress of American and Scottish children who began to read before school entry. While they appeared somewhat reassured when told of this research, they still expressed concern that she might not fit into the classroom. The day care teachers seemed to be pleased with Kathy's reading and urged her to read for them and other children. Nevertheless, both parents and teachers need to learn more about how children develop as readers and writers before instruction so that the entry into formal instruction can build upon the children's development. Teachers were not aware, for instance, that Martin was reading independently prior to Study IV and they were trying to 'teach the sounds' to him when he was already using knowledge of letter–sound relationships proficiently.

Martin brought two books from home for Study IV, and like Kathy, he recited them in a low and rapid voice. His reading was so rapid that it was unintelligible in stretches. One of the books was *The Berenstain's B book* (Berenstain, 1973), which sounded like a tongue-twister filled with /b/, /b/, /b/. The mini-experiment for Martin was to ask him to identify words in isolation and drawn at random from the book, to ask him to identify words with initial consonant substitution. He handled these tasks easily. He could segment *breadbasket* into its two component parts (in contrast with Matt who claimed that the whole of *button my buttons* was found in each individual part) and he could also read the 'hardest page' slowly, a technique used in our studies of rereading from one's own writing (Sulzby, 1982; Sulzby, Barnhart, and Hieshima, in press). The reading slowly task was intended to decide whether he had over-depended on his memory for the text, a feat hard to accept since the text of this 'storybook' was alliterative lists like 'big brown bear, blue book, beautiful new boat, biking backwards,' etc. He also read printed items in the room pointed out at random.

In two kindergarten studies (Sulzby, 1981, 1985a), each containing 24 5-year-olds, only one child was reading independently from storybooks in the fall (this typically varies from one to four children in middle-income classrooms). The current study contained one 5-year-old, Martin, reading, along with one 4-year-old, Kathy. Both of these children were middle-income, similar to the kindergarten samples; however, Joleen, our case-study child from low-income background, was rapidly approaching independence at the conclusion of the study and began to read conventionally during the subsequent months.

### Levels suspected but not included

By examining the children's independent re-enactments of storybooks in detail, we have uncovered orderly changes with development. However, the data also include dependent re-enactments which have not been worked into the analysis scheme sufficiently. At this point, they cannot be due to variability in examiner elicitations; a descriptive look at the data (Otto, 1985) suggests that there is a relationship between the child's speech in these instances and his/her speech in independent re-enactments.

In a few cases we found clues about how children incorporate the questions that adults asked in parent-child or teacher-child interaction (see also Cox and Sulzby, 1982; Teale and Sulzby, 1987). Jack (4 years 2 months) took charge of both his storybook re-enactments for Study II. Notice that Jack both asks and answers his own questions. His language includes both 'labelling and commenting' and 'action-governed' characteristics, but in interaction with the adult he lets us know that he has an understanding that the book, *The Berenstain Bears and the Missing Dinosaur Bones* (Berenstain and Berenstain, 1980), contains a story and that he remembers specific vocabulary terms from that story, like 'museum mummy case' and 'Indian totem pole.'

*Example 11*

CHILD: (*Pages silently to page 13 and points to picture.*)
What's that called?

ADULT: Well, what do you think it's called?

CHILD: I think it called a, a museum mummy case.

ADULT: Could be, yeah, I bet that's right.

CHILD: Hey, you know what—/look it/this thing—that cuckoo gonna come out. (*Referring to picture, turns and looks at adult.*)

ADULT: (*Laughs*) Oh, really.

CHILD: Yeah. (*Turns pages to page 20.*)
Hey, you know what's up in here? (*Picture of tower.*)

ADULT: (*Laughs*) No, tell me.

CHILD: I'll show you. (*Turns to page 22*) Here's what's up in there. See. Look it. That's the same guy.

Jack's language was highly contextualized, with much use of deictic terms and ambiguous pronouns. If we remove the adult speech and connect all of Jack's for his total story, the re-enactment sounds like level three. We cannot assume, however, that he could have done independently what he did in verbal interaction with the adult. Vygotsky's (1978) theory of social interaction claims that children first perform in social interaction before they internalize speech into thought which can be used independently. Jack's re-enactment is a further indication that research in parent–child interaction and research looking at independent emergent reading attempts needs to be combined (Sulzby and Teale, 1987).

Other kinds of reading attempts were not covered, some of which can be seen in children as young as 8 months (Ninio and Bruner, 1978; Ninio, 1980) in parent–child interaction and as young as 18 months (personal observation) in spontaneous independent attempts in the home. Certainly, the research looking at the interactive speech of parents and children in the home (Ninio, 1980, 1983; Snow, 1982; Teale, 1985; Teale and Sulzby, 1987) needs to be included; it points to which features to look for independent attempts. Even in the home, however, children take part in independent re-enactments that were not observed here, due to the age of our subjects. A number of children have been observed using 'babbling' with an intonation like reading, while paging sequentially through a storybook, at ages as young as 18 months. At 21 months, one child could be heard to use different phonological patterns when 'reading' *Three Billy Goats Gruff* than she used in her normal babbling patterns. After a week of using only this kind of babbling, she was heard to insert a threatening-sounding, 'Eat you!' at intervals in the book, a repetition of the troll's words as he came after each Goat Gruff.

Social-class differences cannot be understood without comparing the use of storybooks in the home with what the children do independently. In the current study, low-income children showed as much variation as did middle-income children although their performance as a whole was lower than that of the middle-income children. For those low-income children who showed high performance, like Joleen, there was evidence that the parents read to the children a lot and that books were available in the homes. However, cross-cultural research like that of Heath (1982), Ninio (1980), and Teale (1985) indicates that we must study the home reading patterns in greater detail.

### 'Favorite storybooks' and parents

This study was begun by using the term 'favorite storybook' based upon parents' and children's folk definitions and upon previous research in which children seemed able to select 'favorites'. In the winter of 1983, the parents of the children present for Study IV were interviewed as part of a thesis study (Robinson, 1983; Robinson and Sulzby, 1984). The interviewer asked parents about their children's behaviors with the books that had been sent in as favorites for Study IV. These parents confirmed the operational definition that we had been using: children ask for these books to be read repeatedly; they correct parents' departures from the text, as it had been established in early readings by the parent; and, they attempted to read these books independently. (Parents also stated spontaneously that they became tired of reading a given book so many times but did it anyway!)

## CONCLUSION

The study reported herein presents evidence that children aged 2 through 4 show developmental patterns when attempting to read from storybooks which they have selected as 'favorites.' Furthermore, these behaviors show stability at points in time as well as developmental growth over time with the same children. The patterns of 'reading' contain evidence of children's developing distinctions between written and oral language. Books that are selected by children as 'favorites' appear to have an importance in 'natural' reading development in the home that warrants further research, particularly research comparing parent–child interaction with children's independent performances.

Children's entry into independent or conventional reading is not from a position of no knowledge but from a position of long patterns of development. It is speculated that those patterns just prior to independent reading may interact detrimentally with some kinds of formal instruction.

Further research needs to point in two directions: downward in age, including both parent–child interaction and children's independent functioning; and more intensively into the period of just before independent or conventional reading. If the developmental patterns continue to be detected, particularly cross-culturally, research in emergent reading of storybooks suggests important implications for theory and practice in child development and education.

## ACKNOWLEDGMENTS

This chapter is a revision of a paper presented at the biennial meeting of the Society for Research in Child Development, Toronto, Canada, April 1985. I am particularly grateful to the Spencer Foundation for its support of the research reported herein. Additionally, I thank the children, parents, and teachers at Wesley Day Care Center in Glenview, Illinois, for their generous participation; and the director, Arlene Cohen, for her enthusiastic cooperation and guidance throughout the study. Dr David Cordray of Northwestern University offered design and statistical advice and Dr William H. Teale of the University of Texas, San Antonio, gave careful thought to ideas and read several drafts of parts of this report. Thanks to many students and staff members at Northwestern University, particularly Dr Beverly Otto (now of Northeastern University), Fay Robinson, Ann Branch, Matt Juinte, Alison Holmes, Francine Hsieh, Harriet Rabenovets, Sam Tarkington, Laura Winslow, Christa Reuning, and Liliana Barro for their help in interviewing, videotaping, transcription, scoring, support, and good thinking. I am also particularly thankful for the support of careful readers of subsequent drafts, including Tony Pellegrini, Denny Wolfe, Tom James, Jana Mason, JoBeth Allen, Stephen Dunning, Camille Blachowicz and, of course, Bill Teale. P. David Pearson reminded me of principles of parsimony and parallalism in helping me relabel the subcategories of the Classification Scheme for Emergent Reading of Favorite Storybooks.

Permission to quote sections from *Are you my mother?* by P.D. Eastman (Copyright © 1960 by P.D. Eastman) was kindly provided by P.D. Eastman and Random House, Inc.

## REFERENCES

Amarel, M. (1977, December). *An approach to the study of beginning reading: Longitudinal case studies.* Paper presented at the National Reading Conference, New Orleans.

Amarel, M. (1981, April). *Qualities of literacy: The personal dimension.* Vice Presidential presentation of the American Educational Research Association, Los Angeles.

Anderson, A.B., Teale, W.H., and Estrada, E. (1980). Low income children's preschool literacy experiences: Some naturalistic observations. *The Quarterly Newsletter of the Laboratory of Comparative Human Cognition, 2,* 59–65.

Berenstain, J., and Berenstain, S. (1971). *The Berenstains' B book.* New York: Random House.

Berenstain, S., and Berenstain, J. (1975). *The bear detectives.* New York: Random House.

Berenstain, S., and Berenstain, J. (1980). *The Berenstain bears and the missing dinosaur bone.* New York: Random House.

Bruner, J.S. (1978). Learning the mother tongue. *Human Nature*, 43–48.
Chafe, W.L. (1982). Integration and involvement in speaking, writing, and oral literature. In D. Tannen (ed), *Spoken and written language: Exploring orality and literacy*. Norwood, N.J. Ablex.
Clay, M.M. (1972). *Sand: Test booklet*. Auckland: Heinemann.
Clark, M.M. (1976). *Young fluent readers*. London: Heinemann.
Clay, M.M. (1979). *Reading: The patterning of complex behavior*. 2nd edn. Auckland: Heinemann.
Clay, M.M. (1982). *Observing young children: Selected papers*. Exeter, N.H. Heinemann.
Cochran-Smith, M. (1982). *The making of a reader: A case study of preschool literacy socialization*. Unpublished doctoral dissertation, University of Pennsylvania.
Collins, J. (1981). Differential treatment in reading instruction. In J. Cook-Gumperz, J. Gumperz and H. Simons, *School-Home Ethnography Project*. Final report to the National Institute of Education (NIE-G-78-0082). Washington, D.C.: National institute of Education.
Cox, B., and Sulzby, E. (1982). Evidence of planning in dialogue and monologue by five-year-old emergent readers. *National Reading Conference Yearbook*, **31**, 143–150.
Doake, D. (1981). *Preschool book handling knowledge, or book experience and emergent reading behavior*. Unpublished manuscript, Acadia University, Wolfville, Nova Scotia.
Doake, D. (1982). *Book experience and emergent reading behavior*. Unpublished doctoral dissertation, University of Alberta.
Downing, J. (1979). *Reading and reasoning*. New York: Springer-Verlag.
Durkin, D. (1966). *Children who read early*. New York: Teachers College Press.
Eastman, P.D. (1967). *Are you my mother?* New York: Random House.
Feitelson, D., Kita, B., and Goldstein, Z. (1986). Effects of listening to series stories on first graders' comprehension and use of language. *Research in the Teaching of English*, **20**, 339–356.
Ferreiro, E. (1978). What is written in a written sentence? A developmental answer. *Journal of Education*, **160**, 25–39.
Ferreiro, E. (1986). The interplay between information and assimilation in beginning literacy. In W.H. Teale and E. Sulzby (eds), *Emergent literacy: Writing and reading*. Norwood, N.J.: Ablex.
Ferreiro, E., and Teberosky, A. (1982). *Literacy before schooling*. Exeter, N.H.: Heinemann.
Freeman, D. (1978). *A pocket for Corduroy*. New York: Viking Press.
Goodman, Y.M. (1980). The roots of literacy. In M.P. Douglass (ed), *Clarement Reading Conference Forty-fourth Yearbook*. Claremont Reading Conference.
Green, J.L. (1977). *Pedagogical style differences as related to comprehension performance: Grades one through three*. Unpublished doctoral dissertation, University of California, Berkeley.
Harste, J.C. Woodward, V.A., and Burke, C.L. (1984). *Language stories and literacy lessons*. Portsmouth, N.H.: Heinemann.
Harste, J.E., and Burke, C.L. (1977). A new hypothesis for reading teacher research: Both teaching and learning are theoretically based. *National Reading Conference Yearbook*. **26**.
Haussler, M.M. (1982). *Transition into literacy: A psycholinguistic analysis of beginning reading in kindergarten and first grade children*. Unpublished doctoral dissertation, University of Arizona.

Heath, S.B. (1982). What no bedtime story means: Narrative skills at home and school. *Language in Society,* **11,** 49–76.

Heath, S.B. (1983). *Ways with words: Language, life, and work in communities and classrooms.* Cambridge: Cambridge University Press.

Hoff, S. (1957). *Sammy the seal.* New York: Harper & Row.

Holdaway, D. (1979). *The foundations of literacy.* Sydney: Ashton Scholastic.

Lesgold, A.M., Resnick, L.G., Roth, S.F., and Hammond, K.L. (1981, April). *Patterns of learning to read: A longitudinal study.* Paper presented at the Biennial Meeting of the Society for Research in Child Development, Boston.

Luria, A.R. (1983). The development of writing in the child. In M. Martlew (ed), *The psychology of written language: Developmental and educational perspectives.* New York: John Wiley.

Martlew, M. (1983). Problems and difficulties: Cognitive and communicative aspects of writing development. In M. Martlew (ed), *The psychology of written language: Developmental and educational perspectives.* New York: John Wiley.

Mason, J.M., and Allen, J.B. (1986). A review of emergent literacy with implications for research and practice in reading. In E.Z. Rothkopf (ed), *Review of research in education,* **13,** Washington, D.C.: American Educational Association.

McCormick, C.E., and Mason, J.M. (1986). Intervention procedures for increasing preschool children's interest in and knowledge about reading. In W.H. Teale and E. Sulzby (eds), *Emergent literacy: Writing and reading.* Norwood, N.J.: Ablex.

McDermott, R.P. (1976). *Kids make sense: An ethnographic account of interactional management of success and failure in one first-grade classroom.* Unpublished doctoral dissertation, Stanford University.

Ninio, A., and Bruner, J. (1978). The achievement and antecedents of labelling. *Journal of Child Language,* **5,** 1–15.

Ninio, A. (1980). Picture-book reading in mother-infant dyads belonging to two subgroups in Israel. *Child Development,* **51,** 587–590.

Ninio, A. (1983). Joint book reading as a multiple vocabulary acquisition device. *Developmental Psychology,* **19,** 445–451.

Otto, B. (1985). *Evidence of emergent reading behaviors in young children's interactions with favorite storybooks.* Unpublished doctoral dissertation, Northwestern University.

Papandropoulou, I. (1978). An experimental study of children's ideas about language. In A. Sinclair, R.J. Jarvella and W.J.M. Levelt (eds), *The child's conception of language.* New York: Springer-Verlag.

Pellegrini, A.D. (1985). Relations between preschool children's play and literate behavior. In Galda, L. and Pellegrini, A.D. (eds), *Play, language and stories: The development of children's literate behavior.* Norwood, N.J.: Ablex.

Pellegrini, A.D., Brody, G., and Sigel, I. (1986). Parents' bookreading habits with their children. *Journal of Educational Psychology,* **77,** 332–340.

Robinson, F. (1983). *Parents' descriptions of young children's behaviors toward favorite storybooks.* Unpublished M.A. thesis, Northwestern University.

Robinson, F., and Sulzby, E. (1984). Parents, children and 'favorite' books: An interview study. *National Reading Conference Yearbook,* **33,** 54–59.

Rossman, F.P. (1979, November). *Young children's understanding of graphic lines as letters, words, and pictures.* Paper presented at the annual conference of the National Association for the Education of Young Children, Atlanta.

Sendak (1963). *Where the wild things are.* New York: Harper & Row.

Snow, C.E. (1982, March). *Literacy and language: Relationships during the preschool years.* Paper presented at the American Educational Research Association, New York.

Snow, C.E., and Ninio, A. (1986). The contracts of literacy: What children learn from learning to read books. In W.H. Teale and E. Sulzby (eds), *Emergent literacy: Writing and reading*. Norwood, N.J.: Ablex.

Sulzby, E. (1981). *Kindergarteners begin to read their own compositions: Beginning readers' developing knowledges about written language project*. Final report to the Research foundation of the National Council of Teachers of English. Evanston, 111.: Northwestern University.

Sulzby, E. (1982a, December). *A scale for judging emergent reading of favorite storybooks*. Paper presented at the 32nd National Reading Conference, Clearwater Beach, Florida.

Sulzby, E. (1982b). Oral and written mode adaptations in stories by kindergarten children. *Journal of Reading Behavior*, **14**, 51–59.

Sulzby, E. (1983). *Beginning readers' developing knowledges about written language*. Final report to the National Institute of Education (NIE-G-80-0176). Evanston, 111.: Northwestern University.

Sulzby, E. (1985a). Children's emergent reading of favorite storybooks: A developmental study. *Reading Research Quarterly*, **20**, 458–481.

Sulzby, E. (1985b). Kindergarteners as writers and readers. In M. Farr (ed), *Advances in writing research, Vol. 1: Children's early writing development*. Norwood, N.J.: Ablex.

Sulzby, E. (1986). Writing and reading: Signs of oral and written language organization in the young child. In W.H. Teale and E. Sulzby (eds), *Emergent Literacy: Writing and reading*. Norwood, N.J.: Ablex.

Sulzby, E. (1987). Children's development of prosodic distinctions in telling and dictating modes. In A. Matsuhashi (ed.), *Writing in real time: Modelling production processes*. (pp. 133–160). Norwood, N.J.: Ablex.

Sulzby, E., Barnhart, J.E., and Hieshima, J. (in press). Forms of writing and rereading from writing: A preliminary report. In J. Mason (ed.), *The Reading/Writing Connection*. Boston: Allyn and Bacon.

Sulzby, E., and Otto, B. (1982). 'Text' as an object of metalinguistic knowledge: A study in literacy development. *First Language*, **3**, 181–199.

Sulzby, E., and Teale, W.H. (1985). Writing development in early childhood. *Educational Horizons*, **64**, 8–12.

Sulzby, E., and Teale, W.H. (1987). *Young children's storybook reading: Longitudinal study of parent-child interaction and children's independent functioning*. Final report to the Spencer Foundation.

Taylor, D. (1983). *Family literacy: The social context of learning to read and write*. Exeter, N.H.: Heinemann.

Taylor, D. (1986). Creating family story: 'Matthew! We're going to have a ride!'. In W.H. Teale and E. Sulzby (eds), *Emergent literacy: Writing and reading*. Norwood, N.J.: Ablex.

Taylor, M. (1975). *Henry explores the mountains*. New York: Atheneum.

Teale, W.H. (1981). Parents reading to their children: What studies of early readers tell us. *Language Arts*, **55**, 902–910.

Teale, W.H. (1984). Reading to young children: Its significance in literacy development. In H. Goelman, A. Oberg and F. Smith (eds), *Awakening to literacy*. Exeter, N.H.: Heinemann.

Teale, W.H. (1986). The beginnings of literacy. *Dimensions*, **13**, 5–8.

Teale, W.H. (1986). Home background and young children's literacy development. In W.H. Teale and E. Sulzby (eds), *Emergent literacy: Writing and reading*. Norwood, N.J.: Ablex.

Teale, W.H. (in press). Emergent literacy: Reading and writing development in early childhood. *National Reading Conference Yearbook,* **36.**

Teale, W.H., Martinez, M.G., and Glass, W.L. (1987). Describing classroom storybook reading. In D. Bloome (ed), *Learning to use literacy in educational settings.* Norwood, N.J.: Ablex.

Teale, W.H., and Sulzby, E. (1986). *Emergent literacy: Writing and reading.* Norwood, N.J.: Ablex.

Teale, W.H., and Sulzby, E. (1987). The cultural practice of storybook reading: Its effects on young children's literacy development. In D.A. Wagner (ed), *The future of literacy in a changing world.* New York: Pergamon.

Vygotsky, L.S. (1978). *Mind in society: The development of higher psychological processes.* Cambridge, Mass.: Harvard University Press.

Zion, G. (1958). *No roses for Harry.* New York: Harper and Row.

Psychological Bases for Early Education
Edited by A.D. Pellegrini
© 1988 John Wiley & Sons Ltd.

CHAPTER 4

# Children's Oral and Written Language

MARGARET MARTLEW

> I shall begin with a premise that is already familiar: that the medium of exchange
> in which education is conducted—language—can never be neutral, that it imposes
> a point of view not only about the world to which it refers but toward the use of
> mind in respect of this world.
>
> (J. Bruner, *Actual minds, possible worlds*
> *1986, p.121)*

Interest in oral language has a long tradition, stretching from early diary studies (Leopold, 1939; Taine, 1877), through the normative studies fashionable in the middle of the century (McCarthy, 1954), to the variety of investigations that have used experimental or observational means to investigate hypotheses in more recent times. From all these studies we have a massive amount of data about children's grammatical development and how formal changes in structure are interlinked with communication skills and the expression of meaning. This wealth of evidence has made possible the generation of numerous theories. These have differential biases to linguistic, cognitive and social explanations to account for how and why children acquire spoken language (see Aitkinson, 1982, for a critical review). In contrast, we have a very limited amount of descriptive data to work on when it comes to considering the acquisition of written language. When we come to define differences, or what we mean by literacy, particularly in the stages of emergent literacy, we have both a less rich literature to draw on and a less clearly defined notion of what we are looking at or for, despite the recent surge of interest in this area.

Oral and written language are obviously related but the category boundaries for establishing and defining the relative importance of the differences between them remain somewhat fuzzy. Debates on these distinctions often begin from different standpoints. Snow (1983), for instance, defines literacy from a contextual stance, as skills directly related to print, while oral language is 'simply all forms of spoken communication'. On the other hand, Tannen (1985) talks about ways of using language such as 'involvement features' that can occur in either spoken or written discourse. To take a simplistic approach, obviously written language does not have to be written. It can be dictated just as oral addresses can be written (Gould, 1978). Whether 'involvement' discourse is adequate for conveying writers' intended meaning other than within a limited context is a different question relating to what fits the communicative situation.

Vachek (1973) highlighted the functional norms of speech and writing. Both serve to communicate but appropriately fit different situations. Speech is flexible, transient, immediate. What is meant by the speaker is more important than what is said, and meaning is given by paralinguistic cues and context as well as by the words used. Generally, written language is more abstract and isolating (Vygotsky, 1962). Readers are generally in a different place, at a different time, from when the text was written. They are often unknown to the writer so in addition to not sharing the immediate context, they also may not have much shared world experience. The writer has to create a rapport with the reader through the text, taking account in a very abstract sense of what can and what cannot be assumed as shared knowledge.

Children are much more conscious of learning to write than learning to speak, largely because for them, writing is produced indirectly by a tool that makes marks which signify speech sounds. They have to learn how to manipulate pencils to make recognizable strokes that reproduce standard letter forms and interpretable spelling. Spelling, punctuation, etc., need eventually to conform to rule-governed conventions. Many children acquire some of these skills before they go to school and in the process they are learning ways of using language to talk about language. They have a basis for early education, not only in being able to use pencils and possibly being able to produce letters and words, but they also have concepts about print and about 'literate' uses of language.

The question of what we are looking at or for in written language varies in relation to the stage of development. The purpose of this chapter is to consider oral and written language as a basis for early education. Children all over the world, in a variety of cultural backgrounds and home environments, acquire spoken language. Spoken language is universal, as are its characteristic features. In all spoken languages, small, meaningless units of sounds combine to make meaningful words. This is not the case with written language. There is not a universal direction for writing script, and some written languages are not intrinsically related to spoken forms. There are more illiterate than literate societies and many people in literate societies acquire only minimal literacy skills at school, some even leave school without being able to read or write.

When children enter school, they are not expected to be able to read and write but they are assumed to have a fairly good command of basic language skills. Despite differing circumstances children do seem to achieve these basic linguistic and communicative goals. There are, however, differences in children's ability to use language and in particular to use language which is going to make it easy for them to adapt to the educational system (Rice, 1983). These issues will be considered by looking at what develops in children's oral language, what kind of environments are conducive to expanding children's use of language and how this affects and interacts with the development of written language.

When discussing the development of written language, illustrative material from a single case study of writing development will be used. This is taken from videotaped observations made of my niece Ruth from when she was 15 months old to the present, when she is just over 5 years and attending school. The observations were made in both her home and mine. I found there were many advantages to being a distant, yet familiar observer. Ruth's mother has an MA in Librarianship and a keen interest in children's literature and she took part in most of the recording sessions.

## THE ACQUISITION OF ORAL LANGUAGE

Children learn language in social contexts and when they learn it they use it as a tool to express meaning, to refer to objects and events and to take part in conversational exchanges. Each of these levels, the syntactic, semantic and pragmatic, is interlinked and each contributes to the development of the others. They will be looked at separately to consider factors affecting their development and their relative significance for coping with language-related tasks in school.

### Syntactic development

Structural linguistic knowledge branches out from other kinds of knowledge established in infancy but has within its own development a precursor period, a transition stage, followed by the emergence of basic competence. These progressions are reflected in other aspects of both oral and written language.

Single constituent utterances begin to emerge towards the end of the first year but it is not until the middle or latter end of the second year that children start to combine words into two and then multiword combinations. Many children have their first encounters with books when they are beginning to produce single words. Dore (1985) characterizes four stages as the child progresses from proto-communicative signals to being able to combine two words. These are interesting because they have parallels with the emergence of written language and observations made on Ruth begin in the first stage. Initial proto-communicative signals are often phonologically idiosyncratic in sound. As these sounds are used consistently in relation to situation, parents can

usually interpret their intended meaning. The child then progresses to approx-
imations to conventional words, which are less affect-centred but not yet used
in a clear referential manner. In the third stage the child begins to use
denotative symbols, word-like forms based on adult language which can be
used for a variety of functions. During this stage there is a rapid explosion in the
rate of acquisition of new words. Finally the child shows the ability to predicate
comments about topics and moves into being able to combine two words.

After the combination of two utterances, children seem to be well on the
way to 'cracking the linguistic code' when new forms are consolidated and
rapid advances made in establishing structural rules for ordering words and
adding morphemes and auxiliaries. The sequential ordering of three or more
constituents brings the first complete syntactic clause structures. There is
increasing complexity in the acquisition and use of grammatical features up to
the age of 5 years. Children progress from using simple constructions, for
example, 'Mummy break cup'/'That no dog', to more complex constructions
using auxiliaries and conditionals. Wells (1985a) gives a detailed description
of the syntactic and functional changes that take place over this period. By
the age of 5 years, children who have reached what Wells classifies as levels
9/10, will be producing such forms as 'They shouldn't have put that purple
in should they' (S+aux+neg+aux=V+X) or 'Don't you know why it did'
(aux+neg+S+V+X).

Although there are differences in the time at which children begin to use
word combinations and attach appropriate morphology etc., the sequence of
this development follows a fairly consistent pattern. Differences do occur as
has been demonstrated by Slobin (1973) but these result from differences in the
organization of different languages. When Brown (1973) examined the acquisition of fourteen grammatical morphemes, he could support explanations for
the order of their emergence in terms of both syntactic or semantic complexity
but found no basis at all for an environmental explanation.

With qualifications, Wells (1985a) also finds strong evidence to support
complexity as determining the order in which features emerge, though children
vary in the age at which they acquire new features. Wells draws up what he
terms a 'tentative' table of age norms, constructed from his data. He uses these
measures to investigate possible environmental influences on language development, taking frequency of use by adults, complexity of items and an
interaction of the two as his measures. He then proposes an interactional
explanation. He depicts the relationships between relative linguistic complexity and input frequency as one of reciprocal causality. He suggests that parents
encode in their speech the meanings, functions and forms that their children
already produce or they think they understand. What children learn, therefore,
is to some extent affected by the relative frequency of features that they hear.
There is a tendency for features to show an increase in relative frequency
slightly before they are used by children which could indeed reflect the fine

tuning of parents to their child's comprehension abilities. Cross (1978), for example, found correlations between adults' speech and children's comprehension skills.

A great deal has been written of the way mothers adapt their speech to their children's developmental level (Snow and Ferguson, 1977). 'Motherese', by its simplification, heightened pitch, adjustments, etc., can focus children's attention on a variety of features (Conti-Ramsden and Friel-Patti, 1984; Cross, 1978; Cross, Nienhuys, and Kirkman, 1983). Mothers need to be sensitive however and not overload children with too much information. Nelson, Denniger, Bonvillian, Kaplan, and Baker (1984), for instance, found the most effective adjustments in mothers' speech were simple rather than complex. Children showed higher syntactic growth when they heard more simple rather than complex recasts or continuations of their own utterances. Children have to relate form to meaning and too much syntactic or semantic change in the language they hear may deter rather than enhance their abilities to analyse, consolidate and progress.

Is syntactic precocity important as a basis for early education? Relationships have been demonstrated between the complexity of linguistic structures and the use of abstract verbs which seem to be associated with the acquisition of reading skills (Torrance and Olson, 1984) but further investigations are needed to elaborate on the rationale for this relationship. Kroll (1983) found only a weak relationship between the complexity of oral syntax children were using before going to school and their success in writing at age 9 years. Parental interest in literacy was a more powerful predictor.

Syntax is a tool. It provides children with an increasingly powerful and more flexible system for making themselves understood. They do not learn language for the sake of acquiring syntax, however, they acquire syntax to express meaning. Wells (1985b) claims that semantic and pragmatic distinctions emerge before syntactic expressions are available to children. What seems important is the use to which language is put in context (Bruner, 1983) to provide children with opportunities for consolidating relationships between form and meaning.

## The development of semantic and pragmatic knowledge

Structural linguistic knowledge represents only one level of language learning and its acquisition is facilitated by concepts acquired in the pre-verbal period (Bates, Benigi, Bretherton, Camaoni, and Volterra 1979; Bruner, 1973, 1973). While acquiring linguistic knowledge, children are also extending their ability to refer, to express meaning and to do this in a socially appropriate way. The ways in which mothers encourage the development of meaning and communicative skills even before language is a time when the seeds can be sown for the development of literate uses of language.

Many of the supportive techniques that mothers use in the pre-verbal period extend into later language learning and some have particular significance for the acquisition of literacy. From the earliest days of a baby's life parents encourage him to exchange shared meanings and throughout the period of infancy mothers and infants work together to achieve communicative goals. Mothers have various strategies for helping their children to achieve shared meaning which have obvious implications for the ways in which written language can be acquired, although some parents are more effective than others.

(1) They provide scaffolding frameworks (Bruner, 1973; Kaye, 1982) for structuring their infants' role. Initially mothers do most of the work, taking on the baby's role as well as their own, imputing meaning that the baby could not possibly intend. This is similar to the interpretations mothers give to early scribbles. Gradually as the infant gains autonomy mothers withdraw their support and demand more progressive responses from their children.

(2) They establish predictable routines and give contingent reponses and by doing so help their infants to realize the consequences of their own actions. This is very evident in home-based literacy contexts which will be discussed later.

(3) They are sensitive or, at least, adapt to developmental level, using cues from their infants to establish and expand their interactions and the infants' skills. Again this is apparent in specifically literate contexts, particularly where drawing and writing provide the focus of interest.

(4) Mothers can progressively draw their infants into using more conventional signals, encouraging elaboration and complexity of expression as symbolic communication emerges. This too can be seen in mothers' responses to their children's drawing and the rule-governed conventions of written language.

Infants then are learning a lot about communication and how to refer and express meaning before they have language. One of their most significant achievements, particularly when both written as well as oral language is being discussed, is the acquisition of reference. Referring is a communicative event where the speaker signals a topic that he intends another to become aware of. The ability to share a joint focus of attention, an essential prerequisite for referring, is established quite early (Scaife and Bruner, 1975). Early reference is a negotiated exchange where the mother plays an important role in helping to focus attention, establish routines, encourage conventional deictic gestures and give labels. This generally takes place in well-established routines where there is a purposeful exchange, often a game situation created by the mother (Ratner and Bruner, 1978) or in book reading contexts (Ninio and Bruner, 1978). These are situations where relationships are formed between sign and significate. As Bruner (1983) points out, these are social procedures to ensure that the ways in which the sign and significate are linked also overlap with the way they are used by others.

Reference and referential communication provide a useful focus for drawing out relationships between semantic and pragmatic features of language acquisition, particularly as to how they relate to the acquisition of literate language. In 'naturalistic' settings, young children's ability as competent communicators has been well attested (Garvey, 1984; Ochs and Schiefflin, 1983; Waterson and Snow, 1978). They are known to be able to use many of the features present in motherese. Their use of language reflects a realization of the needs of different listeners as has been demonstrated by their ability to take account of age differences, as well as adopting 'role' voices (Martlew, Connolly, and Macleod, 1978; Sachs and Devin, 1976; Shatz and Gelman, 1973). They can change the information content to suit the listener's knowledge of a situation (Maratsos, 1976; Menig-Peterson, 1975). They can also distinguish between old and new information as demonstrated by their use of the definite and indefinite article (Maratsos, 1973) and are able to describe the sequence of everyday events (Nelson and Greundel, 1979).

These are just some of their many skills and seem to flaunt Piaget's (1926) suggestion that children are egocentric in their communication. However, support for Piaget comes from studies of children's referential communication (Glucksberg, Krauss, and Higgins, 1975). Experimental studies which deprive children of a shared context and force them to rely purely on verbal exchanges to interpret meaning show children as either egocentric or failing to make the necessary selection of criterial features to make themselves understood (Asher and Oden, 1976). Young children rely heavily on context and tend to interpret what they perceive as the function of the message rather than the semantic content (Donaldson, 1984). When they do process an utterance at the semantic level, salient features in the proximate environment usually provide a focus for joint attention (Keenan and Klein, 1974).

Context need not necessarily mean the immediate physical context but can include children's mental representations. These too can interfere with their interpretations of the semantic contexts of utterances by creating expectations about meaning based on previous experience. Changing the context to reflect the child's experience, and framing questions to suit the child's needs, can elicit successful responses to tasks similar to those used to demonstrate egocentricity (Donaldson, Grieve, and Pratt, 1983). However, even with the ingenious supporting techniques devised in some of the experiments reported by Donaldson and her co-workers, children still failed at times to interpret the questions asked. They converted them instead to what they computed as an intended meaning based on their assumptions and presuppositions. For instance, when shown four cars, three of which were in garages and asked 'Are all the cars in the garages?', pre-school children answered 'Yes'. They converted the question into a simpler one 'Are all the garages full?' (Donaldson, 1978). Analysing the semantic content of utterances is an abstract task that requires the child to pay attention specifically to what the utterance means, not what the immediacy of context or prior experience suggests.

### 'Literate' dimensions of oral language: a basis for early education?

Olson (1983), in discussing the ways in which children use context to interpret utterances, would describe the children's responses to Donaldson's question as reflecting casual meaning. The children are converting the semantic structure of the utterance to fit the context of their 'possible' world. Meaning, he proposes, has both a semantic structure and a context. Young children tend to produce a gloss of the semantic structure of utterances to fit their own experience and expectations. He cites an example of pre-school children who, when told that 'John forced Mary to eat the worm' and then asked 'Did Mary eat the worm?' replied 'No. Nobody eats worms'. The children were taking the context as invariant and changing the semantic structure to accord with their 'possible world.'

He contrasts casual with literal meaning, where the semantic structure remains invariant and the context is altered to fit with the properties stipulated by the semantic structure. There is a developmental progression as children become aware that meaning can reside in 'the very words' of utterances, divorced from context. Children begin to see that the possible world is not simply invariant and that they can add information to it if it is not compatible with the context or what they know. They can then progress to both revising their possible world and imagining worlds stipulated by the semantic structure.

This approach links the semantic and pragmatic aspects of oral language development very closely to the acquisition of literacy skill. Olson (1984) claims that becoming literate is only indirectly related to reading and writing. It does however involve the knowledge that 'language exists as an artefact, has a structure, is composed of grammatical units including words and sentences, has a meaning somewhat independent of the meaning intended by the speaker and, perhaps most importantly, that its structures may be referred to by means of a metalanguage' (p. 186).

A study by Barnes, Guttreund, Satterly, and Wells (1983) impinges on this context-independent way of thinking, showing its effect on later achievement in school. Looking at data from the Bristol project, they found that the children showing rapid development in their rate of language learning had more utterances addressed to them that were contingent on their own meanings and activities. This child-focused approach allows the child scope for working from his own knowledge base so that he can consolidate and match what he knows and attach what is new to what is established. Expanding the content of previous utterances, adding new information to topics, asking for clarifications, etc., are some of the ways mothers achieve this (Cross, 1978). Directive speech, where mothers control the topic, is less conducive to aiding development (Nelson, 1973). There is more strain put on the child to match an existing representation onto a new one. Directive approaches are likely to have consequences for active mastery or passive responsiveness in the way children are able to acquire new competencies. Hartmann and Haavind (1981) for instance found, on a game instruction task, that mothers who used an 'informing' approach, using justifications, explanations, choices between alternatives, showed a high correlation with their children's active mastery of the task.

Questions can be raised, however, about what kinds of accelerated language learning are most useful for achievement in school. Barnes *et al.* (1983) tested the children who showed rapid language development when they were in the first term in school. These tests, and teacher assessments, predicted that some would be less likely to succeed than others (there was also a high correlation evident between ability and social class). Tests carried out two years later confirmed these earlier predictions. The children who found difficulty in adapting to school tended to be confused in the organized question/answer routines common to classrooms where information is generally elicited for its own sake, not because of its immediate relevance to any practical activity. The more abstract qualities of language use seemed to be lacking in these children, despite their initial advanced rate of language learning.

The importance of the way language is acquired in the pre-school period is all too evident. A similar effect is shown in the descriptions given by children in their first year at school of a film they had seen (Michaels and Collins, 1984). The children fell into two groups; literate-style speakers who used complex syntactic constructions and lexicalization, and oral-style speakers who relied on special intonation patterns, using paralinguistic cues and context. When the task was repeated with the children in the fourth grade, the children in the literate-style group wrote unambiguous prose whereas the other group failed to compensate for connections that could only be made in oral discourse.

Understanding is best fostered in contexts which are already familiar and meaningful to children. Children who do well at school have often learnt something about written language while acquiring spoken language (Kroll, 1983; Wells, 1985b). They have learnt from parents who have provided them with an environment where literacy learning is functional, purposeful and motivating. Their knowledge is usually acquired in well-established routines, where negotiated meaning has already evolved a predictable structure. When parents share picture book reading with their children, for example, there is a focus for developing oral language, particularly semantic and pragmatic features such as encouraging reference, negotiating exchanges, extending vocabulary, etc. It also provides a situation for the emergence of concepts about literate language, as discussed by Olson (1984). This can begin very early in a child's development, as is illustrated by the following extracts from Ruth 'reading' when she was at the single word stage.

There are many features present even in these short extracts which reflect points already made, and more besides. In the first passage, Ruth reacts to pictures as though they *are* the objects they represent. They evoke the same patterns of responses, particularly affective responses, as do the real objects that they depict. Ruth can however extend beyond the book to make denotative comparisons with real objects. It is also worth noting that she chose her own book and sitting position. She sat in front of her mother and turned the pages herself, thereby maximizing eye contact and shared social enjoyment.

### Ruth aged 16 months

MOTHER: Spot's found the crow.

RUTH: (*Looks up from page to corner of the room where there is a stuffed crow*)

MOTHER: Yes, that's like our crow isn't it?
(*Ruth turns the page*)
There's Spot. He's in the pond.

RUTH: Down—whish, whish. (*Makes downward movement with her hand*)

MOTHER: Down—he falls down in the pond with the fish.

RUTH: Awh (*Bends down, kisses the picture of the fish*)

MOTHER: Oh, poor fish, isn't he?
Spot falls in and gets all wet—look at him he's all wet. Poor Spot.

RUTH: (*Turns page, lists flap on page*)

MOTHER: Who's that?

RUTH: Mummy.

MOTHER: Yes. Spot's mummy.

It is obvious that a lot of opportunities for learning are being presented in this situation. Ruth's mother focuses her attention and asks for labels. Ruth gives her own spontaneous contributions which add a comment to the previous topic. In a later session the interactions have been expanded. Ruth is now taking the questioner role, she is imitating her mother in a generative manner. People and objects are now there to be labelled, even though she knows the labels and knows her mother knows them. She can introduce jokes in the context of a well-established routine reading from a familiar book. Interestingly, in the same session she looked at an alphabet book and her responses here are very different. She produced no dialogue, turned the pages of the book (in reverse) and on each page she pointed first to the word, waited for her mother to give a verbal label, looked at the picture and then turned the page. She was controlling a new learning experience in her own way. She is moving to a new kind of understanding from the basis of a meaningful context and beginning to look for new relationships.

### Ruth aged 18 months

| | |
|---|---|
| RUTH: | Oo dere? (*Points*) |
| MOTHER: | That's a man taking his ball for a walk. |
| RUTH: | Ball. |
| MOTHER: | Um. |
| RUTH: | (*Turns several pages, looks briefly at them before passing to next, then pauses at one*) |
| MOTHER: | That's a girl on a swing. (*Ruth looks at her mother*) Going backwards and forwards. (*Mother makes movements*) (*Ruth watches then looks back at her book.*) What's that? |
| RUTH: | (*Points*) ish, ish. (*fish*) (*Points to dogs*) Oo dere? |
| MOTHER: | What are the dogs doing? |
| RUTH: | (*Makes growling noise*) |
| MOTHER: | Yes. |
| RUTH: | (*Turns page*) Eeow. |
| MOTHER: | Cat in the tree. |
| RUTH: | (*Turns page*) Oo dere? |
| MOTHER: | That's Mrs Smith. |
| RUTH: | Oo dere? (*Points to fur collar*) |
| MOTHER: | That's her fox fur collar. |
| RUTH: | (*Looks at mother and smiles*) Eeow. |
| MOTHER: | (*Laughs*) |

### Alphabet Book

| | |
|---|---|
| RUTH: | (*Points to word*) |
| MOTHER: | That's umbrellas for when it rains. (*Ruth looks at the picture*) |
| RUTH: | (*Turns page, points to word*) |
| MOTHER: | That's tractor. (*Ruth looks at the picture*) |
| RUTH: | (*Turns the page, points*) |
| MOTHER: | Sun. (*Ruth looks at the picture, turns the page, points*) Runners. |
| RUTH: | (*Looks very carefully at this picture of several men in running shorts*) |
| MOTHER: | All those men in shorts running. |
| RUTH: | (*Points to the word again*) |
| MOTHER: | Runners. R is for runners. |

Ruth has well-established book routines even though she is only just emerging from the one word stage. She is also acquiring notions about the difference between pictures and print and taking the initiative in expressing an interest in print. Her mother follows the lead Ruth gives and responds to each book differently.

Book routines however, do not inevitably evoke universal patterns of responses from mothers. Teale (1984) points out that there can be many different uses made of book reading contexts with different outcomes. Heath (1982), for example, found differences in two groups of mothers she looked at, one who were teachers, the other working-class. The group of teachers, when reading books with their children, tended to extend the context of the book beyond the event itself, asking for more affective and 'why' explanations. Although doing well initially in school, the working-class children experienced increasing difficulties as they moved through school. This was also reflected in their responses to 'why' rather than 'what' type of explanations of what they had read. These findings are similar to those of Ninio (1980) who found differences in the formats of interactions between two social class groups in Israel, which was reflected in the productive vocabulary of the two groups of younger children.

Indeed, using labelling techniques to extend interactions and functional uses of language is seen as one of the major outcomes of shared book reading and an important facilitator of language learning. What is often conceived of as the mother's role as an almost inevitable 'labeller' is not, however, a universal phenomenon. Studying the Kauli people in Papua New Guinea, Schiefflin and Cochrane-Smith (1984) found these people do not value labelling in their culture. Mothers neither elicit names as part of conversational interactions nor do they instruct their children, either in the initial, or later stages of language development. Schiefflin and Cochrane-Smith were able to make observations on the only mother in the village, out of all those attending an adult literacy course, who looked at books with her child. The mother's reactions and interactions were very different from those expected in a literate society. This was largely because she considered the activity 'to no purpose' which indeed, in a way, it was, for literacy had no function in this society. However, the child, unlike other children in the village, began to elicit the names of household objects and was even on occasion able to draw her mother into interactive sequences based on these elicited names. The initiations came always from the child with the mother generally trying to distract her.

Living in an oral society has consequences for the purposes for which language can be used. Basic words, such as 'word', do not exist in some non-literate cultures, neither does the concept of using the exact words in repeating utterances (Finnegan, 1970; Goody, 1977; Lord, 1960). From literate parents children can acquire words and concepts for referring to language and this metalinguistic awareness has effects on children's developing competence. Knowledge of words such as *sentence, letter, sound,* has been found to be related to children's progress in learning to read (Reid, 1966; Downing and Leong, 1982). Interested literate parents treat language as an object that can be taught, particularly where the focus of the interaction is directly related to such contexts. This encourages children's interest in recognizing that words have meaning and that language has a structure that can be discussed. Gleitman, Gleitman, and Shipley (1972) for instance, cite the question of a 4-year-old who asked 'Mummy, is it AN A-dult or A NUHdult?' In a similar vein, Ruth, also aged 4 years, reported the following incident to me. Her mother had told her brother to 'Go and tell Dad off.' Jack (2 years 8 months) had gone to his father and said 'Off, off'. Ruth's comment on this, which she found very amusing, was 'He's too little. He doesn't know about words like we do.'

Whatever kind of interaction takes place, parents provide models for their children, they create the worlds which their children inhabit in their early years. The objects they present, the people the child meets, the kinds of interactions that take place are all the child has on which to base his hypotheses and influence his ways of learning. Children learn a great deal from their parents, whether parents teach implicitly or explicitly, whether they have deliberate child-focused interactions or not.

In drawing together aspects of children's environments likely to be most conducive to optimizing their use of language as a basis for early education, there are several points to be considered. When mothers positively assist their child's development they have not usually explicitly thought out or contrived their methods. Some mothers are not good at optimizing their children's experience, some are not even interested in doing so. What does seem most facilitating for linguistic and cognitive development in the pre-school years is an affective, sensitive social relationship where mothers draw their children on, by assisting the child to work out his own means for achieving goals. Dore (1985) proposes a set of procedures operating in mother–child dialogues that reflect in general terms how this can be achieved. These are what he calls 'accountability work' which are the 'projecting, orienting and negotiating of forms and functions at several levels' (p. 44). Adults systematically project possibilities of what to do next and introject conventional forms and functions. Affective interactions encourage intimate and reciprocal adjustments where contingent behaviour represents negotiation on several levels of meaning. The sensitive mother will only ask more of her child when she knows her child is competent to give progressive responses. It is requiring of the child the best behaviour he can give, not demanding what is beyond him or of no interest to him, what Ninio and Bruner (1978) refer to as 'upping the ante'.

Children who have benefited from this optimizing kind of interaction are likely to have well-developed skills in all levels of oral language use and be quite advanced in their concepts about written language. Literacy is a difficult topic for a child to sustain a self-generated interest in. All the children referred to in the literature as self-taught, or generating their own questions, have obviously had a lot of parental support to motivate an interest in stories and reading, drawing and writing, and all other print-focused interactions. Children who already have mental representations of 'literate' language will be better able to approach contexts outside the home.

## THE DEVELOPMENT OF WRITTEN LANGUAGE

Written language, unlike spoken language, is not a universal phenomenon, neither does it have universal characteristics. There are vast differences in writing systems which range from pictographic to alphabetic (Diringer, 1962; Gelb, 1963). There is also no universal direction in which languages are written and read. Some languages are written in linear horizontal sequences, others go up and down the page. Western writing imposes one type of arbitrary convention, others impose different constraints. When Clay (1975) asked non-reading children to 'read with your finger' she found they would move in any direction. The children did not seem to show any tendency to produce one pattern more than any other.

The development of writing in children reflects some of the changes seen in the evolution of writing systems from pictographic to alphabetic. Pictographic writing is a representational language where signs closely resemble what they represent. Pictographs do not imply unique identification of spoken units. Haas (1976), in talking about the evolution of writing, claims that writing had to *replace* the mimicry of the external object by that other and purely structural mimicry of a fully developed language (p. 161). In logographic/ideographic writing the signs have become more abstract and formalized. Individual characters stand for individual words, as in Chinese, but these also are not intrinsically related to a specific spoken form. This has advantages in that characters can be read by people speaking different languages but it does mean that each symbol has to be learnt. Syllabic language is a sound-based system where each character represents a symbol. The great legacy of the Greeks was the invention of the alphabet where individual letters can represent sounds. This means from a small set of letters an infinite number of combinations can be generated with depict the sounds of the language.

The development of writing traces some of these evolutionary changes. Children's early writing, for instance, is in a sense pictographic, their early reading is generally of a gestalt, whole word strategy and not until they can build from individual letter forms and recognize sound/symbol correspondence do writing skills emerge in children using alphabetic systems.

There are few data on the acquisition of writing compared with that on the development of speech or even on reading. Much of what there is traces the progression of children over the ages of 4 and 5 years (Bissex, 1980; Clay, 1975; Ferreiro and Teberesky, 1982; Sulzby, 1985). Illustrations from Ruth's development show that many of the changes noted in these older children can emerge earlier as part of shared exchanges where written language is acquired with spoken language. The observations made on Ruth and her mother show how a supportive and interested home environment, where literacy is an opportunity for shared social activity, can encourage pleasure in the acquisition and development of writing alongside oral language development.

For young children on the point of entering school, writing primarily means producing visible signs. Much of their attention is focused on acquiring the technical skills for making their written expressions intelligible. These early technical skills, therefore, are the ones which represent 'writing'. They are a tangible new skill which many children appear to enjoy acquiring, particularly when it has provided a focus for shared activities with their mothers. A firm grasp of what is involved in manipulating symbols, generating sound–sign correspondence and automatizing these abilities provides a facilitating base which will free the child later to devote processing capacity to higher compositional skills.

## Children's notions of the functions of written language

Children already have notions about the functions of writing when they enter school. They know that it can be used to communicate; they have seen parents receive letters; they have often themselves sent and received invitations and many children can read a few shop signs, road names, etc. Children may also realize something of the permanency of writing (De Gòes and Martlew, 1984) and that it can be used as a mnemonic (Luria, 1983). Young children can also show an awareness of writing as 'visible language', by realizing what marks on a page can signify and they can show metalinguistic skills in being able to talk about these. Written language can also be connected with early narratives and the fictionalizing of experience, even with summarization skills. These abilities can develop early and be apparent in children entering school, as will be discussed below.

### 1. The use of metalanguage, and the acquisition of concepts about print

In modern literate societies it is quite difficult for children to avoid print. It surrounds them: signs on shops, programmes on television, numbers on houses, etc. Children's awareness of what these symbols mean develops at different rates according to the kind of support given in the home. Children do not need to be able to read, however, to have hypotheses about print. Ferreiro and Teberesky (1982) studied the criteria used by non-reading children, aged from 4 to 6 years, for making assessments of forms on cards, as to whether they were letters, numbers, punctuation marks; whether they could be read, etc. Interestingly, the children's criteria for selection followed similar patterns, though these patterns were different from what a literate person would use. The majority of the children, when assessing cards with varying numbers of letters, words or numbers on, adopted a minimum number principle. They usually chose cards with at least three to four letters. Most of the children would not select these if the letters were repeated. A few needed to find something they recognized, while print as opposed to cursive writing generated differing hypotheses. Not surprisingly, letters and numbers were initially confused but soon recognized as belonging to different categories. Presumably the limited number of ideographs a child has to associate with the label *number* as opposed to *letter* facilitates this differentiation. The names for letters, numbers, written conventions such as punctuation marks have to be given to children, concepts about them can come quite spontaneously from the child (Gleitman, Gleitman and Shipley, 1972). Coordinating and systemizing knowledge relating to print is part of what the child brings to creating his system of written language.

These concepts can be illustrated from the following extract where I am talking to Ruth (from behind the camera) because her mother has been called away by a visitor. She had been putting magnetic letters and numbers on the radiator, initially playing on her own, and grouping some by letter shape, others by colour.

### *Ruth aged 2 years 10 months*

| | |
|---|---|
| RUTH: | (*Puts 2 on radiator*) |
| MM: | Is that a letter? |
| RUTH: | No, it's just a number. These are letters. (*Points to o and a*) |
| MM: | What's that one? |
| RUTH: | O for octopus and a for apple.<br>(*Takes another letter from box*) Another g. (*Puts it with the other two g's*) |
| MM: | What a lot of g's. How many have you got? |
| RUTH: | (*Points as counts*) One, two, three. |
| MM: | Yes. Are they all the same colour? |
| RUTH: | There's red, there's (*Pauses*) |
| MM: | Purple. |
| RUTH: | There's purple, there's green.<br>(*Puts a 3 on radiator but wrong orientation, looks like m*) |
| MM: | What's that? |
| RUTH: | A number three. |
| MM: | Very good. It's lying down though isn't it? It looks like an m. |
| RUTH: | (*Stands it upright but reversed*) It goes that way round. |
| MM: | No, it goes the other way round. |
| RUTH: | I'll, I'll see in the book. It goes that way round. I'll see in the book. (*Goes to her bookshelf*) |
| MM: | You're going to show me the book, are you? |
| RUTH: | There, about that number (*Looking for book, finds it*)<br>There we are. |
| MM: | This is your 'I can count' book, is it? |

| | |
|---|---|
| RUTH: | Yes. |
| MM: | You show me the number 3 you are going to look at. |
| RUTH: | (*Turns pages and finds 3*) And this is the one. |
| MM: | That's right. |
| RUTH: | (*Looks at book, looks at 3 on radiator*) This goes this way round. |
| MM: | Yes, Do you know which way round it goes now? |
| RUTH: | Yes. |
| MM: | Can you do it? |
| RUTH: | (*Reversing 3*) This way round you mean? |
| MM; | Yes. Is that the right way round now? |
| RUTH: | Yes. |
| MM: | Yes. Very good. |

What is interesting about this episode is not only the concepts Ruth has about print and categorization, but her spontaneous use of print as an authoritative source of reference to check the spoken word.


*2. Narratives and the 'fictionalizing' of experience.*

Contact with print is not essential for developing children's ability to produce self-generated compositions such as the invention of narratives, etc., but it does expand and enrich the contexts of children's worlds in many ways (Moerk, 1985). Literature can take children into 'possible worlds' which generate skills that can generalize to other contexts. Their creative and imaginative responses in 'fictionalizing' experience (Scollon and Scollon, 1981) can play an important role in cognitive development. Progress in later years in school will show ability to adapt to different genres, to take account of readers' knowledge and to be able to produce formal, expository prose if required.

This can be seen in Ruth's development, focusing on one of her favorite books, Maurice Sendak's *Where the wild things are*. She came to know the story almost word for word and enjoyed 'reading' it to her brother using the pictures as a guide to her place in the text.

*Ruth aged 3 years 6 months 'reading' to Jack*

RUTH: he sailed off (*looks at hands*)
in and out of weeks (*looks at book, turns page*)
almost through a year (*turning page*)
to where the Wild Things are (*looks at page, turns page*)
when he came to the place where the Wild Things were—
the Wild Things (*looks at page*)
roared their terrible roars (*looks at fingers*)
and gnashed their terrible teeth and rolled their terrible eyes—
(*Jack leans across the book saying 'eeth, 'eeth*) and rolled their

terrible eyes. (*Looks at me and back to book*)
Be still (*addresses this to Wild Things*)
He tamed them with a magic touch (*looks at picture of Max*)
staring into all their yellow eyes without blinking once (*looks at fingers*)
And they were frightened because they called him Wild Thing. (*Looks at me*)

Ruth invented numerous games based on the book, assigned roles to her brother and they enacted many variants. The language they used was often taken from the book. Both of them derived enormous pleasure from seeing a performance of the opera based on the book, both in the theatre and on television, because it opened up a new and magical way of coming to what was already familiar to them.

Young children's early narratives have been found to be fairly short and the onus is put on the listener to compensate for the 'leap-frogging' nature of their accounts (Peterson and McCabe, 1983). Although their stories are simple and tend to have a one-to-one correspondence between the representation and the original experience, Applebee (1978) claims that the stories they hear are as meaningful to them as anything else that happens. Children do learn to distinguish between literature and life, and are aware of what is fantasy and what is reality as can be seen in their conversations (Garvey, 1984; Martlew, Connolly, and McLeod, 1978). Ruth, aged 4, showed this distinction, when I was reading a story to her and Jack about an enterprising crocodile. I asked what they would do if this crocodile came into their garden. 'Oh, it's only in a story,' she said.

Ruth associated books with the 'literary imagination' and 'literary style'. A few months before this extract, I came across her alone in the attic when she was visiting my house. She was 'reading' a self-generated story, about a little boy and girl who were lost in a wood. The story lacked any cohesion but was read in a 'story voice'. The book providing the stimulus was a King Penguin Book of Spiders, each page having a picture of a spider on it.

## 3. Summarization skills.

These show the ability to represent linguistically what has been abstracted, organized and reproduced about both real and literary experience (Nelson and Greundle, 1979). In ordinary oral discourse children are quite competent recounters of experience (Menig-Peterson, 1975). It is evident from the following extract that these skills can be quite well developed in young children given a supportive and sensitive environment. This episode was recorded one evening when I was looking after Ruth and Jack. Ruth was just 5 but had been attending school since she was 4½-years-old. (Her Local Education Authority's policy is to take children into school in the year in which they are 5.) The school encourages children to take their reading books home and so continue to share book reading with their parents. Those who are able to are also encouraged to write a summary. Ruth read the story, which she had not read before, at a steady pace, asking only about one word, 'clack'. She then wrote her story.

*Ruth aged 5 years 2 months* (Figure 4.1)

RUTH:    (*Reads*) 'Tessa and the Train (*Title of the story*)
         Pipkin is a little girl and Tess is her rag doll'
         —Where's the Wild Thing gone? (*A doll*)
MM:      He's here. He's listening to you.
RUTH:    Oh yes. Let him listen Jack.
MM:      Jack's not stopping him. He's listening too.
RUTH:    'Pipkin is a little girl and Tess is her rag doll. She is a girl doll.'
JACK:    Let your Care Bear listen too Ruth. (*Ruth looks up and nods*)
RUTH:    'Tess sleeps in Pipkin's bed and sits on Pipkin's lap. She is her
         best doll.'

         The story continues for several pages. Tess falls out of a train into
         the mud but is retrieved. The story ends happily.

RUTH:    'You cannot look out of the window said Pipkin, rest on my lap.
         Pipkin and mother and Tess went on in the train. Clatter, clatter,
         clatter and rumble, rumble, rumble went the train.' (*Closes the
         book*)
MM:      Well. That's very good.
RUTH:    I have to write a story now.
MM:      Have you?
RUTH:    What shall I write? (*Looks ahead, not really addressing me*)
MM:      A story about Tess?
RUTH:    Um. Tess. Um. (*Still gazing ahead*)
MM:      Well, what happened in that story?
RUTH:    Pipkin's rag doll got stuck—fell out of the window in the mud.
         (*Looks at me*).
MM:      That's right. Can you write that as your story then?
RUTH:    Er, Pipkin (*looks at the paper*)
MM:      Have you got a pen?
RUTH:    No, a pencil. Here's a pencil.
MM:      Oh good, now what are you going to write?
RUTH:    Pip—how d— (begins to write) Pip—P—Pipkin—K (*pauses*)
MM:      Kin—in—i
RUTH:    Oh no— (*Has put c instead of k. Rubs it out*)
JACK:    Can I write something down?
MM:      Yes. Go and find a pencil.

|       | That's right. You've changed the c into a k. Very good Ruth. What made you think that was wrong, that it should be k? |
| RUTH: | Yes. |
| MM:   | Why did you remember that? |
| MM:   | Because, because in the, in the book (*opens book and shows me*). |
| MM:   | You remembered from seeing it in the book before did you? |
| RUTH: | Yes. |
| MM:   | Now what are you going to put? |
| RUTH: | Pipkin—Pipkin lost—lost (*writes, looks up*). Have I done it right? |
| MM:   | What you have there is lots, lots. So what have you done wrong? |
| JACK: | I want to write now. (*Has returned with paper and pencil*) |
| MM:   | Now can you write 'J' for Jack. (*To Jack*) So now you want to put the 't' and the 's' the other way round Ruth. |
| RUTH: | Yes. (*Does so after rubbing letters out*) Pipkin lost—Tess (*writes*) the (*pause, writes*) little (*pause*) |
| JACK: | I've done it. |
| MM:   | Very good. Can you draw me a picture of mummy and write mummy? |
| RUTH: | little—rag. |
| JACK: | I can't, can't write, write mummy. |
| MM:   | Can you draw mummy? |
| RUTH: | ra—g. |
| JACK: | I can only draw mummy. (*Draws*). |
| MM:   | Ra—g. That's right. (*Ruth has written rag now*) |
| RUTH: | Rag doll. (*Writes d*) Is the 'd' this way? |
| MM:   | That's right. Do you find it hard to remember that? |
| RUTH: | Yes. Doll (*finishes writing, reads what she has written*) little rag doll. |
|       | Pipkin lost Tess the little rag doll. |

The story continued (Figure 4.1), an interesting story in its own right, doubly of interest in that it was a written composition and was treated as such. Ruth wrote and reviewed what she had written at word and sentence level, before progressing to the next piece. Her writing skills developed alongside her interest in reading. Her familiarity with the words in the story facilitated her spelling but she also used sound–symbol correspondence to work out how to spell some words. In families where literacy is encouraged, reading and writing are often integrated activities, children being requested to produce responses to pictures or text, to interpret their drawings and to respond to requests to draw and write specific things. Children are also asked to recount their own experiences. Summarizing what has happened is quite a difficult task for young children. The recalled experience can outstrip the linguistic capabilities. Ruth's

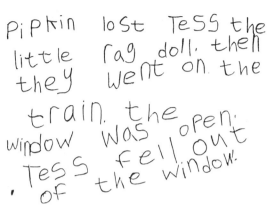

Figure 4.1    Written summary of story *Tessa and the train*. (Ruth aged 5 years 2 months)

account of Guy Fawkes night is a representation of images that were important to her, but she needed supportive prompts to trigger off her recall.

*Ruth aged 3 years 7 months*

MOTHER:     Tell Margaret about the fireworks.
RUTH:           Well James was looking after us from the big booms—bangs. I went outside with Jonathan to play. Well a—two big booms came up and I was scared.
MM:              Wasn't Jonathan scared?
RUTH:           No he just hugged me from the big booms.
MM:              Did all the fireworks make big booms?
RUTH:           Yes.
MM:              Weren't there any pretty ones?
RUTH:           Yes—made lovely lights, green lights, pink lights, red lights.
MOTHER:     Tell Margaret about the sparklers.
RUTH:           And I was a little bit scared of the sparklers but in the end I wasn't.
MM:              What did you do with the sparklers?
RUTH:           Just sparkled them around in the dark, in the very dark. And in the last evening—when—well I was going to go, to go to a bonfire—bonfire in the field—well—all the people came—and we had some food and and Rachel Rachel was there and and (*pause*).
MM:              And did she have some food?
RUTH:           Yes. And Laura had some tea and Rachel had some tea but Anne didn't, Anne didn't.
MM:              Why not?
RUTH           Because, because I didn't see her, she was, she was having any

tea. So after a while my fingers and feet, fingers and feet and toes
were cold. We we both went home.

MM:  Didn't the fire keep you warm?

RUTH:  I just got my little picnic chair and just sat down in it and put my
feet up, and just for a minute, all of a sudden, the fire just
warmed the feet.

Ruth does use several complex syntactic structures but the richness of her
constructed images outstrips her linguistic capacity. Despite that she gives a
description that summarizes events and her responses.

## The emergence of writing

Conceptual abilities, built up from reactions to print, run concurrently with the
emergence of the production of writing. Unlike speech, writing requires an
external tool to produce signs which then have their own, separate existence.
The way children grasp pencils, their stroke direction and efficiency, change
over time (Connolly and Elliot, 1972; Thomassen and Teulings, 1983). Their
early grasps allow for little finger manipulation and often they use both hands
interchangeably. The motor programmes that children build up when using
pens facilitate the establishment of internal representations for forms, first for
letters and then words. These can then be run off without conscious thought
having to be given to their production (Bradley, 1981; Ellis, 1982). This can be
seen even from the earliest stages of children's drawings. Having achieved
skills in producing certain forms they can produce these rapidly, whereas new
forms or combinations of old forms in new relationships take more effort. With
emergent literary skills this applies also to the formation of letter shapes and
eventually to the spelling of words, whether following conventional or idiosyncratic rules.

A lot of attention has been given to the rule-governed aspects of drawing and
analogies have been made between drawing and language (Dyson, 1982;
Goodnow, 1977; Goodnow and Levine, 1973; Von Sommers, 1984). Drawing
and writing are linked in a number of ways. Just as children normally babble
and use gestural communication before they speak, so do they draw before
they write. Initial play with pencils produces gestural-like movements, where
the child moves the whole arm in broad sweeps and circles about the paper,
taking pleasure in the marks created. Vygotsky (1983) proposed that gesture
marked the starting point of written language and that initial scribbles are
manifestations of gestures rather than intended drawings. This has parallels
with play where representational gestures towards objects progress to fantasy
play where the objects can stand for something else. Fantasy play marks a
progression from first- to second-order symbolism. Vygotsky views written
language as second-order symbolism in which signs replace words which are in
turn signs for objects and relations in the real world.

Adults endow children's first scribbles with meaning, in much the same way as they do children's pre-verbal gestural and proto-word forms of communication. They impute intentions which lead children to realize the representational potential of marks on the page. Children then begin to designate scribbles with labels of their own choosing. Children's first interpretations of their scribbles, and indeed their drawings and written words, represent things of interest to them. At first, action and interpretation seem to be embedded in a specific relation, but later extend to other entities. This initial embeddedness reflects Nelson, Engel, and Kyratzis' (1985) observations on the evolution of meanings in contexts. The emergence of these can be seen in the following episode between Ruth and her grandmother.

*Ruth aged 18 months* (Figure 4.2)

GRAN:      What's that you're drawing?
RUTH:      (*Draws circular shape*)
            O—eeow.
GRAN:      A pussy cat. Is that a cat? Draw its tail.
RUTH:      (*Puts a squiggle inside the circle*)

Figure 4.2   Scribbles verbally labelled 'ooeow' by Ruth. Cat drawn by grandmother. (Ruth aged 18 months)

GRAN:       That's its eye. (*Gran draws a cat, labelling each part as she draws it*)
RUTH:       (*Draws round the picture of the cat, stands up and looks at it*)
GRAN:       What's that you've drawn?
RUTH:       Ooeow, ooeow, ooeow.
GRAN:       Shall we draw a spider?
RUTH:       (*Draws another similar shape*)
GRAN:       What's that you've drawn?
RUTH:       OO-eow. (*Takes another piece of paper, fills it in with up and down squiggles*)

Ruth is enjoying filling in the page with marks. No particular part of the scribbles seem to represent a 'cat'. Many of the shared interactions during this episode were spent in exchanging coloured crayons with her grandmother. Her grandmother presumes the drawings are meant to represent something. When Ruth gives a label, she encourages her to add defining features to the main structure. When she draws a model, Ruth draws round it, a very concrete and direct response. Ruth holds her pencils in a palmar grasp, with the pen in an upright position and all her fingers curled round the stem.

A month later the scribbles are more effusive, but Ruth is now willing to 'draw' almost any topic suggested. Notions of print are being incorporated into the activity by her mother. Although Ruth *draws* when asked to *write* 'dad', she is able to roughly identify the words her mother writes.

*Ruth aged 19 months* (Figure 4.3)

MOTHER:     What's that?
RUTH:       (*Rapidly filling the entire, very large, paper*) Eeow.
MOTHER:     Doesn't look like a cat to me. Where's his eyes?
RUTH:       Ooo eow. There.
MOTHER:     You write dad.
RUTH:       (*Continues to draw*)
MOTHER:     Write mummy. (*Mother writes mummy*) What does it say?
RUTH:       Dad.
MOTHER:     No it doesn't. This says dad. (*Writes dad*).
            What does this say?
RUTH:       Dad.
MOTHER:     That's right. Now what does this say? (*Points to mummy*)
RUTH:       Dad.
MOTHER:     No it doesn't. What does it say?
RUTH:       Mummy. (*Looks at mother and smiles*)
MOTHER:     That's right.
RUTH:       (*Draws another shape, leans back*) Ooh. Bird.
MOTHER:     That's a bird. Can you draw a pig?
RUTH:       (*Draws, leans back and makes grunting noises*)

Figure 4.3    Scribbles representing a variety of topics, e.g. Dad, pig, labelled by
mother. (Ruth aged 19 months)

MOTHER:    Is that a pig? Let's write pig on it. (*Writes pig*)
There, that says pig.

Ruth, having just gone through a time of rapid expansion of vocabulary, is
also acquiring the notion that things can be designated by written signs as well
as spoken ones. Although the shapes she draws are very idiosyncratic, there are
the beginnings of differentiation in what they represent. Some of the features
are accidentally produced, as in 'bird' and suggest labels to Ruth which she then
generates herself. What is also apparent in these extracts is the 'accountability
work' from the adults in giving a conceptual base to the activity and encouraging Ruth to move on to further achievements.

Children's early drawings show increasing abilities to represent shapes
similar to the objects they are attempting to depict. They also show the addition
of details which help in representing objects (Ives, Wolf, Fuciana, and Smith,
1981). Perhaps it is because drawings represent objects that children initially
assume that writing can only be used to label, that function words for instance
cannot be written (Templeton and Spivey, 1980). Ruth's drawing at 23 months
of age shows greater pen control (she drew this using both hands but is now
showing the beginnings of a precision grip) and better representational skills.
This drawing also shows the beginning of non-representational additions as

part of the drawing. As Kellog (1970) points out, letters first appear as parts of drawings and this jagged squiggle shape was one of Ruth's first attempts at representing a word.

*Ruth aged 23 months* (Figure 4.4)

RUTH:      (*Drawing with both hands*)
MOTHER:    Draw a house with smoke coming out.
RUTH:      (*Draws a rectangle with curly lines coming from the top*)
MOTHER:    That's lovely smoke coming out. That's beautiful.
           What are you going to draw now?
RUTH:      A yellow one.
MOTHER:    You're going to draw a yellow one.
RUTH:      (*Takes another sheet of paper, draws similar house*)
           There's a yellow one (*speaking while drawing*).
           There's smoke and chimney (*has a pen in each hand*) there's a
           blue one (*draws another*). There's the smoke and the chimney.

Figure 4.4   A house with smoke (Ruth aged 23 months)

Ruth is now able to do several things at once while drawing. She can talk about what she is drawing while producing the representation and generate her own additional ideas for details. She also included the jagged squiggle which represented 'writing'. This gestalt-type pattern was used to represent writing for some time before being replaced by letter shapes. It has its origins in her mother's writing of 'mummy' as one of the first words used to label and introduce the concept of writing. It occurs again, six months later but in a more

Figure 4.5    Two examples of pretend writing and letter strings. (Ruth aged 3 years 5 months and 3 years 7 months)

established and denotative form rather than being part of the drawing. Creative 'pretend' writing occurs much later in conjunction with strings of letters (Figure 4.5). Luria (1983) points out that the transition to a new technique can initially set back the process of writing. Children who have been 'writing' functionally, and representing meaning by scribbles, regress to using alphabetic letters non-functionally in the early stages of acquisition. Letters become part of the drawing. The letter strings and pretend adult writing show private practice and experiments with form that reflect children's experimentation with speech when they are alone (Martlew, Connolly, and McCleod, 1978; Weir, 1962).

Figure 4.6    Drawing 'writing'; b, drawing Dad, 'writing' Dad. (Ruth aged 2 years 5 months)

*Ruth aged 2 years 5 months* (Figure 4.6)

| | |
|---|---|
| RUTH: | (*Draws jagged shape*) |
| MOTHER: | What does that say? |
| RUTH: | Mummy. (*Chooses another colour, keeps changing colours throughout*) |
| MOTHER: | Can you copy this? Can you do a shape like this? (*Draws a circle*) |
| RUTH: | Um. (*Draws a circle*) |
| MOTHER: | Can you do one like this? (*Draws a square. Ruth draws one*) And another? (*Ruth draws this with her left hand*) |
| MOTHER: | What's that um? What's that? (*Ruth gives no response. Draws another shape at the bottom of the page*) What does it say? |
| RUTH: | It says (*continues stroke then looks at it*) 'b'. |
| MOTHER: | It says what? |
| MOTHER: | It says what? |
| RUTH: | It says bath. |
| MOTHER: | Does it? That's a word that says bath? |
| RUTH: | Um. |
| MOTHER: | Can you draw a bath with people in it? |
| RUTH: | I can't mummy draw a bath. |
| MOTHER: | But you can write about it can you. |
| RUTH: | Um. |
| MOTHER: | (*Writes Ruth*) What does that say? |

RUTH:       Ruth.
MOTHER:     Very good. Now can you write Ruth?
RUTH:       No.
MOTHER:     You've not even tried. You don't know. You've not even tried.
            (*Pause*) Draw dad.
            (*Ruth draws*)
            Is that his hair?
RUTH:       (*Indignant tone*) That's his mouth.
MOTHER:     And there's his arms. Those are smart shoes. They are smart
            shoes those. Um, and there's his hands. Very good. That's a
            really lovely dad. Can you write dad then we won't forget.
RUTH:       (*Does smaller version of jagged shape*)
MOTHER:     Does that say dad?
RUTH:       Um.

In moving from first- to second-order symbolism in writing children have to become aware of the possibility that writing can represent speech. Children represent objects before making the basic discovery that one can also draw speech (Vygotsky, 1983) and there is a period in development of writing when the boundaries of what is drawing and what is writing seem somewhat fuzzy for the young child. Children seem to begin by 'drawing' writing. They produce scribbles or mock writing or separate circles and vertical strokes. They confuse write and draw and relate the length of their scribbles to the perceived length of the spoken word, as Ruth does in the above extract. Children tend to confuse 'draw' and 'write' because initially there is nothing to mark an obvious distinction between them (Luria, 1983). Children's conceptualization of the characteristics of drawing and writing was traced by De Gòes and Martlew (1983) using a dictation, copying, and rewriting task. At first children will draw when asked to write. As the realization of the distinction grows they are more cautious about 'writing' but will then attempt to produce identifiable words and show an increasing awareness of the symbolic nature of writing.

In a series of interesting experiments, Luria (1983) shows how the depictive function of writing develops in drawing. When these 'drawn' symbols acquired a functional significance attempts began to be made to use graphic representations. Before this the children, whose ages ranged from 3 to 5 years, would 'write' to a dictated sentence, believing that their scribbles were 'writing'.

When Clay (1975) looked at the writing of 5-year-olds in their first two months at school she also noted that most children began by inventing scribbles or mock writing before they recognized real letters. Again, as others have also noted, she found the first words children write are their own names, often they can write 'mummy', generally writing just the first letter before being able to produce the whole word. Some children will only accept upper or lower case representations, and they tend to be inflexible about the pattern they will accept.

Figure 4.7   Picture of Dad—D for Dad. (Ruth aged 3 years 2 months)

Children follow this by writing strings of letters or even words, an occupation which seems to give a lot of pleasure. They expect adults to be able to tell them 'what it says'. Meaning at this stage seems to rest for the child in his intention for his representation, linked to knowledge that adults can make sense of print in books. Following this they came to realize that writing has to follow certain conventions. This can lead to creative spelling and self-generated captions where children use strategies for mapping the sounds of letters on to known letter forms and combinations (Bissex, 1980; Read, 1986). Some resist spelling unless they can do it correctly with help from adults.

These patterns can be traced in Ruth's progress. By the age of 3 years, Ruth was able to produce most letter shapes, many of them without prompts from her mother. She used these to represent whole words as in the following drawing where she added the 'd' for dad rapidly and without hesitation when asked to write 'dad'. Her drawing of Dad has many distinctive features added such as cheeks, 'eyes inside eyes' and whiskers which she herself commented on while drawing.

Ruth's mother was now encouraging her to join letters into words by persuading her to move beyond using only the initial letter. Ruth's uncertainty about whether 'n' can stand for the whole word 'Nick' is at odds with what is known about pre-literate children's reactions to print. Single letters are not generally accepted as words (De Gòes and Martlew, 1984; Ferreiro and

Teberesky, 1982). Ruth has by now firmly established notions of the difference between writing and drawing. Her drawings are typical in that they represent people from the front which shows their defining features to the best advantage (Ives and Rovet, 1984). Now Ruth has firmly established concepts her mother tries to improve her skills in representing them by persuading her to alter her pen grip, but does not insist.

Ruth aged 3 years 4 months (Figure 4.8)

| | |
|---|---|
| RUTH: | (*Drawing Nick*) |
| | A silly, smiley mouth. |
| MOTHER: | Um. A big smiley mouth. Can you do a 'n' for Nick? |
| RUTH: | (*Looks at mother, writes*) |
| MOTHER: | That's very good. Keep going. Very good. |
| RUTH: | Is that Nick? |
| MOTHER: | Can you do an 'i'? |
| RUTH: | Yes (*writes*) |

Figure 4.8   Drawings with names: Nick, Paul, Margaret. (Ruth aged 3 years 4 months)

MOTHER:  Can you do a 'c' for cat—Nick, 'c' for cat.
RUTH:    No.
MOTHER:  Like this, watch. (*Draws shape with her finger*)
RUTH:    Like that? (*Imitates movement*)
MOTHER:  No, like that. Round and then stop.
RUTH:    (*Writes c*)
MOTHER:  Very good. That's very good. That's lovely.
RUTH:    (*Gets new paper*) Shall I write—shall I draw Paul now?
         (*Nick and Paul are my sons*)
MOTHER:  Yes
RUTH:    I'm very good at writing and drawing.
MOTHER:  Um.
RUTH:    I'm just putting a nose there so I won't forget the nose.
         (*Draws and mother watches*)
MOTHER:  Can you try and hold your pen like I told you to (*Ruth is bunching
         her fingers round the end of the pencil*)
RUTH:    (*Looks at pencil, moves fingers, then moves them back*)
         Can I hold it like this?
MOTHER:  Is it easier?
RUTH:    Yes.
MOTHER:  Remember how I told you to hold it though.
RUTH:    Yes. (*Carries on drawing and produces drawings of Paul and me
         to add to Nick*)

With supportive aid from her mother, Ruth progresses to producing words in
combination as labels for her drawings. Writing is already becoming a more
private activity with fewer exchanges needed to assist in the production of both
drawing and writing. Her later drawings, shown below, were generally produced by Ruth writing alone or only partially attending to ongoing comments.

*Ruth aged 3 years 7 months* (Figure 4.9)

RUTH:    (*Is drawing a cat*)
MOTHER:  Tell Margaret above Mog the cat. (*Mog is a stray cat, recently
         rescued after a road accident, who had to have a leg amputated*)
RUTH:    There's Mog the three legged cat and there's his whiskers and
         there's his hair.
MM:      That's lovely.
MOTHER:  Um, are you going to write Mog?
RUTH:    What?
MOTHER   A big M, then an 'o'—that's right—and then a g—that's an o for
         octopus with a curly tail. That's right. That's beautiful.
RUTH:    Is that the end?
MOTHER:  Do you want to write 'the cat' as well?
RUTH:    (*Leans over paper in preparation*)

Figure 4.9 Drawings of cats with multi-word descriptions: Mog the cat, Bindha the cat. (Ruth aged 3 years 7 months)

MOTHER:    't'— (*Ruth writes*)—and a 'h' and the 'e'. Should have been a little 'e' but never mind. Looks a bit funny. (*Ruth does not look up from page*)
Now cat. Start down here, more room down there.
(*Points to the bottom of the page. Ruth takes no notice*)
'c' and then an 'a' and a 't'. Very good.
RUTH:    Can I write cat again?

*(She then draws a picture of Bindha, their other cat, who has four legs.)*

The bodies of the cats are square. During this period, Ruth made numerous drawings for a builder doing alterations to their house. They all depicted him with a square body, the shape deriving from a book *Mr Brick the Builder.* The square shape generalized to her cats, etc.

Ruth enjoyed practising letter shapes and producing forms that she imagined looked like adult writing (Figure 4.5). She generally attempted to write labels to pictures on her own but would ask for help when she needed it. The beginnings of narrative representation can be seen in her picture of the mummy and the skeleton (which she pronounced—and spelled—skelicton). This followed a visit to the museum where she saw an Egyptian mummy. I explained what it was. We then saw a skeleton which did not have a grave round it but she has merged the two concepts of 'dead people' and generated her own interpretation. Outside the museum, she and Jack played on a large stone made to look like a dinosaur (Figure 4.10).

Ruth now needs less assistance, indeed in this recording some of her requests for help were partly to draw her mother's attention away from Jack who was also drawing.

*Ruth aged 4 years 1 month* (Figure 4.10)

MOTHER: What's that, Jack?

Figure 4.10   Record of museum visit depicting a mummy, a skeleton and a dinosaur.
(Ruth aged 4 years 1 month)

| | |
|---|---|
| JACK: | That's a stick skeleton. |
| RUTH: | I can do skeletons more better than Jack. |
| JACK: | I can do engines. |
| | (*Mother talks to Jack*) |
| RUTH: | There's his hands (*to herself*). |
| | (*Finishes skeleton, leans back*) |
| | There, there's a skeleton. |
| MOTHER: | Can you write his name? |
| RUTH: | (*Not listening—draws circle round skeleton*) |
| | Look, look mum. |
| MOTHER: | Is that his grave |
| RUTH: | Yes. |
| MOTHER: | Now can you write 's' for skeleton |
| | Now a k—k for kangaroo |
| | e— |
| RUTH: | Can you show me a little e (*Mother writes e*). |
| MOTHER: | Remember what I told you about keeping all the letters together so you can tell what words the letters make. |
| RUTH: | Um (*Finishes rest of the word without help while mother talks to Jack*) |
| | (*Finishes, looks at mother and Jack*) |

Ruth is not a good artist but her drawings all depict the contrastive features that distinguish the topic from other entities. Jack, for example, is clearly distinguished from Ruth and the parrot has a stand (Figure 4.11). Ruth labels most of her drawings spontaneously now, usually without assistance (Figure 4.12). As I was present when she drew the picture of me the label 'you' represents a direct piece of communication in print (Figure 4.12).

Ruth's development in both oral and written language shows concurrent changes from the time when recordings began. In the early book reading exchanges she was using proto-communicative words, reflecting her early scribbles, which were tied to representing a limited range of entities. These became more representative of the forms they were intended to depict and features were added that differentiated them from other objects.

Ruth's ability to use language to reflect on her experience, to summarize, to engage in discourse, extends in complexity as does her linguistic ability. Her writing develops from her representational drawings where 'writing' also is initially representational. The beginnings of symbolic communication come with the use of single letters and then combinations of letters forming whole words. In reaching this stage she has had a lot of support from her mother but she can then generate her own words and eventually her own written discourse.

Ruth's progression provides an illustration of the sequence of written language development in an individual child (Figure 4.13). Other children will acquire written language in different contexts, with different degrees of

Figure 4.11   Ruth and Jack at the swimming pool (Ruth aged 5 years 1 month) and a parrot (Ruth aged 4 years 11 months): drawings labelled spontaneously and without assistance

Figure 4.12   Look at Jack in the mud (Ruth aged 4 years 4 months) and 'You' (Ruth aged 5 years 1 month): descriptions added spontaneously and without assistance

support and intrinsic interest and motivation. Although the sequence may well follow broadly similar patterns, it is likely each child develops its own strategies and techniques for coping with both the motoric and conceptual aspects of representation and symbolic communication.

These differences were apparent in a study on young children's writing abilities recently completed by Pat Stanway in Sheffield. The children performed a number of tasks in their last term in a nursery and again in their first

Figure 4.13   Sequence of writing development based on a single case study

1.  (Ruth: single utterance stage)
    Interest in shared book reading, labels items in book and relates items in book to external objects.
    Recognition that pictures are different from print.
    Produces scribbles which adults assume to be intended representations.
    These scribbles are given labels, initially limited in what they can represent but soon extending to a variety of topics. Pen held in palmar grasp.

2.  (Ruth: two years)
    Drawings become more representative of what they are intended to depict. They are drawn with greater fluency and there is the beginning of a precision grip. Descriptions of the drawing are given while the drawing is being produced. Begins to draw 'writing' imitating writing as a 'gestalt', but no distinction between writing and drawing.

3.  (Ruth: two and a half years)
    Many details are added to drawings as distinctive characteristics. Although still drawing 'writing', recognition of the size of words (for example, 'dad' written as a small squiggle, 'mummy' as a larger one). There is the beginning of sound correspondence to graphic symbols and a knowledge of the letters of the alphabet (even of using books as sources of reference).

4.  (Ruth: three years)
    Shows the ability to produce many letter shapes without assistance. Writes words with mother's help and aligns letters together. Realizes letter arrangements follow conventions. Can write her own name and is prepared to write any words, regardless of length, with mother's support.

5.  (Ruth: three and a half years)
    Begins to write multi-word description to drawings. Letters are now run off easily and her attention is focused on words. These have clear spaces between them. Practices writing, producing imitations of 'cursive script' and often uses letters as decorative strings, etc.

6.  (Ruth: four years)
    Generates her own words using sound to symbol correspondence. Begins to correct idiosyncratic letter forms. Writing used for a variety of functions; to label, to send invitations, greetings cards, to write lists.

7.  (Ruth: four and half to five years — attending school)
    Ability to write some words without having to devote a lot of time to thinking about spelling. When writes connected discourse, as in summary, shows recognition that written language is a visible artefact that can be reviewed, changed and re-read as a source of generating further ideas. She has acquired basic literacy skills.

term in school. We found their responses to these tasks varied enormously but there was considerable individuality in the way they wrote and drew which persisted over the four- to five-month interval. Figure 4.14 shows a selection of children's names written on the two occasions, showing marked similarity within

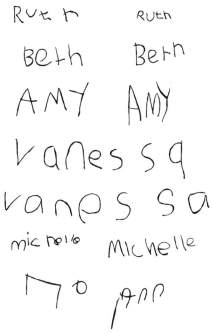

Figure 4.14   Names written by six children at two different times. 1. in their last term in a nursery; 2. in their first term at school

individuals, particularly in the better writers. These established techniques for forming letters and representing people are also evident in the way they wrote and drew mummy (Figure 4.15).

The children in both groups come from middle-class backgrounds, there was no significant difference between them in their performance on the Peabody Picture Vocabulary Test, but in many of the tasks, the Sheffield group were superior. The Sheffield group attended a nursery with a child-focused social orientation. The other group attended a nursery in a small mill town that had a didactic approach and 'taught' some literacy skills. Interestingly, in mother-child play sessions, the Sheffield group spent 57 per cent of their time in 'literacy' activities—reading, drawing etc—while the other group spent only 19 per cent. Time in this group was almost equally divided between playing with bricks, jigsaws, and threading toys. This observation is only suggestive but does support the efficacy of a social and motivating context for supporting children's early learning.

## CONCLUSION

'The roots of literacy lie in how one learns to talk' (Olson, 1984, p. 189). Children's talk, in their early years, is generally acquired and developed in

Figure 4.15    Drawing and writing 'mummy' by six children. 1. in their last term in a
nursery; 2. in their first term at school

the home. The environment that parents provide for their children is the
one their children learn from. It can help or hinder their ability to be active
participants in their own learning. It can provide rich or impoverished contexts.

Not all children learn in the same way or at the same rate but there seem to be
consistent patterns of interactions which correlate with children's ability to
enjoy and benefit from the literate environment of school. Parents who talk to
their children in the ways discussed earlier, show sensitivity to their children's
ability but draw them on to more and more complex behaviours. Children then
are more able to be masters of their own progress, supported by these affective
and cognitively stimulating interactions.

As Vygotsky (1962) says, it is more interesting to know what a child can do
with support than what he can do unaided. Young children have great
capacities for learning. The way language is learnt, from the earliest stages of
acquisition, can affect the uses to which it is put. In homes with an interest in
literacy, children can acquire notions about written language, both conceptual

and technical, while learning oral language. As their spoken language skills develop they can also be acquiring the bases for the 'detachment' features of literate language, alongside the 'involvement' features of immediate conversational discourse.

There is a strong case, therefore, for the facilitating effects of pre-school experience on later achievement in school (Martlew, 1986). This is not simply reiteration of the importance of early experience, particularly mother–child interactions, for later development, not that the home is the only influence on the pre-school child. It is generally, however, a major influence. Homes that are supportive before school tend to continue being supportive when children attend school. So there is every chance of those already having an enriched experience getting richer, while those with an impoverished beginning get poorer for many interacting reasons. The right kind of pre-school environment is vital therefore for such children; one which can provide a socially sensitive awareness of individual children's interests and by providing clear guidelines draw them into extended uses of language. This needs a context where children can feel motivated, curious about their world, and interested in learning.

Understanding develops in contexts that are familiar and well-established. Once skills and mental representations are built up in these contexts, children are able to generalize to novel and more decontextualized situations. They have more scope for creating their own contexts and generatively extending their own learning experiences. The contexts for acquiring and developing written language overlap with oral language development from its earliest stages. Children acquainted with written language, or with 'literate' uses of language, before school have an established basis for the way language is likely to be used in school. The most important basis for early education is having flexibility to use language appropriately over a range of contexts to serve an extended range of functions. Language is the child's tool for expressing meaning. If this tool is inadequate progress will be impeded. A sophisticated tool can feed back to extend the child's range of meanings and concepts.

Literacy provides an excellent focus for such extensions. Literature, according to the Formalists' viewpoints, 'deforms' language (Eagleton, 1983). The language of literature, they claim, is not that of ordinary conversation. If extrapolations can be made from this to children's acquaintance with 'literate' language, then children in literate contexts are being given a different way of using language, a mis-match against which to test their hypotheses and generate 're-formed' uses, thus extending both their formal control and their creative experience.

## REFERENCES

Aitkinson, M. (1982). *Explanations in the study of child language development.* Cambridge: Cambridge University Press.

Applebee, A.N. (1978). *The child's concept of story*. Chicago: University of Chicago Press.

Asher, S.R., and Oden, S.L. (1976). Children's failure to communicate: an assessment of comparison and egocentrism explanations. *Developmental Psychology,* **12,** 132–139.

Barnes, S., Gutfreund, M., Satterly, D., and Wells, G. (1983). Characteristics of adult speech which predict children's language development. *Journal of Child Language,* **10,** 65–84.

Bates, E., Benigi, L., Bretherton, I., Camaoni, L., and Volterra, V. (1979). *The emergence of symbols: communication and cognition in infancy.* New York: Academic Press.

Bissex, G. (1980). *GNYS AT WRK. A child learns to write and read.* Cambridge, Mass.: Harvard University Press.

Bradley, L. (1981). The organization of motor patterns for spelling: an effective remedial strategy for backward readers. *Developmental Medicine and Child Neurology,* **23,** 83–91.

Bruner, J. (1973). From communication to language—a psychological perspective. *Cognition,* **3,** 255–287.

Bruner, J. (1983). *Child's talk: learning to use language.* Oxford: Oxford University Press.

Bruner, J. (1984). Language, mind and reading. In H. Goelman, A. Oberg and F. Smith (eds), *Awakening to literacy* (pp.193–200). London: Heinemann.

Brown, R. (1973). *A first language.* London: George Allen & Unwin.

Clay, M. (1975). *What did I write?* Auckland: Heinemann.

Connolly, K.J., and Elliott, J.M. (1972). The evolution and ontogeny of hand function. In N. Blurton-Jones (ed), *Ethological studies of child behaviour,* Cambridge: Cambridge University Press.

Conti-Ramsden, G., and Friel-Patti, S. (1984). Mother–child dialogues: a comparison of normal and language impaired children. *Journal of Communication Disorders,* **17,** 19–35.

Cross, T.G. (1978). Mothers' speech and its association with rate of linguistic development in young children. In N. Waterson and C. Snow (eds), *The development of communication.* Chichester: John Wiley.

Cross, T.G., Nienhuys, T.G., and Kirkman, M. (1983). Parent–child interaction with receptively disabled children: some determinants of maternal speech style. In K.E. Nelson (ed), *Children's language,* Vol 5. New York: Gardner Press.

De Gòes, C., and Martlew, M. (1983). Young children's approach to literacy. In M. Martlew (ed), *The psychology of written language: developmental and educational perspectives.* Chichester: John Wiley.

De Gòes, C., and Martlew, M. (1984). Beginning to read and write: an exploratory study of young children's understanding of metalinguistic terms and graphic conventions. *First Language,* **5,** 121–130.

Diringer, D. (1962). *Writing.* London: Thames and Hudson.

Donaldson, M. (1978). *Children's minds.* London: Fontana.

Donaldson, M. (1984). Speech and writing and modes of learning. In H. Goelman, A. Oberg and F. Smith (eds), *Awakening to literacy.* Exeter: Heinemann.

Donaldson, M., Grieve, R., and Pratt, C. (1983). *Early childhood development and education.* Oxford: Basil Blackwell.

Dore, J. (1985). Holophrases revisited: their 'logical' development from dialogue. In M. Barrett (ed), *Children's single word speech* (23–58). Chichester: John Wiley.

Downing, J., and Leong, C.K. (1982). *Psychology of reading.* Toronto: Macmillan.

Dyson, A.H. (1982). The emergence of visible language: interrelationships between drawing and early writing. *Visible Language*, **16**, 360–381.

Eagleton, T. (1983). *Literacy theory: an introduction*. Oxford: Blackwell.

Ellis, A.W. (1982). Spelling and writing (and reading and speaking). In A.W. Ellis (ed), *Normality and pathology in cognitive functions*. London: Academic Press.

Ferreiro, E., and Teberesky, A. (1982). *Literacy before schooling*. New Hampshire: Heinemann.

Finnegan, R. (1970). *Oral literature in Africa*. Oxford: Oxford University Press.

Garvey, C. (1984). *Children's talk*. London: Fontana.

Gelb, I.J. (1963). *A study of writing*. Chicago: University of Chicago Press.

Gleitman, L., Gleitman, H., and Shipley E. (1972). The emergence of the child as grammarian. *Cognition*, **1**, 137–164.

Glucksberg, S., Krauss, R.M., and Higgins, E.T. (1975). The development of children's referential skills. In F. Horowitz (ed), *Review of child development research*. **4**, Chicago: University of Chicago Press.

Goodnow, J. (1977). *Children's drawings*. London: Fontana.

Goodnow, J., and Levine, R. (1973). The grammar of action: sequence and syntax in children's copying. *Cognitive Psychology*, **4**, 82–98.

Goody, J. (1977). The *domestication of the savage mind*. Cambridge: Cambridge University Press.

Gould, J.D. (1978). An experimental study of writing, dictating and speaking. In J. Requin (ed), *Attention and performance, Vol VII*. Hillsdale, N.J.: Lawrence Erlbaum.

Haas, W. (1976). Writing: the basic options. In W. Haas (ed), *Writing without letters* (pp. 131–208). Manchester: Manchester University Press.

Hartmann, E., and Haavind, M. (1981). Mothers as teachers and their children as learners: A study of the influence of social interactions upon cognitive development. In W.P. Robinson (ed), *Communication in Development*. London: Academic Press.

Heath, S.B. (1982). What no bedtime story means: narrative skills at home and school. *Language in Society*, **11**, 49–76.

Ives, N., and Rovet, J. (1984). The role of graphic orientations in children's drawings of familiar and novel objects at rest and in motion. *Merrill-Palmer Quarterly*, **25**, 281–292.

Ives, W., Wolf, D., Fucigna, C., and Smith, N. (1981). *Origins of graphic representation at ages two and three years*. Paper presented at annual meeting of the American Psychological Association, Los Angeles, September 1981.

Kaye, K. (1982). *The mental and social life of babies*. Cambridge: University of Chicago Press.

Keenan, E., and Klein, E. (1974). *Coherency in children's discourse*. Paper presented at the Summer Meeting of the Linguistic Society of America, Amherst, Massachusetts.

Kellog, R. (1970). *Analysing children's art*. Palo Alto: National Press Books.

Kroll, B. (1983). Antecedents of individual differences in children's writing attainment. In B. Kroll and G. Wells (eds), *Explorations in the development of writing*. Chichester: John Wiley.

Leopold, W. (1939–49). *Speech development of a bilingual child*. Evanston, Illinois: Northwestern University Press.

Lord, A.B. (1960). *The singer of tales*. Cambridge, Mass: Harvard University Press.

Luria, A.R. (1983). The development of writing in the child. In M. Martlew (ed), *The psychology of written language: developmental and educational perspectives*. Chichester: John Wiley.

Maratsos, M. (1973). Non-egocentric communicative abilities in preschool children. *Child Development*, **44**, 697–700.

Maratsos, M. (1976). *The use of definite and indefinite references in young children: an experimental study in semantic acquisition.* Cambridge: Cambridge University Press.

McCarthy, D. (1954). Language development. In L. Carmichael (ed), *Manual of child development.* New York: John Wiley.

Martlew, M. (1979). Young children's capacity to communicate. In K.J. Connolly (ed), *Psychology survey,* vol. 2. London: George Allen & Unwin.

Martlew, M. (1986). The development of written language. In K. Durkin (ed), *Language development in the school years.* Beckenham: Croom Helm.

Martlew, M., Connolly, K.J., and McCleod, C. (1978). Language use, role and context in a five-year-old. *Journal of Child Language,* **5,** 81–99.

Menig-Peterson, C. (1975). The modification of communicative behaviour in preschool aged children as a function of the listener's perspective. *Child Development,* **46,** 1015–1018.

Michaels, S., and Collins, J. (1984). Oral discourse style: classroom interaction and the acquisition of literacy. In D. Tannen (ed), *Coherence in spoken and written discourse.* Norwood, N.J.: Ablex.

Moerk, E. (1985). Picture book reading by mothers and young children and its impact upon language development. *Journal of Pragmatics,* **9,** 547–566.

Nelson, K. (1973). Structure and strategy in learning to talk. *Monographs of the Society for Research in Child Development,* **38.**

Nelson, K.E. Denniger, M.M., Bonvillian, J., Kaplan, B., and Baker N. (1984). Maternal input adjustments and non-adjustments as related to children's linguistic advances and to language acquisition theories. In A. Pellegrini and T. Yawkey (eds), *The development of oral and written language in social contexts.* Norwood, N.J.: Ablex.

Nelson, K., Engel, S., and Kyratzis, A. (1985). The evolution of meaning in context. *Journal of Pragmatics,* **9,** 453–474.

Nelson, K., and Greundel, J. (1979). At morning it's lunchtime: a scriptal view of children's stories. *Discourse Processes,* **2,** 75–94.

Ninio, A. (1980). Picture-book reading in mother-infant dyads belonging to two sub-groups in Israel. *Child Development,* **51,** 587–590.

Ninio, A., and Bruner, J. (1978). The achievements and antecedents of labelling. *Journal of Child Language,* **5,** 1–15.

Ochs, E., and Schiefflin, B. (1983). *Acquiring conversational competence.* London: Routledge & Kegan Paul.

Olson, D. (1983). Writing and literal meaning. In M. Martlew (ed), *The psychology of written language: developmental and educational perspectives,* (41–65). Chichester: John Wiley.

Olson, D. (1984). 'See. Jumping.' Some oral language antecedents of literacy. In H. Goelman, A. Oberg, and F. Smith (eds), *Awakening to literacy.* Exeter: Heinemann.

Peterson, C., and McCabe, A. (1983). *Developmental psycholinguistics: three ways of looking at a child's narrative.* New York: Plenum.

Piaget, J. (1926). *The language and thought of the child.* London: Routledge & Kegan Paul.

Ratner, N., and Bruner J. (1978). Games, social exchange and the acquisition of language. *Journal of Child Language,* **5,** 391–402.

Read, C. (1986). *Children's creative spelling.* London: Routledge & Kegan Paul.

Reid, J.F. (1966). Learning to think about reading. *Educational Research,* **9,** 56–62.

Rice, M. (1983). Cognitive aspects of communicative development. In R. Schiefelbusch (ed), *The acquisition of communicative competence.* Baltimore: University Park Press.

Sachs, J., and Devin, J. (1976). Young children's use of age appropriate speech styles. *Journal of Child Language,* **3,** 81–98.

Scaife, M., and Bruner, J. (1975). The capacity for joint visual attention in the infant. *Nature,* **253,** 265–266.

Schieffelin, B.B., and Cochrane-Smith, M. (1984). Learning to read culturally: Literacy before schooling. In H. Goelman, A. Oberg, and F. Smith (eds), *Awakening to literacy,* (pp. 3–23). London: Heinemann.

Scollon, R., and Scollon, S.B.K. (1981). Cooking it up and boiling it down: abstracts in Athabaskan children's story retellings. In D. Tannen (ed) *Spoken and written language.* Norwood, N.J.: Ablex.

Shatz, M., and Gelman, R. (1973). The development of communication skills: modifications in the speech of young children as a function of the listener. *Monographs of the Society for Research in Child Development,* **38.**

Slobin, D. (1973). Early grammatical development in several languages. In W. Weksel and T.G. Bever, (eds), *The structure and psychology of language.* New York: Holt, Rinehart & Winston.

Snow, C.E. (1983). Literacy and language: relationships during the preschool years. *Harvard Educational Review,* **53,** 165–189.

Snow, C., and Ferguson, C. (1977). *Talking to children: language input and acquisition.* Cambridge: Cambridge University Press.

Sulzby, E. (1985). Kindergarteners as writers and readers. In M. Farr (ed), *Advances in writing research. Vol 1. Children's early writing development.* Norwood, N.J.: Ablex.

Taine, H. (1877). Acquisition of language by children. *Mind,* **2,** 252–259.

Tannen, D. (1985). Relative focus on involvement in oral and written discourse. In D. Olson, N. Torrance, and D. Hildyard (eds), *Literacy, language and learning.* Cambridge: Cambridge University Press.

Teale, W.H. (1984). Reading to young children: its significance for literacy development. In H. Goelman, A. Oberg, and F. Smith (eds), *Awakening to literacy.* Exeter: Heinemann.

Templeton, S., and Spivey, E. (1980). The concept of word in young children as a function of level of cognitive development. *Research in the Teaching of English,* **14,** 265–278.

Thomassen, A.J.W.M., and Teulings, H.L. (1983). The development of handwriting. In M. Martlew (ed), *The psychology of written language: developmental and educational perspectives.* Chichester: John Wiley.

Torrance, N., and Olson, D.R. (1984). Oral language competence and the acquisition of literacy. In A. Pellegrini and T. Yawkey (eds), *The development of oral and written language in social context.* Norwood, N.J.: Ablex.

Vachek, J. (1973). *Written language: general problems and problems of English.* The Hague: Mouton.

Von Sommers, P. (1984). *Drawing and cognition: descriptive and experimental studies of graphic production processes.* Cambridge: Cambridge University Press.

Vygotsky, L. (1962). *Thought and language.* Cambridge, M.I.T. Mass: Press.

Vygotsky, L. (1983). The prehistory of written language. In M. Martlew (ed), *The psychology of written language: developmental and educational perspectives.* Chichester: John Wiley.

Waterson, N., and Snow, C. (1978). *The development of communication.* Chichester: John Wiley.

Weir, R. (1962). *Language in the crib.* The Hague: Mouton.

Wells, G. (1985a). *Language development in the preschool years.* Cambridge: Cambridge University Press.

Wells, G. (1985b). Preschool literacy-related activities and success in school. In D. Olson, N. Torrance and A. Hildyard (eds), *Literacy, language and learning.* Cambridge: Cambridge University Press.

CHAPTER 5

# Beyond A, B, and C: a Broader and Deeper View of Literacy

DENNIS WOLF, LYLE DAVIDSON, MARTHA DAVIS, JOSEPH WALTERS, MATTHEW HODGES AND LARRY SCRIPP

## INTRODUCTION: OLDER AND NEWER VIEWS OF LITERACY

We usually confine the meaning of the term 'literacy' to the ability to read and write, using it to name the capacity to inscribe and interpret alphabetic scripts. As familiar and well-grounded as this usage is, it brings a problem in its wake. As human beings, we are prolific symbol-users; we inscribe and interpret far more than texts—we create music notations, maps, diagrams, and graphs as records of our experience or means of communicating what we know to friends, colleagues, or future generations. Even in 'reading' as ordinary and straight-forward a record as a newspaper, a reader decodes more than words. She or he needs to know how to make sense of a number of different kinds of text: a table of contents, an editorial, a help-wanted page, the conversation 'bubbles' in a comic strip. Equally, he or she must be able to understand a range of graphic symbols: a photograph of a proposed building site, a political cartoon, the slope of the Dow–Jones graph on the financial pages; a pictogram about US imports; a diagram in a science article on waste conversion.

In other words, a fundamental characteristic of human symbol use is the capacity to tune our forms of representation—whether words or graphic forms—to particular purposes. Thus, to speak of children as becoming readers and writers is insufficient. To be literate in the profoundest sense is to be able to

This research was supported by a grant from the Carnegie Corporation. The work was carried out both in the Cambridge Public Schools and at the Cambridge Friends School. We are grateful to the teachers, children and parents who helped us to pursue our interest in redefining literacy. We would like to thank Howard Gardner and Courtney Cazden for their thoughtful reading of earlier versions of this and related papers.

create and extract meanings from any number of symbol systems, not just alphabets. Moreover, even literacy *within* a symbol system is varied: alphabets can be used to create outlines, poems, or charts; numerals go into lists, formulae, and computer codes; shapes compose drawings, diagrams, and maps. Each of these records uses a code in a particular way: the numerals in a list and a code neither signify the same kind of content, nor accomplish their reference according to the same rules. Consequently, it may be not only wise, but critically important, for psychologists, educators and families to think in terms of children acquiring a *broad notational competence* or a fluency in recording or interpreting experience in a variety of symbolic languages and genres.

There is a second problem with the customary concept of literacy. This problem lies with a 'shallow' view of literacy which is focused too sharply on an individual's ability to use a code like the alphabet—to the exclusion of other centrally important skills. Even the most ordinary and informal notations draw on much more than the ability to encode and decode. As simple as the grocery list pictured in Figure 5.1 appears, it implies a complex and conceptual organization underlying its almost overly familiar form and content. At the broadest level of organization, the list is set up into three 'fields,' or types, of information: the items to be *bought*, the items which have to be *brought* on the trip (e.g. bags, cash, calculator), and the items that have to be bought separately at other stores (the circled items at the top right). But that division only skims the complexity in this everyday notation. Within the list, items are grouped by type (e.g. all the items that come from the bakery and produce sections of the supermarket are written in the same area of the page). Within these areas items are subdivided into smaller groups: the produce is broken down into vegetables and fruits. Looking at the list in still another light, other kinds of literacy-related processes become apparent. Reflecting on the list, the maker entered question marks by items that might not be available. Checking, or editing, the list led to underlining still other items. Just as in a chess game, where the observable moves are backed up by invisible reflection, projection and decision-making, the apparently simple act of writing a grocery list demands that a maker select relevant kinds or dimensions of information, organize that information systematically, reflect on and even edit information. Thus, whether we are concerned with reading and writing texts, numerical symbols, maps or music, full-bodied literacy includes much more than being able to transcribe or read back information. While there is no question that basic code knowledge is essential, it is far from sufficient. Even at the earliest stages of literacy learning, we need to look at the development of a much more complex, or *deeper,* repertoire of skills.

In the remainder of this chapter we will use longitudinal data to discuss and rethink the nature of early literacy learning. We will examine the concept of *broad literacy* by looking at children's ability to create different types of symbol

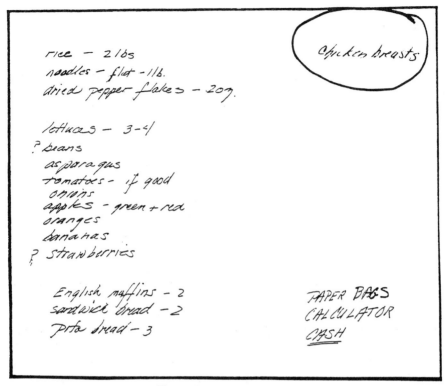

Figure 5.1  A grocery list

systems. First, we will describe how 5- to 7-year-olds come to distinguish between making a map and a drawing of a terrain. Extending the concept of *broad literacy* we will look at the ways in which a particular symbol system (like language) can be tuned to specific purposes (such as performing a puppet show or telling a story). In a second section, we explore the concept of *deep literacy*. There we discuss how, even in the earliest phases of literacy learning, children spontaneously develop a repertoire of literacy-related skills that far exceeds encoding and decoding. To illustrate this, we examine how 5- to 7-year-olds change in their ability to select relevant dimensions of information and their skill at organizing and representing the structure of information.

Based on these observations, we suggest that when educators limit children's notational experience to numbers and letters, they are radically narrowing the range of what children can learn about recording their experience. Further, when educators treat code-knowledge and transcription skill as necessary prerequisites, rather than companion abilities, to skills like organizing and representing information, they make early literacy learning shallow where it should be deep.

## THE NOTATIONAL STUDY

Any number of studies of early development indicate that children between the ages of 1 and 5 take tremendous strides in acquiring the range of symbol systems used in their culture: language, gesture, drawing, music, or numerical terms (Brown, 1973; Davidson, 1985; Golomb, 1974; Gelman and Gallistel, 1978; Wagner and Walters, 1982; Werner and Kaplan, 1967; Wolf, 1985a, b). In fact, many 5-year-olds command some of the most basic rules of narrative, counting, singing, as well as two- and three-dimensional forms of symbolization (Wolf and Gardner, in preparation). In other words, they have a rich knowledge of the problems or issues their culture 'says' are central in particular domains.

In addition, many children have a rudimentary hold on what it takes to *record* this kind of domain knowledge. Although extensive experimentation with different types of record-making may be especially prevalent in middle-class children, 3- and 4-year-olds living in settings where their exposure to records comes chiefly through labels and advertising, also use dots, slashes, simple drawing elements, even bottle caps, to create primitive 'records' of events, quantities, game scores, or debts (Ferrerio, 1978; Landsmann and Levin, 1985; in press; Vasco, 1984). Thus, it is critical to recognize that even young children are learning that different types of information (quantities, songs, spatial relations, etc.) may require different sorts of notational systems.

At the same time, as documented by White (1965, 1970), between the ages of 5 and 7 children exhibit some dramatic increases in the way that they segment and proceed through tasks. In these same years the extent to which children use their symbolic abilities to guide and reflect on their own behavior shifts dramatically (Kendler and Kendler, 1970). Moreover, their ability to pay attention to the particular task at hand increases. Finally, their ability to 'see through' distracting physical appearances to the underlying facts increases (as in conservation of number tasks).

With these kinds of issues in mind, we initiated a longitudinal study of children's ability to record, read back, and reflect on four quite different kinds of information: narrative events, quantitative relations, spatial information, and music. In a three-year study, we followed two highly contrastive populations of children from kindergarten through second grade. One group of middle-class children (11 boys, 15 girls) attended a school which provided them with an exceptionally rich environment in which to make the transition from informal to formal symbolic learning. A second group of children (13 boys, 12 girls) came from working-class backgrounds and attended a school where the climate for notational learning was comparatively impoverished. Each school year, we worked individually with children, exploring what they knew and what they could record in each of these domains. The data from the study include: direct observations of children's processes, their final products, as well as clinical interviews about what they were trying to accomplish. It is from these varied domains and types of information that the concepts of *broad* and *deep* literacy have emerged.

## BROAD LITERACY

When we speak of *broad literacy* we refer to the ability to 'tune' a particular kind of notation or record to a specific purpose. In language, it is often referred to as the control of register or genre (Pellegrini, Galda, and Rubin, 1984; Scholes and Kellogg, 1966). It is this skill that gives human symbol use or record-making capacities tremendous scope and flexibility.

### Broad literacy: developing a range of symbol systems

If we were to describe the diversity of literacy strictly in terms of recording information taken from different domains, we would miss another aspect of broad literacy: our ability to format the 'same' information variously for different purposes. By way of illustration, consider the several different renditions of houses and hiding places made by a 7-year-old and reproduced in Figure 5.2 below. Although her notations may not yet be fully conventional, this child already understands the constraints and rules of different symbol systems. She records the 'same' information about 'hiding places' differently depending on whether she is using words in a text, distance within a bar chart, pictorial shapes in a drawing, or labeled and simplified shapes within a map. It is also important to see that she understands how to use the same symbol system (for example, language) in a variety of ways: richly and descriptively in her story or in a trimmed-down label format within her graph and map. It is this ability to adapt record-making to particular types of information and tasks that gives us both a varied repertoire of approaches to record-making and the ability to tune our record-making continuously to newly emerging purposes and tasks (Scribner, 1983; Scribner & Cole, 1981).

Even these informal attempts at reworking the same information for different purposes suggest that the domain of graphic representation is a rich area in which to study how individuals learn to adapt information to varied cultural formats. Clearly, this differentiation only becomes increasingly important as the symbolic tasks an individual undertakes multiply. Consider, for instance, how differently an individual might render visual information about the 'same' landmarks in a map or a drawing of a neighborhood. Someone making a sketch is likely to include much of the visual information about landmarks in their natural setting as seen from a particular point of view. In that drawing the house at # 23 Union Street might appear as a three-story, gray-shingled, Victorian structure with a Mansard roof and syringa bushes in the front yard. However, if the same person were making a map of the neighborhood, she or

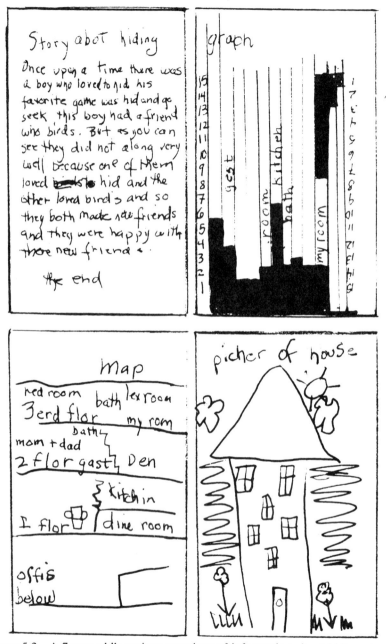

Figure 5.2    A 7-year-old's various notations of information about hiding places

he would set down a different set of visual 'facts,' in a distinct format. In all probability, the maker would draw the area as seen from a bird's-eye perspective and strip down the information to the location of major buildings, landmarks, and thoroughfares. The house would appear as a square, set back one half-inch from the double line labeled 'Union.' Clearly, the process of becoming visually literate involves learning to discriminate among the varied graphic formats in which we can record our concepts or knowledge, whether that information is carried in graphs, diagrams, drawings, or maps (Balchin and Coleman, 1965).

This notion of mapping skills as a part of visual literacy contrasts with more familiar ways of thinking about the development of mapping skills. Typically, children's maps have been used as a means to investigate other aspects of cognition such as children's knowledge of a particular space (Hart, 1979; Siegel, 1981), their perspective-taking skills (Piaget and Inhelder, 1956); memory (Verdonik, 1986); or individual differences in patterns of development (Feldman, 1980). Only recently have researchers documented the development of map-reading and map-making as skills *per se* (Bluestein and Acredolo, 1979; Liben and Downs, 1985). However, the question of how maps differ from other forms of graphic representation, has, until now, been an investigation reserved chiefly for philosophers and semioticians (Downs, 1985; Goodman, 1968).

In order to look at the development of mapping as a distinct form of visual literacy, we presented children to kindergarten, first and second grades with the small model terrain pictured in Figure 5.3. Given a small set of props, each child was asked to make a smaller, but still three-dimensional, reconstruction

Figure 5.3   A sketch of the model terrain used in the Notation Study

of the model terrain. Only after completing this task, were they given paper and pencil and asked to make a map, showing 'what each item in the town is and where it is.'

By first grade, children understand the raw materials required for success at the mapping task. Perceiving the number, size and location of items in the town is not a problem for them: all of the children were able to reconstruct the model on a smaller scale with reasonable accuracy. Similarly, encoding *per se* poses no problem. Asked to make a tree, a house, or a road, all these children are able to produce very readable, and even sophisticated, renditions of the objects. But what develops more slowly is children's ability to tune their record-making to the particular demands of map-making as compared to drawing.

*Differences between maps and drawings.*

Although maps and drawings both render the spatial relations between objects and landmarks, the two forms of graphic representation can be distinguished along at least two major dimensions. To begin, they differ in *faithfulness*. In a drawing, a maker is free to select among landmarks and even to invent features. In a map, a maker must render all major landmarks and may not introduce fictional items. Moreover, the two types of spatial renditions differ in the way they depict the size of landmarks and areas. In a drawing, the maker has the option of playing with the way in which she or he represents the relative size of items and areas in order to highlight the most interesting or important. This is not the case in maps, where objective proportional representation of sizes is crucial. Further, in a drawing, a maker may play with the spatial relations among landmarks and their orientations, creating a scene which is most commonly anchored to the bottom of the page. In a map, the spatial arrangement of items and the distances between them must not be distorted.

Maps and drawings may also differ in *economy*. For instance, in most maps, only major landmarks and geographical features are represented, whereas in drawings, grass, trees, fences and mailboxes often appear. Moreover, even the representations of major landmarks are likely to differ across drawings and maps. Within a map a hill might be rendered using a stylized curve, a house might be designated with a simple square. In a drawing these items might include a rich amount of detail. In the interest of preserving accuracy of spatial lay-out in an economical way, maps most typically present a bird's-eye view of both terrain and landmarks. In a drawing, the volume of objects is depicted by presenting all of an object (front, sides, etc.) that can be seen from a particular vantage point. Consequently, in drawings, items 'speak for themselves,' while map-makers often provide labels and legends to insure the clarity of their representations.

Across the several years of the study, children's reponses to the mapping task shifted on these dimensions in regular and significant ways. A repeated measures ANOVA on dichotomous outcome variables was used to assess the effect of time on children's renditions of the model terrain. For example, on the dimension of what is included in the map, children became increasingly 'faithful' to the model. Not only did they include all major landmarks, but they resisted the temptation to invent compatible but fictional ones ($F(2,76) = 3.08$, $p = 0.052$). With respect to depicting the relative size of buildings and hills, children increasingly follow a system of proportional representation ($F(2,76) = 7.92$, $p < 0.001$). In the area of spatial arrangement, fewer second-graders arranged items in local groups, clustered them at the bottom on the page, or took liberties in the placement of items as they might in their drawings. Instead, by the age of 8, almost all of the children represented the items in correct topological relations ($F(2,76) = 43.17$, $p < 0.001$).

Children also came to approach drawing perspective in quite distinct ways. Across the three years, they exchanged their reliance on frontal views for the more efficient aerial perspective ($F(2,76) = 3.77$, $p = 0.027$). Their renditions of terrain items also became more economical, as they gradually reduced the amount of detail in their symbols to one or two defining features. Thus, across a number of measures there is a shift in the number of children employing mapping vs. drawing strategies.

*Case studies of the emergence of map-making.*

By looking closely at children's maps as they change between the ages of 5 and 7, it is possible to see the gradual evolution of a specialized and distinct approach to recording spatial information in highly economical and faithful formats. Although the children described here are the same chronological age, the second child begins his development where the first child leaves off. By looking across these two individuals, we get a full view of the spectrum of mapping development possible during the early elementary school years.

When 5-year-old Jordan made a map, he borrowed on his already well-established picture-making skills and created a landscape of the town. He anchored items to the bottom of the page, distorted sizes and location, and included quite a bit of detail. He even added non-existent details like a chimney on the middle building (cf. Figure 5.4a). Jordan's first-grade product is more faithful, and thus, more map-like than his kindergarten version. The roads and stream became more prominent and the sizes of other items are proportionally reduced (cf. Figure 5.4b). He also used space in a markedly different way, arranging items in a way that more closely matches the model. However, he still lined up major items in a horizontal array, seemingly unable to break away from the notion of the top of the page as the sky and the bottom as the ground. Jordan continued to include realistic as well as fictional detail in his representation and relied on frontal perspective characteristic of many children's drawings at this stage of development—both indications of a lack of concern for

Figure 5.4a, b, and c    Jordan's maps at ages 5, 6, and 7

economical symbols. By second grade, Jordan's approach to mapping had changed in two major ways. First, he came to use the space on the page more effectively, positioning items in reference to the roads and each other, rather than relating them to a horizontal ground line. Secondly, Jordan began to shift his drawing angle. By the age of 7 he rendered the several faces of each building, including the roofs. He dropped all fictional embellishments on the buildings, yet continued to include a great deal of realistic details. Thus, he had not begun to abstract his map symbols into iconic forms (cf. Figure 5.4c).

A longitudinal look at the maps of a second child, Daryl, suggests what may occur between the ages of 5 and 7 for the graphically sophisticated child. Even in kindergarten, Daryl positioned items throughout the page in correct topological relation to one another. He faithfully included all items in the terrain and

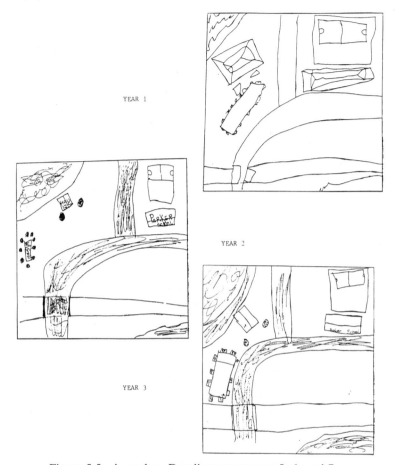

Figure 5.5a, b, and c    Daryl's maps at ages 5, 6, and 7

only those in the terrain. Like Jordan in his later maps, Daryl began to shift to a bird's-eye view. He 'squashed' each building in order to show both the roof and each of the four sides (cf. Figure 5.5a). By first grade, Daryl had abandoned the transitional mix of perspectives and was able to create a map from a consistent bird's eye view. He compensated for the fact that the resulting simple rect-angles were hardly identifiable as rooftops by adding labels (cf. Figure 5.5b). In second grade, the faithfulness of Daryl's spatial arrangement and proportion rivalled that of an adult (cf. Figure 5.5c). He had started to break free of the obligation to render items realistically, as evidenced by the square, economical icons used to represent bushes around the left-most house. It is this level of abstraction that is likely to make him increasingly aware of the need for and power of labels and even a legend within his maps.

It might appear that the changes evident in Jordan and Daryl's maps can be explained by an overall increase in children's skill at any type of graphic representation. However, data from an additional study indicate that children are constructing the distinctive rules of several different graphic systems. In this study, children were asked to draw *both* maps and drawings of the same terrain. Findings suggest that there is an early period during which children produce the same basic product in response to a request to make either a map or a drawing. These 'generic' representations are simply not guided by the rules belonging to any one particular function. It is in a second phase of representational development that children's maps and drawings emerge as distinct forms. It is only at this time that children make maps which are both rigorously faithful to the spatial information they portray, yet highly economical in the way that information is rendered. By comparison, their drawings become increasingly inventive, detailed, and concerned with at least the illusion of rendering three-dimensional space.

**Broad literacy: tuning a symbol system to a particular purpose**

The process of tuning a symbolic form to a particular use is not limited to the case of map-making. In fact, human beings often take the very same symbol system and adapt its content and form to highly specific purposes. Consider the case of language use. Children as young as 2 and 3 alter their speech when talking to babies (Berko-Gleason, 1973; Dunn and Kendrick, 1982). Pre-school children speak differently when they build with blocks and engage in dramatic play (Pellegrini, 1985).

As a part of the notational study, we looked at children telling the 'same' story in a number of different formats. After they were shown a short, silent film about three boys teasing each other with a yellow hat, children retold the events of the film as an oral narrative or as 'show' using small figures. Across these two formats, children vary their language quite systematically. In telling narratives, children create accounts in which they are quite faithful to the events of the film, whereas in their shows, children invent and elaborate. While retelling the film events, children put together 'autonomous narratives' in which they speak as an observing narrator, using the third person and the past tense and not interacting at all with their audience. Their shows are often described in an 'on-line sportscaster style.' Finally, while children are careful to put all of their story information into words, during their shows they leave at least some action implicit in actions, sound effects, and the set-up of their scenes (Wolf, 1985a, b). Figure 5.6 presents excerpts from one child's story and show.

While these performances occur in spoken language, they are indicative of similar distinctions that children make in written language. In recording their 'stories,' children write words from left to right so as to form sentences. However, they often keep another sheet where they try out more difficult

STORY

Once there was a little boy/
and his name was Alex/
Alex was walking through the park one day/
and then his shoe came untied/
so he bent down and tied it/
then/when he put his head up/
he found a hat/
so he put the hat on/
but/the/for some reason/
the hat made him twirl and twirl and twirl around/
until he fell down/on the ground and bumped his head/
so/he got up/and took the hat off/
then he started to walk through the park again/
then his hair felt funny/
his hair stuck out/
and he did not like the way it looked/
so/he dropped the hat/and combed his hair/
but/there/there were two boys/hiding behind the bushes/
and the two boys/took the hat/and ran back behind the bushes/
(transcript continues)

SHOW

| Child Vocalizations | Actions | Adult Contribution |
|---|---|---|
| | | E. asks her to tell the same story of the movie, but as a puppet show, setting up figures in a theatre |
| This show is called//the// | | |
| This show is called// | | |
| | ya//the . . . | |
| the mystery of the magic hat/ | | |
| | places white and green figures behind bush | |
| | blue to left in front | |
| blue: Hum de dum de dum/ | | |
| I'm walking along . . . | | |
| through the park/what a wonderful day/ | | |
| oh/my shoe's untied/ | | |
| guess I'll have to tie it/ | | |
| | blue kneels to tie | |
| | white throws hat out | |
| blue: huh? how did that hat get here? | | |
| oh well/probably somebody's that's lost/ | | |
| that's a nice yellow hat/with/strange wings/ | | |
| | puts hat on blue | |
| eh/there we go/I think I'll put it on/ | | |
| haaah/this thing makes me turn around/ | | |
| | twirls blue in place | |

Figure 5.6 (continued overleaf)

```
hahhh/I am getting dizzy/
haahh/I'm going to take this off/
I don't wanna/get so dizzy that I won't be able to walk straight/
                    pops hat off of blue
Hmmm, my hair feels kinda funny/
I think I'll comb it/
I'll just put the hat right there/
                    places hat on ground
humming sd. effects as
                    blue makes combing gestures
white:   (whisper) hey/look/
green:   (whisper) what?
white:   (whisper) he dropped the hat/
now we can get it back/
green:   (wh) hmmm/ya/
white:   (wh) I'll hide behind/I'll hide behind these/those
   bushes/
green:   (wh) okay/
                    white darks out/grabs hat and
                    rushes back behind a sec set. of bushes
(transcript continues)
```

Figure 5.6  Excerpts from a child's 'story' and 'show' based on the same narrative information

words before writing them into their texts. It is no accident that the two kinds of writing take different forms on the paper—they are tuned to distinct purposes: that of a text and that of a list. This finding echoes that of a number of other researchers (Ehri, 1979; Ferrerio, 1978) who have noted how many 4- and 5-year olds have already caught on to the different formats of signs, menus, grocery lists, and the running text of stories.

## Acquiring broad literacy

Ironically, school—as it is presently conducted—can be a difficult place in which to acquire broad literacy. Typically, children are engaged in using only two (letters and numerals) of the many ways in which it is possible to record experience. Instead, classrooms should be packed with examples of the various ways in which it is possible to record experience: graphs, maps, timelines, charts, diagrams, musical scores. Even more important, children need the opportunity not only to study, but to become involved in generating maps and drawing, texts and lists. In addition, children need the chance to see the ways in which the 'same' set of symbols can be used differently. Instead of meeting numerals chiefly in the context of calculations, children should have the chance to use numbers to make ordered lists, to measure, and to code information.

Finally, children need a climate which fosters the explicit examination of the way notations work. Rarely, if ever, do they compare maps and drawings of the same terrain. Yet, as the findings above indicate, 5- to 7-year-olds are still working out the differences between these two kinds of spatial renditions. Similarly, children whose most familiar forms of discourse are conversation and story-telling, are often assigned reports. Implicitly, they are being asked to deal with information in an expository, *not* a narrative manner. But rarely do teachers explicitly address the differences between telling 'stories' about what happened in a science lesson and portraying the observations and conclusions of the lesson in an expository manner. Such differentiations are not beyond the reach of children—the observations and analyses presented here insist just the opposite. The point is rather that children's initial and spontaneous explorations of these issues deserve constant and thoughtful encouragement.

## DEEP LITERACY

Thus far, we have talked about reconceptualizing literacy chiefly in terms of the range of products it is vital for children to understand and be able to produce. There is, however, another aspect to our redefinition—one that deals more centrally with the range of cognitive processes, which although invisible, are essential for productive, generative literacy. By way of illustration, consider what happens as a 7-year-old makes a book in which she recreates the narrative events she originally saw in a movie about several boys playing in the park. As she works, she does more than transcribe some kind of inner narrative into a series of words. In fact, she organizes a larger notational system in which words are only a part. Using spacing, underlining, and positioning, this young writer either reflects (or articulates on the spot) a conception of the several dimensions of narrative meaning (organizational comment, narrator observation, character speech) and their interrelations.

Figure 5.7 shows how she used heavy underlining to set off the title ('The Boy'), from a picture caption (This is the boy who . . .), from the story proper (The boy has . . .). In this way, she created a distinction between organizational and narrative text. By positioning her words either in an illustration or in the running text, this young writer made a further distinction within the narrative text: whether each event is portrayed from the narrator's point of view or through a character's speech. Because the words 'O boy' show up under the illustration of the boy and the hat, we know both that the boy has found a wonderful hat and what he exclaims. Even this short sample of writing reveals that children's texts—if carefully studied—provide evidence for a range of conceptual and organizational skills that are necessary complements to children's knowledge of letter forms, spelling, and punctuation. A closer look at two such skills, the ability to select relevant dimensions and the ability to organize a notation, will provide a clearer sense of both their importance and their widespread occurrence in the various forms of literacy available even to young children.

Figure 5.7    A 7-year-old's organization of narrative information in a book

## Deep literacy: the skill of selecting dimensions

Music exhibits a number of interacting dimensions which must be heard, isolated, and notated in a way that reflects how they intertwine. Even at the level of foot-tapping, music has 'that swing,' which musicians recognize as the *underlying pulse*. The pulse, in turn, supports another dimension of rhythm, the grouping of longer and shorter durations which make up the music's *surface pattern*. Independent of this temporal dimension, there is the melodic contour of the song, made up of individual pitches taken from particular scales, and organized into phrases. A musical 'moment,' therefore, consists of the inter-action between at least these temporal and melodic frameworks.

Since music is clearly a multi-dimensional domain, its notation requires a great deal of skill in integrating the various symbols for the different dimen-sions with one another. In fact, it is rarely enough to be able to translate the temporal and melodic aspects onto the two-dimensional space of a piece of paper. For example, additional remarks like 'allegro' or 'andante' track an expressive dimension. A look at a young musician's personal score indicates that at its most complex, musical performance, and consequently musical notation, has still more dimensions (cf. Figure 5.8). Pencilled throughout the printed music are marks which track changing dynamics (a set of widening and diminishing angles); emphasis (circled notes); and phrasing (lines tying notes).

As part of our study of notational skills, we asked young children to make notations of the well-known song. 'Row, row, row your boat,' with an additional introductory phrase. Altogether this tune consisted of five phrases and might be conventionally notated as in Figure 5.9.

Figure 5.8   A young musician's personal score, marked for additional dimensions of musical information

Previous research (Bamberger, 1982; Upitis, 1985) suggests that in clearly-structured tasks children can invent surprisingly articulate notations of rhythmic fragments and are sensitive to training with musical notational symbols (Walker, 1978, 1981). However, with this study we deliberately presented children with open-ended instructions: 'Write down this song so that someone else who doesn't know the song can sing it back,' in order to look at the dimensions which children would *spontaneously* select as relevant. In addition, we presented them with a whole musical piece—one that would ask them to

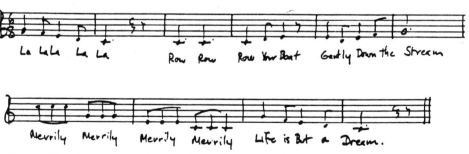

Figure 5.9   A conventional musical notation of the song used in the Notation Study

make numerous decisions about which of the many available dimensions (sound-silence, lyrics, surface and underlying rhythm, etc.) were most important to capture. As a reflection of our interest in a 'deeper' view of notation, we examined development changes within and across the musical dimensions that children recorded.

Our analyses show that, without training, and using a wide variety of invented and borrowed symbols, elementary school children can extract musically relevant dimensions and create notational formats which show an increasingly sophisticated ability to record events within and across these dimensions. All children's notations were scored for the ways in which they recorded rhythms and pitch relations. These analyses indicated both the increasing sophistication with which children deal with each of these dimensions and their growing ability to discern and record multiple dimensions throughout a song. For example, in their initial trials, most children record some simple aspect of the rhythmic structure of 'Row, row, row your boat.' The majority of 5-year-olds portray how the song consists of different phrases by separating each new phrase from others with an open space on the paper. Children first record the song's phrases. This is followed by notations that record individual notes (or syllables). Later notations indicate underlying pulse and eventually record the units according to surface pattern. Scoring notations according to this progression—phrase, note, pulse, surface rhythm—over the three years of the study produced a significant test statistic (Friedman test of repeated measures, chi square $= 34.51$, $df = 2$, $p = 0.000$).

Between the ages of 5 and 7, most children exhibit a parallel developmental progression in their ability to isolate and notate the melodic dimension of the song. Once they have mastered the notation of phrases and units (syllables) they next encode the contour of the pitches (e.g. the rising and falling motion of the melody), and finally, the scalar organization that underlies the whole piece (Friedman test of repeated measures, chi square $= 37.21$, $df = 2$, $p < 0.000$).

Looking across these two dimensions, it is clear many children also show a steady increase in their ability to notate a number of musical dimensions at once. All children begin by encoding the phrase structure (e.g. a picture denoting each phrase of the song). When they add a second dimension, children break up their earlier phrase-based song renditions in order to show the units of the song—usually in terms of the individual syllables which typically carry a beat of the song. Thereafter, while children continue to add dimensions, they do so according to much less universal patterns. The third dimension to appear in some children's songs is underlying pulse, for others it is surfaces rhythm, for still others it is the melodic contour of the song. There is equal variety in the fourth dimension—some children turn their attention to encoding pulse plus surface grouping, others begin to notate the scalar organization underlying individual pitches. Despite this diversity, children regularly increase the number (1–4) of independent musical dimensions they encode in

Figure 5.10a, b, and c   Arietta's song notations at ages 5, 6, and 7

their song notations (Friedman test of repeated measures, chi square = 18.5, *df* =2, *p*= 0.000).

*Case studies in the development of musical notations.*

Both the increasing number of dimensions and the individual emphases among these dimensions become evident when we look carefully at individual children's notations. At the age of 5, Arietta represents the entire song with a sprawling set of icons. This notation is lean, it merely indicates the presence of the 5 song phrases (cf. Figure 5.10a). A year later, at 6, there is a huge jump in her notational ability; she elaborated the structure of the song by showing *units* within the phrases, plus occasional *groupings* of the surface rhythm patterns. In this way, she showed the remarkable ability to extract simultaneously three dimensions of the song—its lyrics, indications of its phrase structure, and the rhythmic groupings characteristic of the surface patterns (cf. Figure 5.10b). At the age of 7, Arietta developed a notationally efficient, yet even richer approach to encoding the musical dimensions of the song. Employing abstract symbols, she consistently showed four distinct dimensions of the song: *phrase structure, units, pulse or rhythmic grouping,* and *melodic contour* (cf. Figure 5.10c).

It is important to note that these dimensions emerged without any explicit request on the part of the observer to put down words, rhythms, or pitch patterns. Left on her own. Arietta extracted these critical dimensions. Moreover, having picked out these dimensions, Arietta did not set them down individually. Rather, she created a densely-packed record of a series of musical moments. The marks representing each of these moments is modulated—at once—in several ways. Its position within a larger spatial group indicates in which song phrase it occurs, its relative position to other marks indexes its value within both surface rhythms and pulse, its height on the page indicates its place within the melodic pattern of the whole song. It is to this ability to understand and record the complex structure of information that we now turn.

### Deep literacy: recording the structure of information

The notations we make rarely track single or independent lines of information. Even the simplest and most familiar notation, such as calendars, portray the *relations* between different types of information, such as the *interaction* between the day of the week and the date within the month. In fact, as in calendars or music, most notations make extensive use of both symbols and graphic features (such as size, color, location on page) in order to portray the intersections of various dimensions of information. When asked to record a song, children not only define particular dimensions—lyrics, rhythms across time, relative pitches—they invent systems that portray the coordination of these dimensions into a series of musical moments or events. In a different situation, that of recording a clearly defined quantitative event, we were able to analyze more precisely how children organize information within and across what they see as relevant dimensions.

In order to investigate how children come to reflect (and perhaps even realize) the relations between interacting lines of information in their notations, we asked children to participate in a 'Bus Trip.' In that trip, an experimenter pushed a cardboard bus along a paper road and placed small and large 'riders' on the bus at different 'stops.' The child's task, as the 'conductor' was to keep track of what happened. At the end of the trip, the 'conductor' called up the 'Boss' (who had not seen the trip) to report how many adults and how many children got on at each stop. To make this report accurately, children made a written record of the bus trip.

Unlike many other studies of early number development, we were not centrally concerned with children's ability to count and calculate accurately (Gelman and Gallistel, 1978) or their use of the conventions of place value (Kamii, 1981). Nor were we concerned with monitoring the kinds of class inclusion errors (Inhelder and Piaget, 1964) or the development of more intuitive collections (Markman, 1979; Markman and Siebert, 1976). In addition, we were interested in examining children's spontaneous and untutored ability to *organize* any kind of marks (numerals, tallies, icons) into a system that either reflected or realized the *structure* of the information they were attempting to record. For us, these organizational abilities constitute a major, though a neglected, aspect of learning to use numerals (or any other code) to save and communicate information.

*Fields in early number notations.*

Just as children had to find a way of describing any given musical moment simultaneously in terms of pitch and rhythmic values, they eventually discovered that any adequate notation of an event in the bus trip must include information from two distinct dimensions—information about how many riders got on at *each stop* and information about how many riders of *each type* (adults and children) got on and off at each stop.

These two dimensions, *stops* and *types*, are, in turn, composed of 'fields' of information. Each of the four *stop* fields (Star, Rainbow, Acorn, and Pine) is defined in terms of all the activities occurring there (adults on, children on). Each of the *type* fields (children and adults) is defined in terms of occurrences across all four stops. What is critical is that these fields intersect. If '3 adults get on at Rainbow Street,' the '3' must somehow be a part of both the field for Rainbow Street and the field for adults. It is this overlapping nature of fields that yields notational challenge to the task. Not only must a child represent the quantities observed in the event, but he or she must also capture, as efficiently as possible, the *relationships* among these quantities. For example, the child must determine the quantity of riders of each type that get on at a particular stop. In creating the notation, the child must represent these basic classes; but when asked, 'How many children got on the bus?' the child must also be able to form a superordinate set, 'all riders of the type children from all stops.'

*Developmental findings on the emergence of organizational abilities.*

Children's notations are not simply transparent records of the way they apprehend and organize information. Clearly, there is a symbiotic relation between concepts and their representation in a notation. As concepts emerge, the ability to notate them changes; and as notational abilities grow, the concepts embodied by them are reinforced. We know that as notational systems become deeply ingrained as ways of recording particular kinds of information, our very perception of that information is shaped (Kaput, 1986; Menninger, 1969). Nevertheless, children's notations give us an observable behavioral record from which to infer possible changes in their underlying ability to organize information.

To describe children's development across the three years of the study, we scored their ability to organize their notations of the Bus Trip into systems that reflected the existence and the interrelations among numerous dimensions or fields of information. We found that the most primitive notations exhibited no fields at all—for instance, a child might simply create a running total of riders by erasing a previous amount and writing in a new one after each stop. Slightly more sophisticated notations represented the fields of a single dimension (e.g. just the total number of riders at the various stops). Still more developed notations represented both dimensions, but lacked any explicit organizational devices (labels, columns and rows, etc.) indicating that children grasped the structure of the relationship between dimensions. Alternatively, children's notations included marks to differentiate just one of the two dimensions of information included. At their most developed, some notations differentiated and explicitly marked both dimensions of information. The Friedman repeated measures test verified that children's scores improved significantly across the three years of the study (chi square $=32.09$, $df = 2, p. = 0.000$). This significant upward trend suggests that the ability to *organize* a notation constitutes a fundamental aspect of even beginning literacy.

*A case study in the organization of notations.*

The written records made by one child in kindergarten, first, and second grade, suggest how much more than the ability to translate numbers of riders into numerals is required in order to record the events of a 'Bus Trip.' In kindergarten, Arietta used numerals to represent accurately the number of riders getting on at various stops; but she did not organize the numerals on a page or label them in a way that detailed how these quantities were related to one another (cf. Figure 5.11a).

In first grade, Arietta's notation became more organized. She labeled specific rows of numerals. Within each row, she used spatial organization to keep track of which numerals refer to 'adults' and 'children': the right-hand numeral regularly stands for adults, the left-hand figure denotes children. At

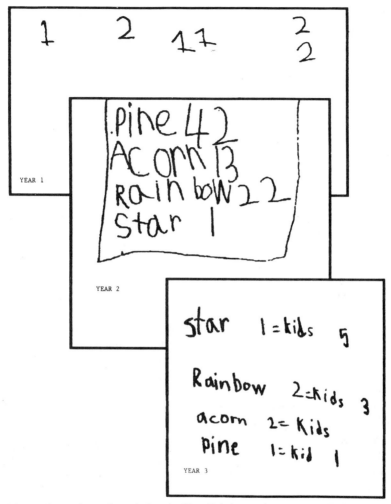

Figure 5.11a, b, and c   Arietta's 'Bus Trip' notations at ages 5, 6, and 7

the last stop, where no children got on the bus, Arietta was careful to move the adult numeral (1) to the right, using an empty space to denote the absence of younger riders. This effort at place-holding is a striking illustration of how clearly she grasps the interrelations between the various lines of information she is encoding: the numeral indicating the number of adult riders *cannot* occur in the place in the system reserved for the numeral indicating the amount of children getting on the bus (cf. Figure 5.11b).

In second grade, Arietta used two sets of labels; one marks the individual rows with names for 'stops' and the other differentiates the 'children' numeral from the 'adults' numeral within each row (cf. Figure 5.11c).

**The power of deep literacy: the place of dimensionalizing and organizing information**

Too often, in their first years of school, we restrict children's literacy learning to learning and practicing codes—alphabets, numerals, and sometimes musical notes. Yet our findings on the processes of selecting dimensions and organizing information systems show that other skills are not outside the reach of 5- to 7-year-olds. As the invented 'Bus Trip' and song notations indicate, children can judge dimensions and organize information, long before their control of conventional codes is complete.

Despite these spontaneously-available skills, it is rarely that children are asked to engage in the larger or deeper exercise of their encoding skills. Workbook exercises of the kind pictured in Figure 5.12 may make children fluent in numerical labels, but they keep children's other skills at bay. Fluency in numeral use is essential, but it needs to be complemented by tasks that demand children think about how numerals (or letters or icons) operate, what relevant information needs encoding, and how those categories of information interact. By comparison with the workbook page, consider the teacher of a mixed first and second grade classroom who asked her students how they could figure out how many blades of grass there were in the outdoor playing field. Across the next several days, children argued out the relevant dimensions of the task: the length of the field, the width, the fact that the grass was thick in places, thin elsewhere, and just plain absent in muddy zones. Later, they worked out how much grass in a square foot of each type of field and surveyed how much of each kind there was using cardboard templates. Then they worked out a system which reflected the way they organized (or understood) the structure of the information they were collecting. Each 'researcher' entered his or her totals in columns marked 'Thick,' 'Thin,' and 'Mud,' subtotals were circled and the 'grand total' was boxed.

As much as children need to know how to make numeral forms and how to handle column addition or subtraction problems, they ultimately need to understand how to *use* numerals (or icons or musical notes). Any robust notion of use must include abilities such as isolating relevant dimensions and organizing those dimensions so that they reflect or help to realize the structure of information. At the same time, it is equally important to recognize that the processes of selecting dimensions or organizing notations are not the only skills that children need in addition to code use. As the example of book-making shown in Figure 5.7 indicates, full-fledged literacy also includes the ability to reflect and to edit.

## THE ROLE OF EDUCATION IN EARLY LITERACY LEARNING

The data presented thus far suggest that both broad and deep forms of literacy

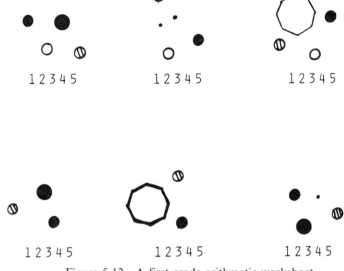

Figure 5.12   A first-grade arithmetic worksheet

learning unfold smoothly, even vigorously, in many children between the ages
of 5 and 7. Given this kind of robust developmental data, even in areas like
mapping and music where children receive almost no instruction, it is tempting
to see little role for education other than exposure.

**Literacy learning: an active, not an imitative process**

Much as in language development, children need models—finished maps,
outlines, musical scores—in order to acquire broad and deep literacy skills.
However, the acquisition of complex literacy skills demands far more than the
simple borrowing of forms or imitation of strategies. Our observational data
suggest that children rarely come to the paper knowing exactly what they want
to record, instead they engage in considerable questioning, experimentation,
and redrafting until they 'recognize' possible solutions. Moreover, children
show us forms of recording they have never seen in adult models. For example,
on their way to working out the rules of aerial perspective, children invent
bird's-eye views of roofs to which they attach the front and side faces of
buildings, thereby creating anomalous 'squashed' renditions which fit the
demands of both mapping and drawing. Similarly, on their way to learning to
use quotation marks, children denote character speech by placing utterances
inside illustrations, next to their speakers. Finally, the children within the study
exhibit many individual approaches to solving the same problem. Thus, some
individuals denote children and adults in the bus task using large and small stick

figures, 'C' and 'A,' taller and shorter tally marks. Again, such observations suggest that what we observe is an active learning process, not a simple parroting of adult forms.

The role that education can—and ought to—play becomes clear if we look at group differences in early literacy development. Perhaps the most striking variation takes the form of the significant differences in the performances of the two groups of children we studied—differences which appeared in all four of the domains, and across the three years of the study. At the broadest level, children in the school which encouraged them to explore varied kinds of recording and to ask searching questions about how to capture information, consistently out-performed children whose early learning at most contained attention to the more rote aspects of letters and numbers. However, there were children from the poorer school who shone—who took on the novel demands of new kinds of record-making with zest and insight. Frequently, these children came from homes where, despite the level of income or education, there was enormous interest and pleasure in literacy and learning. These children went to the library weekly, their parents had shown them the transit map while riding on the subway, they marked off special days on calendars that hung in their kitchens. Such findings suggest that the role of early education (as opposed to just exposure or rote learning) might be to provide a wider group of children with consistent opportunities to observe and engage in the kinds of activities that fuel an understanding of and an interest in literacy.

**Variation in the achievement of literacy**

The performances of three additional groups of children also speak to the need for thoughtful, explicit, early training in literacy skills. Each of these groups is 'at risk' for missing the kind of broad and deep symbolic learning that provides the foundation for higher-level literacy skills. First of all, in the classrooms we visited roughly 10 percent of the children scored in the lowest 15 percent across the full range of tasks. These are clearly the most endangered children—ones, who will not, on their own, access either the range of symbol-using skills or the kinds of conceptual and organizational abilities that make notations powerful. Again looking across tasks, we discerned a second group of children whose transition to literacy is likely to be other than typical. These are children who exhibit what we term 'jagged profiles of skill.' They may excel in one area, while performing at average or lower levels in other areas. Almost a quarter of the children we observed exhibited marked differences in performances across different types of notations (e.g. their rank-order dropped by as many as 10–15 places across tasks). That many children again exhibited somewhat milder differences in their abilities across domains. Such findings suggest that one purpose of early literacy training might be to use an individual's strengths in one domain to build deeper or broader skills in novel, or less-developed, areas.

There is a third group of children for whom current forms of literacy training are often poor and insufficient. These are children whose cultural backgrounds give them assumptions about communication, symbol use or literacy that differ from the ones that prevail in instruction and textbooks. In our data, for example, we find that children can exhibit quite different approaches to the tasks of telling and writing narratives. Children who come to school with an 'oral style' (many of whom are speakers of Black English) differ from children whose style is more 'literate' (like written text). Oral speakers emphasize the performance qualities of language (stress, rhythm, repeating patterns, different character voices). Moreover, they build on the expectation that speakers and listeners are intimates who share and ought to acknowledge a significant fund of common experience. By comparison, children with literate styles emphasize the lexical power (e.g. the precise referential options) of language. Moreover, they frequently speak as if speaker and listener were strangers, reintroducing well-known background information. But despite these contrasting approaches, our data indicate that children of both styles understand much that is crucial to eventual writing skill: the notion of sequencing events, portraying causality, combining narrator comments and character speech, the ability to adapt a narrative to different tasks and audiences (Wolf, 1985a, b). Even so, in many classrooms there remains considerable confusion over whether these children exhibit a 'deficit' (a failure in understanding) or a 'difference' (an equally powerful, but distinct approach to the task). As a result of this confusion, culturally-different children are at risk for sometimes unjustified remedial work, which keeps them from exploring the more demanding and rewarding aspects of literacy learning.

## CONCLUSION: THE NEED FOR A MORE COMPLEX MODEL OF LITERACY LEARNING

In many elementary classrooms, teachers and students work toward learning how to record experience in just two ways—through the alphabetic and the arithmetic codes. Music, maps, diagrams and graphs simply wait until middle school (or later). Even within the realms of alphabetic and numerical information, there is little explicit exploration of the different ways in which texts or numbers capture information. Children meet stories, essays and outlines, column addition, measurements, and ordinal lists—but there is little talk about the ways in which language and numbers can be tuned to different kinds of tasks. Moreover, much language and mathematical learning occurs within a *ladder model* where instruction occurs in a strictly ordered way: alphabet skills, sound-letter knowledge, word-writing, sentence-writing, punctuation, editing; numeral names, numeral formation, counting, addition facts, etc. In accordance with this strongly sequential model, children do not progress to the 'next' skill until they master the previous one(s).

The concepts of broad and deep literacy presented in this paper suggest we need quite a different model for early literacy. First, as the cases of music and map-making illustrate, the range of symbolic forms children can use far exceeds letters and numerals. In fact, a major lesson of early literacy might be that of learning to make thoughtful choices about just how to record a particular experience. Second, even 5- to 7-year-olds, who are still very much in the course of learning to shape letters and numerals, are simultaneously engaged in thinking about other issues such as the selection of relevant dimensions to record and inventing ways to reflect the structure of information. Such findings point away from a ladder model of literacy learning; they point toward something much more like a complex grid of literacy skills. One dimension of that grid refers to *broad literacy*, or learners' access to the many forms which records may take: texts, maps, matrices, scores. The complementary dimension of the grid refers to *deep literacy* or learners' possession of a repertoire of skills that include not just code knowledge but the ability to select relevant information; grasp the structure of information; edit and proof-read. While such a model may not be surprising as a vision of sophisticated adult literacy, the data and observations presented here argue that such a complex view of literacy ought to apply to the learning of children just entering school.

It will take careful work in laboratories and classrooms to substantiate the developmental and instructional nature of this more complex form of early literacy. However, unless we adopt such a model, we will provide children with the literacy skills of scribes, not thinkers.

## REFERENCES

Balchin, W., and Coleman, A. (1965). Graphicacy should be the fourth ace in the pack. *The Times Educational Supplement.*

Bamberger, J. (1982). Revisiting children's drawings of simple rhythms: a function for reflection.in action. In S. Strauss (ed), *U-shaped behavioral growth* (pp. 191–26). New York: Academic Press.

Berko-Gleason, J. (1973). Code switching in children's language. In T.E. Moore (ed), *Cognitive development and the acquisition of language* (pp. 159–168). New York: Academic Press.

Bluestein, N., and Acredolo, L. (1979). Developmental changes in map-reading skills. *Child Development,* **50,** 691–697.

Brown, R. (1973). *A first language: The early stages.* Cambridge, Mass.: Harvard University Press.

Davidson, L. (1985). Tonal structures in children's early songs. *Music Perception* **2,** 3, 361–374.

Downs, R. (1985). The representation of space: its development in children and in cartography. In R. Cohen (ed), *The development of spatial cognition* (pp. 323–346). Hillsdale, N.J.: Lawrence Erlbaum.

Dunn, J., and Kendrick, C. (1982). The speech of two- and three-year-olds to infant siblings: 'baby talk' and the context of communication, *Journal of Child Language,* **9,** 579–595.

Ehri, L.C. (1979). Word consciousness in readers and pre-schoolers. *Journal of Educational Psychology,* **67,** 204–212.

Feldman, D.H. (1980). *Beyond universals in cognitive development.* Norwood, N.J.: Ablex.

Ferrerio, E. (1978). What is written in a written sentence: a developmental answer. *Journal of Education,* **160,** 25–39.

Gelman, R., and Gallistel, C.R. (1978). *The child's understanding of number.* Cambridge, Mass.: Harvard University Press.

Golomb, C. (1974). *Young children's sculpture and drawing: a study in representational development.* Cambridge, Mass.: Harvard University Press.

Goodman, N. (1968). *Languages of art: an approach to a theory of symbols.*

Hart, R. (1979). *Children's experience of place.* New York: Irvington.

Indianapolis, In.: Bobbs-Merrill.

Inhelder, B., and Piaget, J. (1964). *The early growth of logic in the child.* New York: Harper and Row.

Kamii, M. (1981). Children's ideas about written number. *Topics in Learning and Learning Disabilities,* **1,** 47–59.

Kaput, J. (1986). *Towards a theory of symbol use in mathematics.* Unpublished paper.

Kendler, H.H., and Kendler, T.S. (1970). Developmental processes in discrimination learning. *Human Development,* **13,** 65–89.

Landsmann, L.T., and Levin, I. (1985). Preschoolers' written language: representations of phonetic and semantic similarities and differences. Paper #52, Tel-Aviv University Unit of Human Development and Education.

Landsmann, L.T., and Levin, I. (in press). Writing in preschoolers: an age-related analysis, *Journal of Applied Psycholinguistics.*

Liben, L., and Downs, R. (1985). Children's understanding of maps. The Center for the Study of Child and Adolescent Development Scholarly Series, Report No. 8, Pennsylvania State University.

Markman, E. (1979). Classes and collections: Conceptual organization and numerical abilities. *Cognitive Psychology,* **11,** 395–411.

Markman, E., and Seibert, J. (1976). Classes and collections: Internal organization and resulting holistic properties. *Cognitive Psychology,* **8,** 561–577.

Menninger, K. (1969). *Number words and number symbols.* Cambridge, Mass.: MIT Press.

Pellegrini, A. (1985). The narrative organization of children's fantasy play: The effects of age and play context. *Educational Psychology,* **5,** 1, 17–25.

Pellegrini, A., Galda, L., and Rubin, D. (1984). Context in text: The development of oral and written language in two genres. *Child Development,* **55,** 1549–1555.

Piaget, J., and Inhelder, B. (1956). *The child's conception of space.* New York: Norton.

Scholes, R., and Kellogg, R. (1966). *The nature of narrative.* New York: Oxford University Press.

Scribner, S., and Cole, M. (1981). *The psychology of literacy.* Cambridge, MA.: Harvard University Press.

Scribner, S. (1983). Invited address. The biennial meeting of the Society for Research in Child Development. Detroit, Mi.

Siegel, A. (1981). The externalization of cognitive maps by children and adults: in search of ways to ask better questions. In L. Liben, A. Patterson, and N. Newcombe (eds), *Spatial representation and behavior across the life span* (pp. 167–194). New York: Academic Press.

Upitis, R. (1985). Children's understanding of rhythm: the relationship between development and musical training. Unpublished doctoral dissertation. Harvard University.

Vasco, C. (1984). Learning elementary school mathematics as a culturally conditioned process. Unpublished paper. Universidad Nacional de Colombia. Department of Mathematics. Bogata, Columbia.

Verdonik, F. (1986). Reconsidering the context of remembering: the need for a social description of memory processes and their development. Unpublished paper. City University of New York Graduate Center.

Wagner, S., and Walters, J. (1982). A longitudinal analysis of early number concepts: From numbers to number. In G. Forman (ed), *Action and thought: from sensorimotor schemes to symbolic operations.* (pp. 137–164). New York: Academic Press.

Walker, R. (1978). Perception and music notation. *Psychology of Music,* **6,** (1), 21–46.

Walker, R. (1981). Teaching basic musical concepts and their staff notations through cross-modal matching symbols. *Psychology of Music,* **9** (2), 31–38.

Werner, H., and Kaplan, B. (1963). *Symbol formation.* New York: Wiley.

White, S.H. (1965). Evidence for the hierarchical arrangement of learning processes. In L.P. Lipsett and C.C. Spiker (eds), *Advances in child development and behavior,* Vol. 2. New York: Academic Press.

White, S.H. (1970). Some general outlines of the matrix of development changes between five and seven years. *Bulletin of the Orton Society,* **20,** 41–57.

Wolf, D.P. (1985a). Ways of telling: narrative discourse repertoires. Paper presented at the annual meeting of the American Anthropological Association, Washington, D.C., December 1985.

Wolf, D.P. (1985b). Ways of telling: Text repertoires in elementary school children. *Journal of Education,* **167** (1), 71–87.

Wolf, D.P., and Gardner, H. (in preparation). *The making of meanings: The course of early symbolic development.*

# Affective and Social Dimensions of Early Education

In the preceding section of this volume children's cognitive development and literacy were discussed. These chapters, though they concentrated primarily on cognition, did note that social factors influenced children's cognitive development and the acquisition of literacy. For example, the effects of different mother–child interaction patterns on children's literacy were stressed by both Sulzby and Martlew. On a more general level, Malkus *et al.* suggested that culture has a potent effect on the different domains of intelligence. This discussion of the interrelation between children's social and cognitive processes is currently the *Zeitgeist* in early education and developmental psychology. The new scholarly areas of socio-cognition and social competence are evidence of this trend. Scholars again realize that cognitive and social processes are indeed interdependent.

The first chapter in this section addresses the interrelation among cognitive, social, and emotional processes in children. Case portrays child development as a process in which cognitive, social, and emotional processes are integrated. This chapter does, however, like the chapter by Malkus *et al.*, recognize individual differences in children; a child's development in each of these areas may be arrested or accelerated. Also like the Malkus *et al.* chapter, Case's chapter is useful to educators and psychologists in what it tells us about children's individual differences.

In the next chapter, Martin examines a common individual difference in young children, temperament. Like Case, Martin examines both social and cognitive dimensions of children's behavior. For example, children's school adjustment and attention span are reviewed. Like other contributors to this volume, Martin recognizes that individual differences in children exist and that they are affected by both biological and cultural factors. Martin's chapter provides psychologists and educators with a critical examination of the construct of temperament in school settings. For educators, the chapter points out ways in which adults relate to children with different temperaments. This information should be useful in understanding the ways in which temperament affects children's performance in school settings.

The last chapter in this section, by Peter K. Smith, examines the role of children's play in development. In keeping with the other chapters in this section, both the social (e.g. social participation and role-playing) and cognitive (e.g. problem-solving and creativity) dimensions of children's behavior are discussed. A separate chapter on children's play is necessary because of the importance assigned to it in early education: Many educators and developmentalists assign an important role in young children's socio-cognitive development. As such, it can be used as an instructional strategy or as a window into children's developmental processes. These, and other, assumptions about play are critically evaluated in this chapter.

In summary, chapters in this section examine social and affective aspects of children's development. The effects of genetic and social processes on these variables are examined. Taken as a whole, these chapters help us to view the child as a being wherein social, emotional, and cognitive processes are integrated.

Psychological Bases for Early Education
Edited by A.D. Pellegrini
© 1988 John Wiley & Sons Ltd.

CHAPTER 6

# The Whole Child: Toward an Integrated View of Young Children's Cognitive, Social, and Emotional Development

ROBBIE CASE

During the past twenty years, psychoanalytic theory has moved from a drive based theory of psychopathology to a view that is based on onject relations. One of the central tenets of object relations theory is that much, if not all, adult psychopathology has its origins in a disturbance of the child's relationship with its first love objects (e.g. Klein, 1957; Mahler *et al.*, 1975). As this view has taken hold, psychoanalytic writers have begun to describe the nature of children's first relationships in considerable detail (see Stern, 1977; Schaeffer, 1977). They have also begun to describe the vital issues that must be negotiated at different stages of development, if these early relationships are to form a basis of healthy functioning in later life (Sander, 1975). Finally, they have begun to focus on the way in which children represent and resolve these issues, thus ultimately forming either a normal or an abnormal model of themselves and the world around them (Kernberg, 1976: Stern, 1983).

At the same time as these developments have been taking place in psychoanalytic theory, an interesting set of developments has been taking place in cognitive-developmental theory. The first of these has been a move toward studying children's representation of their social world, using the same theoretical and empirical tools as were once reserved for studying children's representations of their physical world (e.g. Damon, 1977; Turiel, 1983; Flavell and Ross, 1981; Serafica, 1982). The second has been a move away from classic Piagetian stage theory, toward theories that are more environmentally and contextually sensitive (see Case, 1985; Fischer, 1980; Pascual-Leone and Goodman, 1979). Finally the third and most recent trend has been a move away from studying children's cognitive development in isolation from their emotional and/or psychosocial development (see Fischer, 1981; Fischer and Pipp,

1985; Case, Hayward, Lewis, and Hurst, 1987.

Whereas the phenomena and questions that were pursued by psychoanalysts and cognitive-developmentalists showed very little overlap as recently as twenty years ago, then, it would appear that they are currently converging on a number of common questions. Two of the most important are (a) How do children represent the affectively powerful transactions that take place with their earliest caretakers? and (b) How do these representations evolve in the course of children's development? Given that these two questions are of common interest to both disciplines, it would appear that a unique opportunity exists for work in each discipline to profit from work in the other. In particular, it would appear that cognitive-developmental theory is in a unique position to benefit from the insights of contemporary psychoanalytic theory in regard to (a) the role of powerful emotional forces in shaping children's earliest transactions with their primary caretakers, (b) the way in which individual children differ in representing, dealing with, and/or defending against, these powerful experiences, and (c) the importance of such individual differences for children's subsequent cognitive and affective growth. At the same time, it would appear that psychoanalytic theory is in a good position to benefit from the insights of current cognitive-developmental theory in regard to (a) the general form of children's representations at different points in their development, (b) the way in which these forms constrain and shape children's experience of their first social relationships, and (c) the processes by which these representations are transformed, as further development takes place.

The goal of the present chapter is to illustrate the potential contribution that cognitive-developmental theory can make to psychoanalytic theory, not the reverse. Thus, it is the latter three issues that will be addressed. Moreover, since this is a volume on pre-schoolers and their education, it will be confined to this age range. Before beginning, however, something must be said about the particular theoretical perspective that will be brought to this endeavor.

## DIALECTICAL CYCLES IN THE PROCESS OF HUMAN DEVELOPMENT

For the past ten years, the author has been engaged in a research program whose aim is to reinterpret the classic concepts and data in the field of intellectual development in the light of the concepts and findings of contemporary cognitive science. What has emerged is a new theory of cognitive development, together with a new data base (Case, 1985). A central construct in this theory—and the one to be applied in the present chapter—is the notion of a dialectical cycle.

This construct is best introduced by means of a concrete example. Consider, therefore, the following changes that take place within the context of Western industrial culture between 4 and 10 years of age. By the age of 4, if they are

DIMENSIONAL STAGE

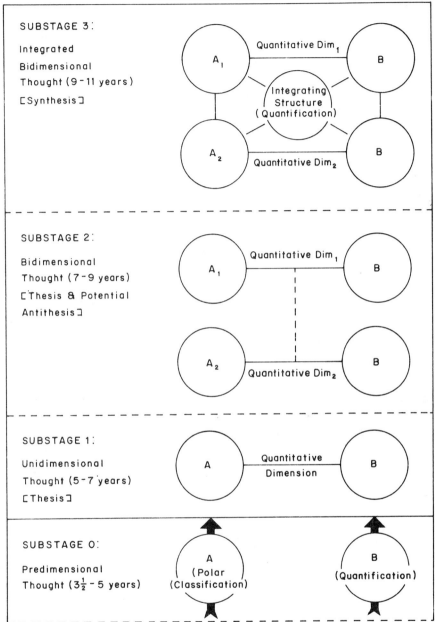

Figure 6.1   Abstract model of logico-mathematical progression during dimensional stage. Solid lines indicate major transition in thinking. Dotted lines indicate more minor transition, as the field of centration expands and implications of major transition are worked out. (Note: The general form of notation in this figure is taken from Fischer (1980). The particular representation of substage 3 thought is taken from Pascual-Leone (1969) )

allowed to play with a balance beam, most children soon realize that the side with the heavy weight on it goes down, while the side with the light weight goes up (Liu, 1981; Marini, 1984). The same children can also count small sets of objects, and realize that the set with the bigger number contains more objects, while the set with the smaller number contains less (Gelman, 1978; Case and Sandieson, 1986). While they can execute either of these operations in isolation, however, they are as yet incapable of combining them. Thus, they are not able to think of weight as a continuous variable, or to predict that the side of a balance with a slightly greater *number* of weights on it will go down. This capability emerges at about 6 years (Siegler, 1976), and heralds children's entry into the dimensional stage. By the age of 8, children can consider two quantitative dimensions rather than just one. They can thus predict that, when the number of weights on each side of a beam is equal, the side whose weights are at a greater distance from the fulcrum will go down (Siegler, 1976). Finally, by the age of 10, children can consider two quantitative variables in a more systematic or integrated fashion. They can thus solve certain problems where weight and distance are set in *conflict* with each other, and one must notice not just the direction in which each variable is acting, but also its magnitude (Inhelder and Piaget, 1958; Marini, 1984).

The general progression in children's scientific thought during this age range is depicted in Figure 6.1, using the graphic form of representation developed by Fischer (1980). In our recent work, we have begun to examine the validity of this model for tasks which involve artistic rather than scientific thinking (Case, Marini, McKeough, Dennis, and Goldberg, 1986). As is shown in Table 6.1, the surface elements of such thought are quite different. Nevertheless, there is an underlying progression that is virtually identical. On each task, the following developmental sequence is observed: (a) at 4, children can apprehend either of two relational systems (A or B) in isolation; (b) by 6, they have coordinated these two systems, with the result that some new and higher order unit of thought has emerged; (c) by 8, two rather than one unit of this new sort can be considered; (d) finally, by 10, a mental procedure for integrating these new units is available, with the result that conflicts arising from their juxtaposition can be resolved. The dialectical cycle in Figure 6.1 can therefore serve as a very general model for the transformation that takes place in children's thinking during middle childhood.

In addition to probing the validity of this model across a range of different intellectual endeavors, we have begun to explore its validity across a range of different age groups. What this work has revealed is the presence of two very similar cycles prior to the age of 4 (from birth to 2 years, and 2 years to 5 years) and one additional cycle between the ages of 11 and about 19 years (Case, 1985). The full model to which we have been led is thus a four-stage one, as is illustrated in Figure 6.2. Note that what constitutes the end point of one cycle simultaneously constitutes the starting point for the next. In short, the cycle is recursive.

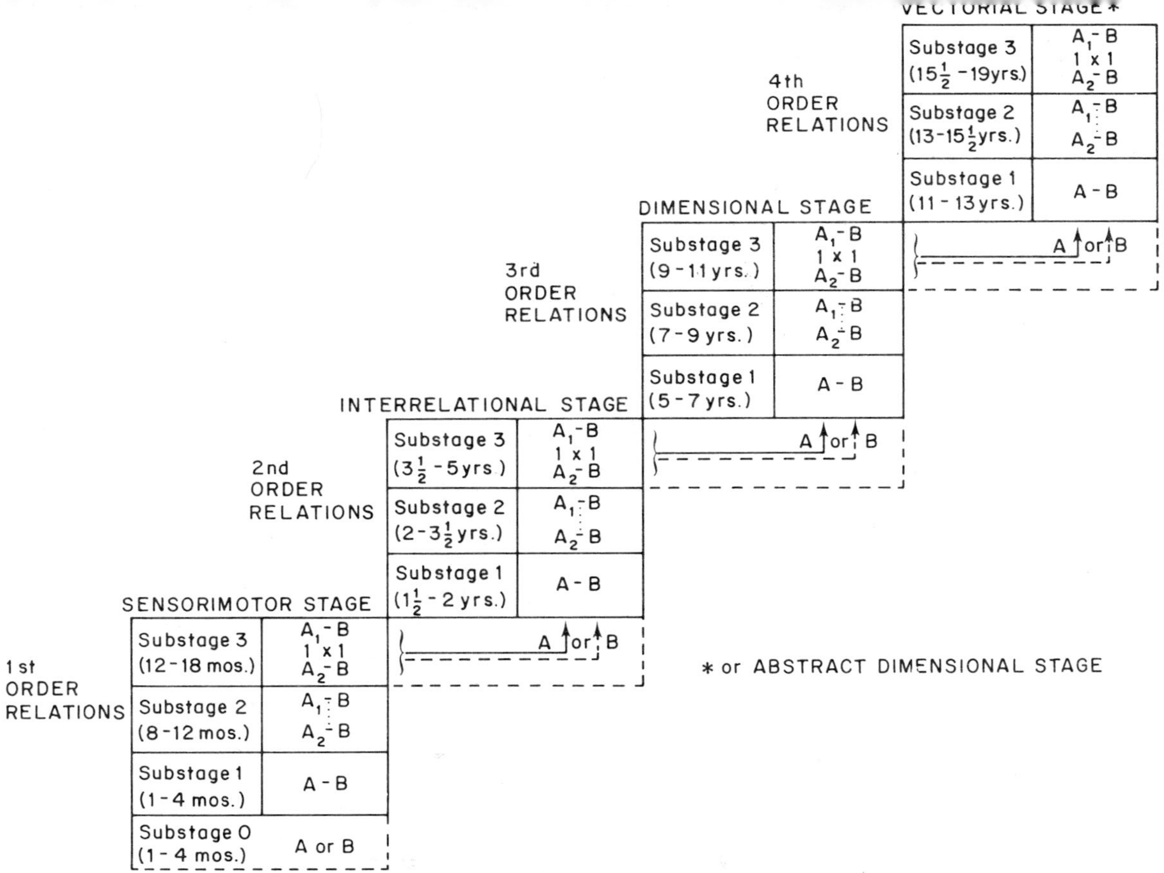

Figure 6.2   Abstract model of the recurrent dialectical cycles that take place in intellectual development, between the ages of 4 months and about 20 years of age. Note that each cycle naturally feeds into the next, in the sense that two qualitatively different systems or relations at one level, when coordinated, generate the new type of relational unit at the next

Table 6.1   Responses of four different age groups to four different tasks

| Age | 2-variable science problems | 2-variable social problems | Story telling | Picture drawing | General characterization of response |
|---|---|---|---|---|---|
| 4 | Child can understand and manipulate simple mechanical relations inherent in operation of multiple piece toy, and can classify various types of initiating events and outcome. Child can also count. | Child can understand, and take advantage of, the relations inherent in a simple social system, and can classify various types of initiating event and outcome. Child can also count. | Child can understand and relate sequences of events whose temporal relations culminate in a 'problem.' Child can also understand problems, and invent a sequence of events that will solve them. | Child can understand and draw basic spatial relations inherent in human figure. Child can also do same for certain inanimate objects such as 'trees' or 'flowers.' | Systems of 2nd order relations are consolidated; products can be treated as a single unit. |
| 6 | Child can coordinate classification of mechanical relations with counting; result is ability to deal with higher-order unit: the continuous quantitative dimension. | Child can coordinate classification of social relations with quantification; result is ability to deal with higher order unit: the continuous (social) dimension or variable. | Child can coordinate construction of event sequences that lead up to, and that resolve, problems. Result is emergence of simple 'plot' as higher-order narrative unit. | Child can coordinate drawing of two or more objects along a single baseline. Result is emergence of 'scene' as higher-order unit in spontaneous drawing. | Two qualitatively different units from previous stage coordinated; result is emergence of a higher-order unit. |

| | | | | | |
|---|---|---|---|---|---|
| 8 | Child can deal with two or more quantitative dimensions in situations where they do not conflict. | Child can deal with two or more social dimensions in situations where they do not conflict. | Child can create stories with simple plot and subplot (consisting of one or more additional problems and resultion-attempts). | Child can draw objects placed with regard to two scenes: one in foreground and one in background. | Two or more higher-order units can now be considered, albeit in a somewhat unintegrated fashion. |
| 10 | Child can now deal with two quantitative dimensions, in an integrated fashion. Dimensional conflicts can be resolved via 'Quantification of differences.' | Child can now deal with two social variables in an integrated fashion. Dimensional conflicts can now be resolved via various 'tradeoffs.' | Child can now deal with major and minor problems in an integrated and pre-planned fashion. Result is new coherence in stories, with plot/subplot structure. | Child can now coordinate construction of foreground and background scenes, often via introduction of objects in middle ground. Result is appearance of coherent 3-dimensional scene. | Two or more higher-order units can now be considered and related to each other, in an integrated fashion. Result is elimination of conflict or inconsistency, and consolidation of system or 3rd-order relations. |

How can a theory of this sort be applied to the task of understanding the child's first relationships with its primary love objects, and the way in which these relationships are experienced? At first glance, it would appear that the answer to this question is that it cannot. There is good evidence that, from the first few months of their lives, infants experience their inanimate world in a different fashion from their animate world. The types of events to which they orient in each domain are different, the type of affect they display is different, and the nature of their responses appears different as well. It would seem dangerous, if not disastrous, to apply a theory that was developed in one domain to the other.

While recognizing the hazards of such an endeavor, the assumption on which the present chapter is based is that the two different types of experience are nevertheless subject to certain common general constraints, which are a function of children's general level of cognitive development. In particular, it is assumed that the *level of relationship* children can encode, and the *complexity of event* they can understand which entails such a relationship, increase with age in each domain at approximately the same rate, and according to the same epigenetic schedule, namely the one indicated in Figure 6.2. Once this assumption is made, the principal challenge which must be faced is that of suggesting how this epigenetic schedule might manifest itself in the domain of object relations.

It is this challenge to which the balance of the present chapter will be addressed. What we shall do is consider each one of the dialectical cycles indicated in Figure 6.2 in sequence. After sketching some of the major changes that take place in children's behavior toward their physical world during the time period in question, we shall then consider such data as are available concerning the concurrent changes that take place in their object relations. Finally, we shall try to show how both sets of changes (or at least aspects of them) might be a function of a common underlying change in the type of mental representation children are capable of constructing during the period in question.

## CYCLE 0 (BIRTH TO 4 MONTHS): INITIAL ORIENTATION TOWARDS THE SOCIAL AND PHYSICAL WORLD

Since the model in Figure 6.2 is recursive, it would be possible to consider the period prior to the age of 4 months as a dialectical cycle in its own right. If this were done, then it would be further possible to break the period down into substages in which (a) some sort of basic orienting capability was assembled out of more primitive components (6–8 gestational months); (b) this capability was then extended so that it could be applied to more than one stimulus or aspect of a stimulus in succession (8–10 gestational months); and (c) a further elaboration took place, so that these bifocal orienting structures became more flexible and reversible (1–4 months *post partum*). While this sort of progression may well occur, however, a treatment at this level of detail is beyond the scope of the present article. What is important here is the more global task of specifying the general type of orienting response which children exhibit prior to the age of 4 months, and the most likely cognitive and affective consequences of doing so in the domain of object relations.

Such a task is at least broadly manageable. During the first part of the neonatal period (i.e. birth to 1 month), children's orienting responses are relatively inflexible. Although children can perceive and orient towards more than one sensory stimulus, they tend to do so in a relatively rigid and sequential fashion. Even this rudimentary capability, however, is sufficient to generate sensory expectations concerning the relationship between a variety of stimuli, as well as motor and affective responses to these expectations. And, as a consequence, the child's first cognitive-affective structures are formed.

From the viewpoint of object relations, the most important of these structures are of course those having to do with the primary caretaker. If it is to survive, the infant must develop structures for locating and latching on to the nipple which its mother presents, and for ingesting the milk that the breast contains. Moreover, if it is to come to recognize its mother as a social being, the infant must also develop some more global representation of her bodily features, particularly the usual features displayed by her face, and the tactile and kinesthetic features of her upper body. During the neonatal period of its life, of course, a considerable portion of the baby's waking time is apt to be spent in nursing, or in scanning its mother's face while resting in her arms; these activities thus constitute the normal context in which the child's first cognitive representations of these features are formed.

At the same time as the baby is engaged in these first orienting activities, it experiences a set of affective states as well as cognitive ones. As it orients towards the nipple that is pressed against its cheek, and attempts to pass from this experience to the experience of feeling the nipple between the lips, the infant may experience a considerable amount of frustration, coupled with gastric pain, high arousal, and diffuse distress. As it succeeds, these sensations will normally give way to feelings of contentment and satisfaction. Assuming that these events recur, a 'schema' or representation will tend to form which includes both sets of information: that is, information regarding the results of the visual and oral orientation, and information regarding the attendant feelings. As a consequence, the sight (or smell) of the mother's nipple will gradually assume a broader 'meaning': that is, it will come to elicit a network of related sensations and feelings.

What is true for the transactions that take place between the newborn and its mother is true to a lesser degree for the other transactions in which the newborn engages as well. The neonate does not spend all its waking hours with its mother. It may spend a considerable portion of its waking time swaddled in a blanket by itself, or being 'talked to' and held by other members of the community. Thus, at the same time as it is developing its first primitive representations (cognitive and affective) of its mother, the infant will also be developing its first primitive representations of the other objects in its physical environment, and its broader family.

During the latter part of the orienting stage (1–4 months) children's motor operations increase considerably in their complexity and flexibility. Infants remain capable of representing and associating different perceptual stimuli. However, they can now integrate the different responses they make to different stimuli in a variety of flexible fashions. For example, in tracking moving objects, infants show their first rudimentary capability for coordinating the movement of their head with movement of their eyes. In scanning stationary objects they show their first capability for moving from one part of a pattern (e.g. the mother's breast) to another (e.g. her face), and then back again. Finally, in the movement of their arms and legs, they show their first capability for connecting one motor response (e.g. pulling the hand out of the mouth) with its reciprocal (i.e. putting the hand back in the mouth).

At the same time as they are executing each one of these operations, infants are still experiencing a variety of affective states. Moreover, the range of affects they experience appears to be more differentiated as well. In addition to diffuse pleasure, interest, or distress, they now appear capable of experiencing such affects as joy (as in the joy of recognition), wariness and rage.

What sort of structural consequences would one expect as a result of applying this more differentiated and reversible set of orienting operations on the one hand, and experiencing a concomitant set of more differentiated feelings on the other? The specific structures would depend on the specific environment to which the infant was exposed, and the particular feelings that he or she experienced in it. Nevertheless, it seems safe to suggest that most infants would gradually come to form a coherent sensory representation of their mothers during this period. While the mother's breast might be experienced as one perceptual object at birth, and her face as another (Klein, 1957; Weininger, 1984), the sort of active visual oscillation mentioned above—from the breast to the face and back again—would insure that these different partial representations were combined into a unified whole by the age of 2 or 3 months. The objects surrounding the infant's cradle or normal resting place would tend to be integrated into a unified 'scene' during this period as well, as would the various observable aspects of the other members of the social community with which the infant had any recurrent form of interaction.

Finally, as each one of the above representations was consolidated, it would assume a distinctive affective tone or charge. The nature of these charges would not only vary from one person to another, they would also vary from one type of interaction to another. Thus, the infant might have one predominant feeling that it associated with its mother in the context of being picked up and put to the breast. It might have another predominant feeling that it associated with its mother in the context of face-to-face interaction games. It might have still another predominant feeling in the context of being placed in its crib for a quiet period, and so on.

As has already been suggested, not all of the above affects would be positive. In the course of the baby's day-to-day life, one would expect that recurrent frustrations would develop, as well as satisfactions. And, as a consequence, the physical or social objects that were associated with these feelings would become invested with these feelings as well. This would be especially true if particular contexts or particular activities in which the infant engaged (e.g. crying) elicited negative feelings in the mother or other family members, and resulted in any sort of agonistic behavior on their part. However, it would be true even in the absence of any direct negative action, simply by virtue of the fact that no environment can perfectly satisfy all the desires or needs of any infant.

In summary: during the first stage of children's development, one would expect that newborns' innate structures would be applied to the task of recognizing and orienting towards the major sensory features of their social and physical environment. One would also expect that a major figure in their mental and emotional lives would be their mother, but that other figures might play important roles as well, with the nature and importance of these roles varying from culture to culture and from family to family. Finally, one would expect that each one of the baby's first structures, both physical and social, would become affectively 'charged' or 'invested', with the nature of this investment varying not only from one person (or object) to the next but from one context or type of transaction to the next as well. Since these investments could be negative or positive, the child would not just acquire a discrete set of structures for orienting towards its physical and social world, it would acquire an overall emotional orientation as well. This orientation might well constitute the roots of the child's later attitude towards its world, and more specifically whether this attitude was one of *trust* or *mistrust* (Erikson, 1950).

## CYCLE 1 (4 MONTHS TO 1½ YEARS): FIRST ACTIVE SENSORIMOTOR EXPLORATION OF THE PHYSICAL AND SOCIAL WORLD

While most innate orienting responses become well differentiated and integrated as entities in themselves during the first few months of life, infants cannot normally coordinate one fully developed orienting structure with another during this period. For example, infants are not normally capable of using one orienting structure as a *means* towards the attainment of an *end* that is specified by another. They are also incapable of maintaining the *record* of one structure's activation in working memory while they are in the midst of applying a second.

At the age of about 4 months, however, these capabilities emerge, and signal the infant's arrival at a new stage of cognitive development. As indicated in Figure 6.2, this stage is typically labelled the 'sensorimotor stage.' It may be divided into a number of substages, which extend from 4 to 8 months, 8 to 12 months, and 12 to 18 months respectively.

### Substage 1: operational coordination (4 to 8 months)

During the first substage, the most obvious motoric change that takes place is that the infant develops the ability to take gross motor actions such as arm sweeping, and put them in the service of eliciting interesting sights and sounds from the objects in its immediate environment. This increased power over the physical world may well be discovered in a very brief time period. It may also be generalized very rapidly, and may result in feelings that the baby never experienced before. One of these feelings may be a form of exhilaration, or delight.

There are at least two 'down sides' to this new capability as well, however. One is that the child may experience new sources of frustration, as it for the first time conceives of goals which it cannot accomplish by using the gross motor movements in its existing repertoire. Another is that the child's newly experienced exhilaration may build up and sustain such a high level of arousal that this, in itself, may be experienced as distress (White, 1975; Sroufe, 1979). Thus, as the child moves into this period, one may temporarily observe a newly emerging crankiness or 'temperamentality' in its interactions with the physical world, as well as a newly emerging sense of power and elation.

At the same time as the baby is experiencing its new potential in the physical world, it will experience its new potential in the social world as well. Whereas the baby could goo and coo responsively during the previous period, and delight at its power to keep the mother smiling and cooing in return, it can now conceive of calling out to the mother while she is in a different room, because whatever activity the baby is currently engaged in (e.g. visually scanning) no longer precludes a memory of the mother's presence. With the arrival at the sensorimotor stage, therefore, the baby can experience a new sense of power over the social world as well, both with its parents and with its siblings or age mates, who can now become genuine sources of fascination.

As with any new capability, this new power has its down side too. As Lewis (1986) has pointed out, the ability to retain an image of the absent mother while scanning an empty room can also give rise to the first genuine experience of loss, and the feelings of fear, anger, or sadness which such a loss can occasion. Since memories of a loss experience may still be present when the mother returns—all smiles—the baby may also encounter its first affective conflict and the anxiety which this entails. In effect, then, the transition to the sensorimotor stage may confront the child with the threats inherent in what Klein has termed the 'depressive position' (Klein, 1957; Weininger, 1984). The child must somehow come to grips with the problem of having representations of its mother that are positive and negative *simultaneously,* and discover some means of controlling the feelings that it experiences as a consequence (Hayward, 1986; Lewis, 1986). A similar consequence can occur as a result of being able to engage in interaction that is genuinely reciprocal: the infant may be exposed to feelings of frustration and/or depression, when the form of interaction it knows to be possible fails to materialize or goes awry.

Taken together, the infant's new capability to reach out with its limbs and actively explore the world, coupled with its new capability for reaching out and actively engaging other human beings, herald an important change in its life situation. Mahler's term 'hatching' captures some of the most important aspects of this change, indicating as it does that the child is emerging from its semi-exclusive and symbiotic relationship with its mother, and setting out on the first steps of what will ultimately become its own life course. It is important to remember however, that as the infant 'hatches' from its first state of equilibrium with its mother, it does not simply move *away* from her, as one would from an egg in which one had been contained. It also moves *closer* to her as well, and builds affectively charged representations of her that are trans-situational.

## Substage 2: Bifocal Coordination (8 to 12 months)

In the second substage of the sensorimotor period, infants become capable of focusing on two action–reaction pairs simultaneously. Or, somewhat more accurately, they become capable of storing a pointer to one action–reaction event or possibility in working memory while they are actively engaging in a second. Although this change does not produce the sort of major qualitative shift in children's experience that appeared at 4 months, it does produce a more minor, or quantitative shift. Moreover, this shift is one that has significant consequences for the development of children's object relations, inasmuch as it permits them to make their first connection between their relationship with their mother, and their relationship with the broader social and physical world.

Consider first the changes that take place in children's play with physical objects. During the previous substage, the world of physical objects became a source of intense interest for young infants, as they utilized their newly acquired potential for prodding it into action, and exploring the properties it revealed in response. As they enter into the period from 8 to 12 months, two interesting changes take place. The first is that the baby becomes capable of playing with two objects or parts of an object at the same time. For example, having seen a drum make an interesting noise in response to being struck by a stick (action–reaction pair 1), it can now set this sort of event as a goal, reach out to the same stick in order to transport it to the drum (action–reaction 2) and produce the same event itself. A second interesting change is that babies' play with inanimate objects becomes interleaved with their activity with their primary love-objects. In the midst of playing with a toy, for example, children may glance over at their mothers and smile or laugh. In addition, having crawled off to investigate this or that object, they will often crawl back to their mother for 'emotional refuelling'.

The above behaviors have often been interpreted in the clinical literature as indicating that the child is using its newly acquired motor capability—that is, its capability for crawling—to practice its first independence from its mother. As a consequence, the period has been referred to as one of 'initial practicing' (Mahler *et al.*, 1975). The problem with this interpretation, however, is that in many respects children practice greater independence during the previous substage: the one in which they are just hatching from their initial symbiotic union with their mother. During the previous substage, for example, children will sometimes show longer periods of object play without maternal eye contact. And, if provided with a 'walker,' they may go farther afield from their mothers and make no obvious attempt to 'refuel'.

Within the present framework, these earlier behaviors do not appear as particularly problematic. Taken together with the later behaviors, they are simply seen as a further indication that, at about the age of 8 months, children make an important substage transition: from a substage where the structures for exploring the physical world, together with the affects that these structures entail, cannot be integrated with their structures for seeking and maintaining contact with their mothers, to a substage where the two different types of structures *can* be integrated, in a tentative fashion. And, as with any substage or stage transition, the above transition is seen as bringing with it a new set of opportunities and a new set of threats.

Among the new *opportunities* which the new substage brings are (a) the opportunity for sharing the positive affects that are experienced in the course of exploring the physical world (i.e. the experience of joy, exhilaration, excitement), with the most significant member of the baby's early social world—thus participating for the first time in the sort of 'socio-affective heightening' of physical experience which is unique to the higher mammals, and on which the motivation for acquiring language may partially depend; and (b) the opportunity for using the positive affect that is experienced in the context of a good parent–child relationship (i.e. the feelings of warmth, containment, and security) to offset the negative feelings that may be encountered in exploring the physical world (e.g. frustration, over-arousal, fatigue)—thus for the first time actively using a member of the older generation as a 'secure base' from which to launch an independent exploration of the physical world.* In the context of the

---

* Note that an inanimate object in which certain similar feelings of warmth and containment have been invested during the previous substage (e.g. a blanket) may also be used for the same purpose at this point in time—thus producing the first use of such objects as blankets to provide 'security.'

present theory, the baby who uses its mother in this fashion is in effect 'taking its mother with it.' That is, it is keeping a pointer to its mother's presence active in its mind, as it turns away from her and crawls out to explore the world.

The new *threats* that are experienced during this substage are simply the inverse of the new opportunities. Thus, for the first time, children will interrupt their play, display clear signs of anxiety, and try to reduce the distance between themselves and their mothers under a number of different circumstances. These include (a) when they are surprised by a wind-up toy which moves towards them, and they are not in their mother's arms; (b) when they are approached by a stranger, who attempts to initiate some form of interaction with them, and they are not in their mother's arms; or (c) when they are playing in a strange environment, and their mother gets up and starts to leave the room. What all these situations share, from the present perspective, is that the baby is first allowed to establish some form of balance between its own exploration and the novelty this generates, and the presence of its mother, and the sense of contentment and safety which this generates. This balance is then disturbed in one of two fashions. Either a novel object approaches the baby on its own, thus increasing the baby's arousal beyond an optimal level, and requiring a parallel increase in the sense of containment or security. Or else the mother leaves, thus reducing the baby's sense of security and the amount of novelty it can seek out. In either case, the result is that the baby feels compelled to re-establish its original equilibrium, by calling out to its mother or approaching her directly.

The foregoing interpretation provides a convenient illustration of the sort of contribution which cognitive-developmental theory might potentially make to research in the area of human ethology as well as object relations. The core assumptions on which the foregoing account depends are (a) that the baby's behavior in the 'strange situation' is just part of a much broader set of cognitive and affective developments; (b) that the things which all these developments share in common is the requirement for tying together two unifocal structures: that is, two structures for regulating some form of action–reaction contingency; and (c) that the reason none of these developments takes place prior to the age of about 8 months is that the elements from which any bifocal structure is assembled must first be consolidated (0–4 months) and then coordinated (4–8 months).

Now if the above three assumptions are correct, it follows that the baby's behavior in the strange situation does not really indicate the beginning of attachment, *per se*, but rather the use of a figure to which the baby is *already* attached, to create a subjectively safe environment in which it can explore the properties of other, less familiar, objects. It also follows that the baby's initial attachments are very probably formed during the period from 1 to 4 months, and that its first attempts to actively regulate its attachment relations very probably take place during the period from 4 to 8 months. Finally, it follows that, if these structures are interfered with in some fashion, one should be able to observe the presence of attachment-related distress a good deal prior to the age of 8 months. For example, one should be able to observe distress at the age of 1 to 4 months under circumstances where, having just quieted her baby's fussing, a mother then hands the baby to another mother who continues the same sort of settling activity. Similarly, one should be able to observe distress at 4 to 8 months under circumstances where, having just engaged her baby in some sort of reciprocal interaction which it finds rewarding, the mother then withdraws without warning to another room.

A test of the latter hypothesis has been conducted by Lewis (1986) and was briefly described in the article to which the present chapter is the sequel (Case, Hayward, Lewis, and Hurst, 1987). For the moment, however, the point is not so much that this hypothesis was confirmed (which it was), but simply that it was *generated*. What this implies is that, by setting the behaviors that have been studied in specific paradigms such as the 'strange situation' in a somewhat broader context, the present theory may have the potential not only to explicate the relationship between these behaviors and other behaviors to which they are related, but also to generate a number of novel and potentially testable predications.

**Substage 3: elaborated bifocal coordination (12 to 18 months)**

During the final substage of the period, a further expansion takes place in children's ability to coordinate their sensorimotor schemes. Children now become capable of executing one bifocal structure, while storing a pointer to a second sensorimotor structure, either unifocal or bifocal. One of the capabilities which this introduces is that for 'reversibility', that is, for executing one operation on an object in order to produce a reaction in a second object, and then 'undoing' this operation to see if the effect is undone as well. Another capability which it introduces is that for complementarity: that is, for executing an action on an object pair which is parallel to that just executed previously— either by the baby itself or by someone else.

In the baby's play with physical objects, the changes which this new capability brings about are quite striking. Babies will often be seen putting one object inside another, only to take it out again, or putting one object (e.g. a block) on top of another, only to knock it down again, and so on. In short, they will often be seen bringing a pair of objects into some particular relationship via one operation, and then 'undoing' that relationship by applying the reciprocal operation. In the baby's interactions with its parents and siblings, the changes which take place are more subtle, but of just as great importance. One change that takes place is that the baby's pleasure in exploring the physical world appears to reach its zenith—often amounting to what is referred to as a 'love affair with the world.' At the same time, the phenomenon of 'emotional refuelling' becomes more frequent. That is, babies will not just glance over at their mother in the midst of their play, but will crawl or toddle over to her and throw themselves in her arms, only to set out for further exploration. In the present framework, these events are once again seen as being intimately linked, and as stemming from the baby's increased ability to imagine two action–reaction structures as being reciprocally related. Thus, as the baby sets out on any exploratory journey, it can not only carry the image of its mother actively with it, it can imagine a return or reciprocal voyage as well, with all the joys of reunion and affective sharing that the rearrival will entail.

It is important to note that the experience of affective sharing itself takes on a more reciprocal or complementary character during this period as well. Infants will now be observed to bring back 'booty' from their journeys. They will drop the object in their parent's laps, as if to say 'See! You try it, too!' Finally, if the parent does imitate the child, the baby will often grasp the object again, re-execute the action that the parent demonstrated, and return the object to the parent. This sort of reciprocal exchange is often accompanied not just by affective sharing, but by careful observation of the parent's action on the object. Moreover, when the parent's action is different from the child's, the child will often alter its own actions accordingly. It is in the course of this sort of imitation, then, that babies develop their first repertoire of actions that derive their meaning not just from the properties of physical objects, but from the use that is made of those objects in their culture. For example, to a 10-month-old, a small teapot would primarily be an object to touch, taste, manipulate, etc. By the age of 1½, however, it would be an object to tilt toward a cup, in the same fashion that 'Mummy does'.

A final point to note with regard to reciprocal interaction is that it often takes place when the child is seated in a parent's lap and no object is present. During the period from 13 to 18 months the baby will for the first time point to interesting objects and/or events during such times and turn to its parent, as if to say 'did you see that?' A parallel development is that the baby will point to a nearby object, lean forward, and babble insistently. Here the message is equally clear, namely 'Hey I want that! You bring it to me!' In the present framework both these forms of interdependence are like those mentioned in the previous two paragraphs, in that they involve a linking on the baby's part between its *own* action and the action of another object on the one hand, and some action of the *parent* and an action of some other object on the other. Moreover, the linking is in each case achieved by the sensorimotor action of pointing, which produces either a complementary experience (i.e. you do—I do too), or a reciprocal experience (you bring—I receive).

What holds for the baby's relationship with its parents of course holds for the baby's relationship with its peers or siblings as well. Whereas the most frequent form of interaction that one witnesses between children at the age of 8 to 13 months is simply glancing over at the other, while each is engaged in parallel play, one now begins to observe a more direct interaction, in which one baby acts on an object in the same particular fashion that it has observed its companion to do, or in which two babies act in a complementary fashion on the same object.

Of course, not all the baby's interactions during this period are positive. The same capability for imagining a 'return voyage' can bring feelings of insecurity and a reluctance to explore with children whose mothers are not sufficiently available to their children. Alternatively, in mothers who are intrusive and overprotective, it may elicit a sense of anger. In these cases exploration may become a tool of either escape or retribution. Finally, in families where parents are abusive, there may be a disturbing sense of anger and fear, which may tie up so much of the baby's psychic resources that very little room may be left over for exploration. As with all stages, what the average infant experiences will probably be a balance of positive and negative emotions, which balance might be referred to with a set of polar terms such as *security* vs. *insecurity*. Once again, then, although a great many developments that are of relevance to the child's sense of security are yet to come, the seeds of the adult sense of security may be planted during this period.

To summarize: having made an initial 'investment' in the physical and social objects in its environment during the first few months of life, and established a tentative positive or negative orientation towards them, the baby then proceeds to explore the ways in which its own actions can serve to initiate, preserve, and/or heighten emotional reactions of this sort, or attenuate them and 'turn them off.' After an initial substage in which the child's explorations of the physical and social world are relatively independent, they become increasingly interleaved, with the result that the baby's sense of curiosity or initiative becomes increasingly a function of the degree of *security* or *insecurity* which it experiences in its relationship with its primary caretakers. Assuming that the baby's initial orientation towards the world was tilted in favor of *trust* over *mistrust*, and that its activity during the sensorimotor period is tilted in favor of *security* and initiative, rather than *insecurity* and doubt (or isolation), then the accomplishments of the sensorimotor period will constitute a firm platform from which the child can launch itself into the next major stage of its development: the one with which the present volume is most directly concerned. As will be seen, however, the transition to this third stage of development is not without its hazards, either.

 CYCLE 2 (1½ TO 5 YEARS): FIRST ENTRY INTO THE WORLD OF PHYSICAL AND SOCIAL SYSTEMS

In the context of the present theory, the stage that follows the sensorimotor stage is referred to as the interrelational stage. Transition into this stage is assumed to take place by a process that is directly parallel to the one that produced the prior stage transitions, namely by the coordination of existing schematic units (by this time representing reversible relations), into units of a higher order. In addition, transition into the stage is presumed to bring with it another qualitative change in children's behavior. Finally, progression *through* the stage is presumed to involve another sequence of substages, as children apprehend first one and then two interrelationships; then finally begin to assemble complementary or opposing relationships into fully integrated systems.

### Substage 1: operation coordination (18 to 27 months)

Children's cognitive capabilities in the first substage are perhaps best illustrated by the newly emerging competence that they display in the realm of 'constructive play.' By the end of the sensorimotor period, children are capable of assembling either of the two following schemes: (a) a scheme for representing and controlling the relationship between a 'marking object' such as a pencil, and a 'background object' such as a piece of paper; and (b) a scheme for representing the relationship between one stationary object and a second (e.g. object A goes along *beside* object B). The first capability permits children to produce scribbles on pieces of paper or other flat surfaces such as sand. The second capability permits them to label a variety of spatial relationships such as 'up', 'beside', 'down', etc.

As they move into the interrelational period, children become capable of utilizing the first sort of scheme as a means towards the generation of a particular type of goal that is specified by the latter sort of scheme. As a consequence, their drawing takes on a qualitatively different character. They can now purposively set out to make a particular *kind* of scribble. Or, if so requested, they can now imitate the particular type of line (e.g. vertical) drawn by an experimenter. The result is that children for the first time enter the world of 'Drawings', that is, the world of geometric systems. This same change is observed in their play with blocks, where they now begin to set one block on another with the intention of producing a particular geometric configuration.

As might be expected, children's new cognitive capability brings with it a new sense of delight, when the patterns that they produce turn out the way they intended. By the same token, however, the same capability often brings with it a new source of frustration, when things do not turn out as anticipated.

At the same time as they are making the abovementioned transition in their independent play, children are making a parallel transition in the realm of object relations as well. However, the set of threats and opportunities that they encounter there is apt to be much more powerful.

Consider first the new set of *threats* to which the growing child may be exposed. During the previous stage, the child became capable of controlling its proximity to its mother, and the feelings of security which this proximity generates. At the same time, the child also became capable of monitoring its mother's relationship with others, and any affective consequences which these relationships happened to generate. What happens as children enter the interrelational stage is that they become capable of recognizing the higher order relationship that exists between these two sorts of relationship. For example, they begin to realize that their mother's engagement in some other relationship can affect her emotional availability for relating to themselves. This realization can give rise to a mixture of fear, anger, and/or sadness, which adults recognize as jealousy (Hayward, 1986). And, in turn, this new feeling can lead the child to escalate its attempts to gain attention via clinging and whining, (or running too far away).

A similar threat to security can be experienced when the child is left in the care of a familiar and loving caretaker, other than the primary one (usually mother). Because the child can now conceptualize the mother's departure and interactions with a different world of objects from those present, at the same time as it can focus on the objects in its immediate environment and the security provided by the substitute caretaker, the child can become capable of experiencing the present—for all its opportunities—as lacking a vital affective quality that was experienced in the past. As a consequence, feelings of anger and/or sadness can be reawakened. Moreover, as Lewis has suggested, the 'manic' defense of simply pitching into some form of object play, under the watchful eyes of whomever remains, can no longer be expected to be completely effective. The reason for this is that the substitute relationship will not displace the primary relationship from the child's working memory. Thus, the result may often be an increase in separation distress, in the very situations and contexts where this sort of event had been easily accepted and even joyfully entered into (via bye-bye routines) just a few months earlier. A period of 'mourning' or depressed play may also follow, during the first 10 or 15 minutes after the mother's departure.

At the same time as the child experiences new threats to its previous security and affective equilibrium, the child may also experience threats to its previous sense of *power*. In fact, this new threat—and the power struggles it occasions—is often taken as a defining characteristic of the stage.

During the previous stage, as already indicated, children normally perfect their ability to issue commands to adults, in order to acquire objects that are beyond their reach. If they do not get what they want, they often fuss or persistently request the object. However, they can normally be appeased by being offered something else of interest. Alternatively, if their request fails, they will often spontaneously turn their attention to something else as the next best alternative (thus defending against their sense of frustration).

As they enter the interrelational stage, however, it becomes possible for children to represent their own relationship with their mother and their mother's relationship with something or someone else as separate cognitive entities, and to coordinate them. And this coordination produces a dawning apprehension and/or fear which cannot be easily defended against by the children or mollified by an adult.

Stated simply, the new fear is that the mother's relationship to the world of objects is beyond the children's ability to control, by manipulating their relationship to the mother; while the children's own relationship to the physical world is completely dominated by their relationship with their mother, and is thus completely under her control. What formerly was perceived as merely the failure to get the mother to provide a new toy, then, can now be perceived as a *loss of control,* or *rejection,* that is, a failure of the child's relationship to its mother to have any impact on her relationship to the world of other objects or an insistence on the mother's part of putting some other relationship before that with her child. Similarly, what formerly was experienced as an unwelcome loss (e.g. when a dangerous toy is replaced by a safe one) can now be experienced as an attempted subjugation of its own will by its mother. It is this change which gives rise to the classic 'tantrum in the supermarket.' It is also this change which produces much of the child's refusal to follow the mother's wishes and continued use of the word 'no'. For in both instances a particular issue becomes subordinated to the larger issue of which this is simply one example: namely the issue of who will dominate whom.

A very similar struggle for dominance can be seen emerging during the same time period in the child's relationship with its peers. Here the desire for control also frequently centers around objects, as the relationship of 'possession' now becomes the focus of the child's attention. It is not at all infrequent during this period to see a child who was quite content just a few months previously to have another child play with its toys (as long as they themselves had their favorite toy) suddenly become angry and possessive, and want to deny their best friend access to any of their toys. As was the case with the mother, the new focus is not the relationship between the other toy and the child directly, nor even between the child itself and its toys, but rather the higher order relationship of power or possession, which the ability to determine both one's own relationship to an object, as well as the relationship of others to the same object, implies.

Many of the changes in the child's relationship with its mother that have been described so far have also been chronicled by Mahler, and labelled the 'rapprochement crisis.' In the context of Mahler's theory, this crisis is seen as stemming from two events: (a) the child's successful attempts, via its increased motor competence, to separate itself from its mother and to invest its love in the world; and (b) the child's growing awareness, as a result of concomitant cognitive developments, of its own separateness from its mother, and therefore its vulnerability. According to Mahler, these changes produce a desire for reunion with the mother on the one hand, and a fear of engulfment with a consequent loss of autonomy on the other.

There is much to be said for Mahler's interpretation. For one thing, it serves to unify a large number of the behavioral exchanges that are observed between the mother and the child during this time period, such as the pattern of alternately clinging or shadowing, and darting away. For another, Mahler's interpretation serves to make contact with adult phantasies that involve total merging of self with another, and/or a return to some prior experience of unity and bliss.

While not gainsaying these advantages, however, one might suggest that the present interpretation offers a number of advantages of its own—ones which are not possible in the context of Mahler's theory. The first and most obvious advantage is that the present theory specifies what *particular* cognitive developments are important, and why they bring the issue of autonomy versus dependence into such sharp focus. The second advantage is that the present theory integrates not only the wide variety of changes that take place in the child's relationship with its mother during this time frame, but also those that take place with its peers and siblings (e.g. possessiveness with regard to toys, struggles for social dominance, etc.). A third advantage is that the present theory does not require the postulation of an initial stage at which the child was incapable of differentiating itself from its mother—which suggestion has been seriously challenged, not just by other psychoanalysts (see Eagle, 1984; Stern, 1983), but by much of the data on infant capabilities. Finally, the present theory enables one to explain a number of the *positive* developments that take place during the period, as well as those that are experienced by both the child and its caretakers as problematic. Stated differently, it enables one to interpret the new emotional opportunities that the child experiences as well as the new threats. Three of the most important of these opportunities are: (a) the opportunity for complementary co-operation; (b) the opportunity for sharing at a distance; and (c) the opportunity for understanding and manipulating the feelings of others.

*1. Complementary cooperation.*

Consider first the opportunity for complementary cooperation. Children between the ages of 12 and 18 months, as has already been mentioned, are capable of imitating a culturally appropriate relationship of the form actor–action–agent (tool) patient (recipient of tool application). As yet, however, they are not capable of focusing on two such relationships simultaneously. As a consequence, they cannot apprehend the higher order cultural patterns of activity or 'scripts' of which these basic actor–action–agent patient relationships are a part (e.g. I pour tea from a teapot into a cup, so that you can pick up the cup and drink tea from it; or I hold a dustpan down beside a pile of dirt, so you can push the dirt on to it with a broom). At about the age of 18–20 months, however, they do acquire this sort of capability, and thus become capable of assuming the complimentary role in such a joint activity. They also become capable of initiating such joint activity, and making their desire for the joint activity apparent via words or gestures (e.g. child brings one chair to a table, while signalling for parent or peer to being another chair to the table, so that they can work/play/eat there together).

*2. Sharing at a distance.*

A second opportunity which the child's arrival at the new stage brings with it is the opportunity for retaining the feeling of connection to someone who is not physically present, and sharing an experience with them. Consider the following interchange between a mother and her son:

| | |
|---|---|
| *Scene*: | *21-month-old boy sitting beside father and looking out of living room window. Mother in kitchen.* |
| CHILD: | *(Quietly pointing at cat outside window)* 'Oh.' |
| CHILD: | *(Turning from window and shouting loudly in direction of kitchen)* 'Mum!' |
| CHILD: | *(Again)* 'Mum!' |
| MOTHER: | *(From kitchen)* 'What is it, love?' |
| CHILD: | 'Cah.' |
| MOTHER: | 'Do you see a cat?' |
| CHILD: | 'Yah' *(smiling contentedly, turns attention back to the cat).* |

Note that the child in the above example has not used any words which are unique to the interrelational stage. Nor has he used the capability for two-word speech (although this is another capability that normally develops during this period). What he has used, however, is his new ability to maintain an interest in one relationship (looking out of window at cat with father), while entering into a second relationship and communicating the results of this first relationship. In effect, then, this new capability is really the positive side of the same coin that is seen when a child's mother really leaves (i.e. not just the room, but the house), and the child remains saddened even in the presence of toys and a positively valued substitute caretaker such as his father. The only difference is that, in the departure instance, the capability for continuing to share with the mother is blocked (and hence ongoing activity takes on a reduced or depressed affective tone), while in the 'talking to the next room' case it is sustained, and the ongoing activity thus takes on an emotionally elevated tone.

*3. Understanding and dealing with feelings of others.*

A third new opportunity which the new stage affords comes as a result of the child's new ability to understand and manipulate the feelings of others. By the age of 1½, children already show a clear responsiveness to the emotions of others, as well as to the emotional exchanges that take place between others and their animate or inanimate environment. A good example is the sort of relationship which leads to feelings of comfort, and which might be symbolized as follows. *Initial State:* Child A Distressed, followed by *Relational Transaction:* Mother of A *encircles* Child A, followed by *Final State:* Contentment. Children will observe such transactions closely, and engage in them themselves, taking either part (e.g. running to mother for comfort when hurt, or attempting to encircle a baby that is crying). At the same time, children can focus on the relational events which lead up to or which follow such emotional transactions. An example of the sort of transaction that might lead to a need for comfort in the first place would be the breaking of a toy or the departure of a loved one. *Initial State:* Child A happy, followed by *Relational Transaction*: Child A's Mother *leaves*. Followed by: *Final State:* Child A cries. Once again, children will observe such transactions carefully, and be influenced in a similar way themselves.

Until the age of 1½, however, children do not appear to be capable of understanding the potential interrelationship between these two events. Thus, one does not see them approaching a child who has been left and is in tears, and bringing it a blanket in order to provide it with comfort. By the age of 2, this sort of empathic behavior is frequently reported in naturalistic situations (see Hoffman, 1978), and can be shown to be present experimentally in the laboratory. Children can use one object to counteract a mood that has been produced in someone by a different object (Marini, 1984). They can also predict what the consequences of particular operations of this sort will be, in the absence of any direct evidence (Bruchowsky, 1984). Once again, then, they are entering the world of physical and social systems, and understanding the coherence of episodes in which particular transactions follow each other in some sort of causally related sequence. This change brings with it a new capability for understanding, entering into, and improving the emotional life of others.

### Substages 2 and 3: (27 months to 3½ years and 3½ to 5 years) bifocal and elaborated coordination

If children remained at the first substage of the new period, they would no doubt learn which situations were and were not genuine threats to their existing relationships with their love-objects. They would also no doubt eventually learn when their environment was prepared to tolerate assertions of their own will and when it was not. Finally, they would no doubt learn to defend against situations which were continued to be perceived as threats, but against which no external action was possible. All of the above changes are given additional impetus, however, by the further changes that take place in children's cognitive development. As was the case with the previous stage, the most important change that takes place is that children become capable of focusing on two interrelations rather than just one.

With regard to children's feelings of jealousy, the result of this new development is that the mother can now set up a second interrelationship, one which excludes the baby but includes her older child, and thus mitigate negative feelings which the older child experiences, due to the fact that it is being excluded from the holding or feeding situation. For example, the mother can ask her older child to draw her a picture, notice the child's progress, and praise him or her for it. By the middle of the interrelational period the older child may appreciate this sort of effort, and not demand to be held or to introduce itself into the feeding situation. In addition the older child will be capable of seeing that the baby is not capable of entering into this sort of 'achieving for mother' interrelationship due to its immature status, whereas the older child *is* capable of entering into a cuddling relationship, and furthermore will probably be allowed to do so as soon as the baby's feeding time is over. In effect, then, both 'deprecation of the rival' and 'anticipation of future consequences' can be used by the older child as defenses, to further bolster its positive feelings.

While space does not permit their detailed portrayal here, it will hopefully be apparent that similar sorts of 'counteracting' relationships can be set up to mitigate the negative feelings engendered by the other triangular situations mentioned in the previous section: that is, having another child use one's own toys, seeing mother temporarily abandoning one for 'work,' and having mother refuse to purchase one's 'heart's desire' in a supermarket.

As children reach the end of the stage, they need even less help from their mother in setting up relationships which will compensate for relationships of temporary exclusion or dominance. Moreover, they can now compare such relationships more flexibly, and appreciate situations in which they are genuinely integrated. Continuing with the jealousy example, children can now appreciate that, while the fact that the mother is comforting a little baby *does* preclude their being held just now, they can adopt a complementary posture towards the baby, such as amusing it with a rattle. By doing so they will not only elicit attention from their mother which will compensate for the lack of being held, they will effectively make themselves 'partners' with her in the endeavor of taking care of the baby. In effect, then, they can be much closer to the mother than the baby can, by entering the system of social relations as 'Mummy's little helper.' Similar solutions can be appreciated or devised to the toy ownership dilemma, the supermarket dilemma, and the dilemma of mother's leaving for work. The result is that the tumultuous events and feelings of the beginning of the stage can potentially (though not inevitably) be avoided.

To clarify the underlying structural progression which is being hypothesized, the changes with regard to the 'rival dilemma' are presented in diagram form in Figure 6.3. Note that the hypothesized progression is based on the assumptions (a) that the potential rival is different from the self in some way which is parallel to the way it differs from the mother; and (b) that the mother is willing to take on a 'partner' in dealing with the potential rival. If either of these conditions is not met—for example, if the potential rival is not in a role relationship with the mother which is different from the child's but rather the same, and/or if the 'rival relationship' shows any true signs of excluding any relationship whatever with the self, children's feelings of jealousy may well be intensified at the end of the period, precisely because children are better attuned to these additional possibilities (Hayward, 1986).

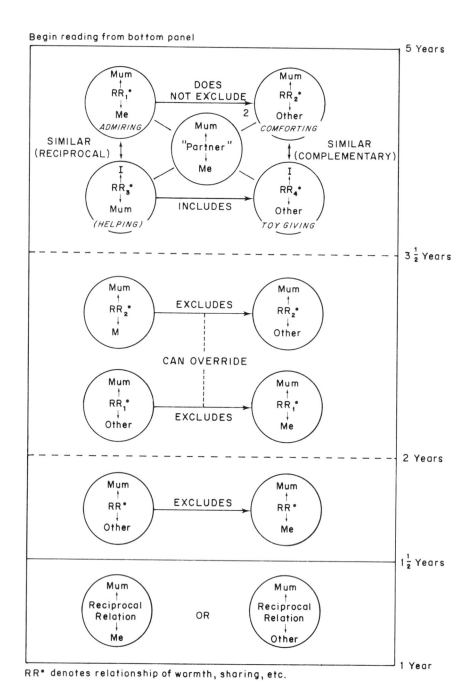

RR* denotes relationship of warmth, sharing, etc.

Figure 6.3    Abstract model of hypothesized socio-cognitive developments during the interrelational stage which first heighten, and then permit the child to overcome, its natural feelings of jealousy towards a young baby when that baby becomes the object of it's mother's attention

To summarize: having made an initial emotional investment in the world of physical and social objects during the orienting stage, and then learned how to maximize its enjoyment and sense of security in relating to these objects during the sensorimotor stage, the child then enters a world in which second-order relations—that is, relations between sensorimotor relations—become apparent. Stated differently, the child enters the world of physical and social *systems*. In our own culture, the new emotional vulnerabilities to which the child is subject as a consequence of making this transition are sometimes more apparent than the emotional opportunities. These include a vulnerability to feelings of exclusion, abandonment, rejection, and domination. That new opportunities are presented as well, however, is evidenced by the child's increased capacity for empathy, communication at a distance, and role complementary. As children move through the stage and begin to assume appropriate (albeit junior) roles in their family and/or peer system, what generally happens is that they use their emerging cognitive abilities to cope with and/or defend against the new threats, and to optimize the opportunities. Just as trust and security predominate over mistrust and insecurity for most children during the first two stages, then, so *assertion* and *control* during the third stage predominate over *doubt* and *loss of control*. Once again, the result is that a secure platform is constructed for entry into the next cycle of development.

## CYCLE 3: 5 TO 10 YEARS

The present subject of this chapter is pre-school development, not development during later stages. Still, for those who are charged with the responsibility of actually working with pre-school children, it is important to realize not just where their development has come from but also where it is leading. By way of conclusion, therefore, a brief glimpse of the further cycles in children's growth during the school years is offered. As children enter the dimensional stage (5–10 years) they develop the capacity for ranking themselves relative to others along the new dimensions they apprehend, and realizing that others are doing so as well. The new opportunity this brings is for sharing parents' values and judgments, not just their behaviors, feelings and roles. Possible threats are that children may not fare too well relative to peers or siblings in such comparative judgments, and may thus have to face a new form of rejection. Even their own feelings (e.g. fear, sadness) may be a cause of such rejection in some sex groups in some cultures, and must now be monitored. The period is thus one of greater affective control, as the new structures that are formed in effect come to function as the Freudian 'superego' and 'ego-ideal.' The period is also one where feelings of social 'embarrassment' come to play a far more significant role in children's lives. Note that conflicts between parents' standards and peers' standards and the potential embarrassments which these occasion will not be resolved (as in any new type of functioning) until the end of the period.

## CYCLE 4: 11 TO 18 YEARS

As children enter the first substage of this cycle and become capable of thinking in terms of abstract dimensions, they also build an abstract model of their own (and parents') traits, and analyze situations in terms of them (Marini, 1984). This may lead to the 'idealizing' of parental figures that Blos (1962) has described (11–12 years) followed by a period of potential conflict as parents are seen as embodying both negative and positive ideals (13–15 years), followed by a period in which some resolution of this conflict is possible (16–19 years).

## CONCLUSION

From its inception, the progressive movement in early childhood education has held as one of its central tenets the notion that we should focus on the 'whole child.' So far, however, the best we have been able to do as researchers and practitioners has been to make sure that we do not neglect one aspect of children's functioning at the expense of another. What we have not been able to do is to appreciate the *relationships* between the various aspects because (as the chapter headings of the present volume amply demonstrate) these aspects have been studied in isolation. What has been attempted in the present chapter, then, is to reverse this trend: that is, to make a start in the direction of integrating what we know about children's competencies at different points in their pre-school development.* The attempt is only a preliminary one, and should not be seen in any sense as 'gospel.' Still, it is hoped that the general model proposed will focus at least some of our attention on the connection between behaviors which co-occur in young children's behavior on an almost day-to-day basis, yet whose interrelationship we have only begun to appreciate.

## REFERENCES

Blos, P. (1962). *On adolescence.* New York: Free Press.

Bruchowsky, M.M. (1984). The development of empathy in early childhood. Unpublished M.A. Thesis, University of Toronto 1984.*

Case, R. (1985). *Intellectual development: birth to adulthood.* New York: Academic Press.

Case, R., Marini, Z., McKeough, A., Dennis, S., and Goldberg, J. (1986). Horozontal structure in middle childhood: cross domain parallels in the course of cognitive growth. In I. Levin (ed), *Stage and structure: reopening the debate.* New York: Ablex.

Case, R., Hayward, S., Lewis, M., and Hurst, P. (1987). Toward a neo-Piagetian theory of cognitive and affective development. *Developmental Review.*

Case, R., and Sandieson, R. (in press). Two cognitive developmental approaches to the design of remedial instruction. *Cognitive development,* in press.

---

* For a demonstration that children's gross motor development is a part of this same pattern, and shaped by the same underlying processes, see Reid (1987).

Damon, W. (1977). *The social world of the child.* San Francisco: Josey Bass.
Eagle, M. (1984). *Recent development in psychoanalysis: a critical evaluation.* New York: McGraw Hill.
Erikson, E.H. (1950). *Childhood and society.* New York: Norton.
Fischer, K.W. (1980). A theory of cognitive development: The control and construction of hierarchies of skills. *Psychological Review,* **87,** 447–531.
Fischer, K.W. (1981). Explaining the Oedipus conflict. *New Directions for Cognitive Development,* **12,** 79–93.
Fischer, K.W., and Pipp, S.L. (1985). Development of the structures of unconscious thought. In K. Bowers and D. Meichenbaum (eds), *The unconscious reconsidered.* New York: Wiley.
Flavell, J.H., and Ross, L. (eds). (1981). *Social and cognitive development.* New York: Cambridge University Press.
Gelman, R. (1978). Counting in the preschooler: What does and does not develop? In R.S. Siegler (ed), *Children's thinking: what develops?* (pp. 213–242). New York: Academic Press.
Hayward, S.W. (1986). *A developmental study of jealousy: The social triangle and its effects on the developing child.* Unpublished doctoral dissertation. University of Toronto (OISE).**
Hoffman, M. (1978). Developmental synthesis of affect and cognition and its implications. In H.E. Howe, Jr. (ed). *Nebraska Symposium on Motivation.* University of Nebraska Press: Lincoln, Nebraska.
Inhelder, B., and Piaget, J. (1958). *The growth of logical thinking from childhood to adolescence.* New York: Basic Books.
Kernberg, D. (1976). *Object relations theory and clinical psychoanalysis.* New York: Aronson.
Klein, M. (1957). *Envy and gratitude: a study of unconscious sources.* London: Tavistock.
Lewis, M.D. (1986). The relationship of separation distress and reunion gaze version to cognitive development in infancy. Unpublished M.A. Thesis, University of Toronto (OISE).
Liu, P.A. (1981). An investigation of the relationship between qualitative and quantitative advances in the cognitive development of preschool children. Unpublished doctoral thesis, University of Toronto (OISE).*
Mahler, M.S., Pine, F., and Bergman, A. (1975). *The psychological birth of the human infant.* New York: Bosie.
Marini, 2.A. (1984). *The development of social and non-social cognition in childhood and adolescence.* Unpublished doctoral dissertation, University of Toronto (OISE).*
Pascual-Leone. (1969). *Cognitive development and cognitive style.* Unpublished doctoral dissertation. University of Geneva.
Pascual-Leone, J., and Goodman, D. (1979). Intelligence and experience. *Instructional Science,* **8,** 301–367.
Reid, D. (1987). Motor development in young children: A test of the vertical structure hypothesis. Unpublished doctoral dissertation, University of Toronto.
Sander, L.W. (1975). Infant and caretaking environment: Investigation and conceptualization of adaptive behavior in a system of increasing complexity. In E.S. Anthony (ed), *Exploration in child psychiatry.* New York: Plenum.
Schaeffer, H.R. (1977). *Studies in infancy.* New York: Academic Press.
Serafica, F.S. (ed). (1982). *Social cognitive development in context.* New York: Guilford Press.
Siegler, R.S. (1976). Three aspects of cognitive development. *Cognitive Psychology,* **4,** 481–520.
Sroufe, L.A. (1979). Socioemotional development. In J. Osofsky (ed), *Handbook of infant development.* New York: Wiley, pp. 462–518.

Stern, D.N. (1977). *The first relationship: Mother and infant.* Cambridge, Mass.: Harvard University Press.

Stern, D.N. (1983). The early development of the schemas of self, other and 'self with other'. In J.D. Lichtenber and S. Kaplan (eds), *Reflections on self-psychology.* New York: International Universities Press.

Turiel, E. (1983). *The development of social knowledge: morality and convention.* New York: Cambridge University Press.

Weininger, O. (1984). *The clinical psychology of Melanie Klein.* Springfield, Illinois: Charles Thomas.

White, B. (1975). *The first three years.* New York: Englewood Cliffs.

Psychological Bases for Early Education
Edited by A.D. Pellegrini
© 1988 John Wiley & Sons Ltd.

CHAPTER 7

# Child Temperament and Educational Outcomes

Roy P. Martin

Professional interest in temperament during the past five years has been something of a phenomenon. Researchers in behavior genetics, infant development, general child development, family process, developmental psychopathology, personality, pediatrics, and child and adult psychiatry have made substantial contributions to the literature. A small group of these researchers has focused on the educational implications of temperament. This group includes child development experts and others who have carried out studies with educational outcomes as one measure of interest, and several researchers whose primary interest has been the effects of temperament on the process of education. The body of research produced by these groups has been small, although it has increased in volume rapidly during the past few years. It is the purpose of this paper to review this research with an eye toward locating promising avenues to be followed in future efforts.

This review is limited in several ways. First, the work selected for inclusion was contributed by persons who labeled their work as temperament research. Most were in the Thomas and Chess tradition in terms of measures used and variables studied. Second, the research reviewed is limited to those English language journals readily available in the United States. Finally, the review is not exhaustive even of this limited subset. It does, however, present what is believed to be a representative portion of the research available.

The review is organized around the six educational processes and products that have been the primary concern of temperament researchers. These include (a) scholastic ability, (b) achievement, (c) observed classroom behavior, (d) school adjustment as rated by teachers, (e) teacher attitudes, and (f) teacher planning decisions. A final section presents research on the effects of goodness-of-fit in the context of education.

185

## RELATIONSHIP OF TEMPERAMENT TO SCHOLASTIC ABILITY

Educators and psychologists have understood for a number of years the genetic foundations of measured intelligence, although the extent of the genetic contribution to intelligence is a hotly debated topic (Jensen, 1973, 1979; Plomin, 1986; Scarr, 1981). Far less clear is the mechanism by which genes influence learning ability. Genes affect learning ability directly through the biochemistry of learning, and indirectly through setting up the behavioral circumstances under which learning can take place. One possible indirect mechanism is that genes may influence behaviors such as attention and distractibility which influence learning rates. Other less obvious connections may also be hypothesized. For example, the tendency to approach in novel situations (rather than withdraw) may bring young children into contact with a greater variety of environmental stimuli which affects the rate of learning. This line of reasoning in combination with the notion that temperament, like intelligence, is inherited has lead some researchers to investigate the relationship between temperament and measured intelligence.

For example, Martin and Holbrook (1985) studied 104 first-grade children correlating first-grade teachers' temperament ratings with Otis–Lennon Mental Ability Test IQ scores. Temperament was rated on the teacher form of the Temperament Assessment Battery (Martin, 1984). Correlations were significant for Adaptability ($r = 0.34$), Approach/Withdrawal ($r = 0.51$), and Persistence scores ($r = 0.41$). In support of the relationship between persistence and intelligence, Palermo (1981) obtained a significant correlation ($r = 0.33$) between a Persistence/Distractibility factor and teacher-rated academic ability.

Matthews-Morgan (1984) and Burk (1980) studied gifted children (IQ greater than 130 on an individually administered intelligence test) in the age range from nursery school through second grade. Matthews-Morgan used the parent form of the Temperament Assessment Battery, and Burk used the Behavior Style Questionnaire (McDevitt and Carey, 1978) as the temperament measure. Matthews-Morgan found very few differences between temperaments when comparing the gifted group of children in the IQ range 100 to 130; only Persistence was significant and it was higher for the gifted children. Burk found that the gifted group was rated significantly higher on Approach/Withdrawal, Adaptability, Mood, and Persistence, as well as significantly lower on Distractibility when compared to the normative group of the Behavior Style Questionnaire. The differences in the results from these studies seem to be related to the range of IQ scores in the comparison group; one can assume a much greater range in the Burk study.

Palermo (1981) and Lerner, Lerner, and Zabski (1985) have looked at the relationship between self-rated temperament and teacher ratings of academic ability. Both used the Dimensions of Temperament Survey (Lerner, Palermo,

Spiro, and Nesselroade, 1982) as the temperament measure. Palermo (1981) found no relationship between self-rated temperament and teacher ratings of academic ability for a sample of fifth-grade students. However, Lerner, Lerner, and Zabski (1985) found self-rated Activity, Adaptability/Approach, and Emotional Reactivity were significantly correlated to teacher ratings of academic ability in their sample of fourth graders, although the level of these relationships was low (in the 0.15 to 0.20 range).

These studies show that the relationship between temperament and scholastic ability is modest. Low to moderate relationships have been found for parent- and teacher-rated persistence and distractibility, with occasional relationships found for adaptability and approach/withdrawal. The results for self-rated temperament are less clear.

One implication of these findings is that researchers who are interested in the relationship of temperament to educational outcomes, and perhaps even social ones, should control for the effects of measured intelligence, particularly when relationships with persistence and distractibility are considered. Future researchers might consider the nature of the relationship between temperament and measured intelligence. One possible explanation for the relationship is that temperament (e.g. persistence) manifested at the time of intelligence assessment is the major contributor to the relationship. An alternative hypothesis is that children who manifest persistence consistently in their day-to-day lives are more likely to learn the material tapped on intelligence tests. Sorting out the variance attributable to these two factors is a worthwhile pursuit and would clarify the nature of the temperament–intelligence connection.

## RELATIONSHIP OF TEMPERAMENT TO ACHIEVEMENT

The arguments presented for the connection between temperament and intelligence are applicable in part to the relationship between temperament and achievement in that measured intelligence is the best single predictor of achievement. However, the importance of the temperament–achievement relationship is most clearly seen when we attempt to understand differences in achievement among children of similar intelligence; that is, when the effects of intelligence are removed. All teachers know that even among the brightest children, some perform well in the classroom and on standardized achievement instruments, and some do not. Perhaps predispositions toward persistence, moderate activity level, adaptability and other factors that are temperamentally based play a role in these achievement differences. If so, then psychologists and educators can make better predictions of achievement outcomes, and can institute specialized programs for children whose predispositions make performance in achievement settings difficult.

Martin and Holbrook (1985) found for a sample of first-grade children that Adaptability and Persistence rated by teachers on the teacher form of the

Temperament Assessment Battery were positively correlated with teacher-assigned grades in reading and mathematics in the range of 0.35 to 0.65. Activity and Distractibility scores correlated with grades in the range of $-0.42$ to $-0.56$. These correlations were lowered only slightly when variance due to IQ was partialled out. In the same study, correlations with standardized test scores in reading were found to be significantly and positively related to Adaptability and Persistence, and negatively to Distractibility. Correlations were somewhat lower than for teacher-assigned grades. Only Adaptability scores were related to standardized mathematics scores.

Martin, Gaddis, Drew, and Moseley (1986) have shown that temperament scores significantly predict school achievement over periods of one, two, and four years. For example, teacher temperament ratings on the Martin Temperament Assessment Battery predicted Metropolitan Achievement Test scores in reading and maths as well as assigned grades in the fifth grade. Distractibility, Persistence and Activity Level significantly correlated with all four achievement variables with variance due to IQ removed. The correlations ranged from 0.26 to 0.41, with the strongest correlations being between Distractibility (a negative relationship) and Metropolitan test scores.

Some support for these findings was obtained by Pullis and Cadwell (1982). They investigated the relationship between teacher estimates of academic achievement and teacher ratings of three temperament factors: Task Orientation (related to persistence and distractibility), Reactivity (related to intensity, mood, and threshold), and Flexibility (related to adaptability and approach/withdrawal). A short form of the Teacher Temperament Questionnaire was used (Keogh, Pullis, and Cadwell, 1982). For their kindergarten through second grade sample, achievement ratings were correlated 0.44 with Flexibility, and 0.76 with Task Orientation.

Burk (1980) attempted to find a relationship between parent-rated temperament on the Behavior Style Questionnaire and standardized achievement scores within a gifted group. This was a stringent test in that variance in achievement was restricted in this generally high-achieving sample. Activity level and Persistence produced a significant multiple $R$ of 0.29. No relationship was found for mathematics achievement. Lerner, Lerner, and Zabski (1985) also obtained low significant correlations for fourth graders between self-rated Activity level (Dimensions of Temperament Survey) and SAT reading ($r = 0.18$). No other self-rated temperament score was related to achievement.

These studies indicate that moderate correlations are often obtained between achievement and selected temperament variables, even when variance due to IQ is controlled. The temperament variables that are most commonly related to are achievement persistence, distractibility, and adaptability. Activity also is sometimes found to be a significant covariate. Relationships are highest when teacher-rated temperament is the predictor; parent-rated and self-rated temperament produce lower relationships. Higher relationships are generally found between teacher-assigned grades and temperament than between standardized test scores and temperament. Grades may reflect the ability consistently to perform in the classroom (regularly doing homework punctually and completely, for example), whereas the standardized test scores may be a more objectively assessed performance skill. Also, larger relationships are obtained between temperament and reading achievement than between temperament and mathematics achievement. It may be that the dominant place of reading instruction in early elementary school creates more variance in reading achievement than the mathematics achievement, or that both parents and teachers are biased in their temperament ratings by knowing the child's reading achievement level. Both of these artifactual effects must be ruled out before a statement can be made about temperament–achievement relationships.

The questions that were raised in regard to temperament effects on intelligence have similar importance for temperament–achievement relationships. That is, persistence manifested at the time of taking standardized and teacher-made tests may account for the relationship between persistence and achievement; alternatively, this relationship may be due primarily to a generalized persistence in classroom learning. Martin, Nagle, and Paget (1983) found that Persistence correlated −0.60 with observed gross-motor inappropriate behavior, and 0.46 with constructive self-directed activity observed in first-grade classrooms. This suggests that children who are rated as persistent exhibit this persistence in the classroom in ways that would enhance learning.

Perhaps a more critical and theoretically important issue concerns the effects of teacher perception of child temperament as a biasing effect in grading, independent of classroom performance. It is possible that adaptable, persistent students are given higher grades based on a halo phenomenon or some similar judgmental bias. Data to be reviewed later indirectly support the hypothesis that such a bias exits and that this phenomenon may account for part of the temperament–achievement relationship.

## RELATIONSHIP OF TEMPERAMENT TO OBSERVED CLASSROOM BEHAVIOR

Understanding the relationship between temperament and classroom behavior is important for several reasons. First, if reliable relationships between specific classroom behaviors and ratings on temperament measures are obtained, this provides an indication of the reliability of the temperament rating. This is an important consideration in that error variance of various kinds is a potential hazard for all rating scales, including those designed to assess temperament (Martin, Hooper, and Snow, 1986).

Second, understanding the relationships between temperament and classroom behavior sheds light on the mechanisms by which behavior predispositions affect achievement-related behaviors. If children who are rated by their parents and teachers as more distractible and more active are found to exhibit more off-task behavior than their peers then the mechanisms by which temperament affects achievement have been clarified.

Finally, if the researcher focuses on teacher–student interactions in the classroom, another potentially important link in the temperament–achievement relationship may be found. It is possible that some temperament variables affect teachers' behaviors which in turn influence the performance of the student.

Billman and McDevitt (1980) observed the peer interaction of pre-school children in the classroom. They also obtained parental ratings of temperament on the Behavioral Style Questionnaire, and teacher ratings of temperament on the Teacher Temperament Questionnaire ( Thomas and Chess, 1977). A number of significant and theoretically meaningful correlations were obtained between both parent and teacher ratings, and peer interaction. Significant correlations for the parent ratings were in the 0.19 to 0.33 range, while for the teacher ratings, they were in the 0.20 to 0.53 range.

Martin, Nagle, and Paget (1983) correlated teacher-rated temperament from the teacher form of the Temperament Assessment Battery (Martin, 1984) with various types of student activity, and task-related behavior for a sample of first graders. A number of significant and practically meaningful relationships were obtained. For example, Activity scores correlated $-0.50$ with constructive self-directed activity, and $0.55$ with gross-motor inappropriate behavior. Adaptability scores correlated $0.49$ with constructive self-directed activity, $-0.40$ with nonconstructive self-directed activity, and $-0.63$ with gross-motor inappropriate behavior.

Two investigations were found that related temperament to observed teacher–child interaction. Keogh and Burnstein (Keogh, in press) observed the student–teacher interaction of a small sample of handicapped children and a nonhandicapped control group. They found that for nonhandicapped children, higher rates of interaction with the teacher were associated with positive temperament patterns while for handicapped children, higher rates were associated with negative temperament patterns. For peer–peer interaction, the number of interactions was associated with positive temperament characteristics for both handicapped and nonhandicapped children.

Paget, Nagle, and Martin (1984) studied the teacher–child interaction of 105 first-grade children using the Brophy and Good (1969) observation system. Teacher-rated temperament scores were obtained from the teacher form of the Temperament Assessment Battery. Three factors were extracted from the temperament ratings: Reactivity (the Activity, Intensity, Threshold scales loaded most heavily on this factor), Social Adaptability (the Adaptability and Approach/Withdrawal scales loaded most heavily on this factor), and Task Attention (the Persistence and Distractibility scales loaded most heavily on this factor). A regression procedure revealed that 19 percent of the variance in the total number of behavior contacts (as opposed to content-oriented contacts) was associated with Social Adaptability scores (negative relationship) and Reactivity (positive relationship). From this pool of behavior contacts, those that were followed by teacher praise were significantly related to Social Adaptability and Task Attention. The beta weights were negative, indicating that more adaptable and attentive children were involved in fewer behavior contacts terminated in praise. Behavior contacts that were terminated in teacher criticism were positively related to task attention. These last two findings were interpreted as indications that teachers adjust their feedback and interactions to the individual style of the child in a compensatory manner. That is, less adaptable, less attentive children tend to be praised for attentive, socially appropriate behavior. Their more adaptable and attentive peers receive much less praise for such behaviors, and tend to be criticized for not exhibiting appropriate behavior in the classroom.

These few studies show that meaningful relationships between temperament and observed classroom behavior have been obtained. However, so few studies of this type have been published to date, it is impossible to make generalizations about the temperament variables that are associated most strongly with various types of interaction (e.g. peer–peer, teacher–student).

Three of the studies reviewed have used teacher ratings of temperament. While for some research questions this procedure is questionable, for others it seems to be appropriate. If, for example, one wishes to determine whether teachers are able objectively to rate the activity level of a child, then obviously using the teacher rating is appropriate. Further, if the question concerns the relationship between the teacher's perception of the child and his/her interaction with the child, again teacher ratings are appropriate. If, on the other hand, the question is one of determining the relationship of behavior outside the classroom to behavior in the classroom, ratings from someone who has observed behavior outside the classroom should be obtained. Future classroom researchers could utilize both parent and teacher ratings, as well as the aggregate of these two in order more completely to determine the effects of rater and setting on temperament–behavior relationships.

## RELATIONSHIP OF TEMPERAMENT TO SCHOOL ADJUSTMENT

Much of the current interest in temperament can be traced to the New York Longitudinal Study of Thomas and Chess (1977). One aspect of this study was an investigation of the relationship of temperament measured early in the child's life to adjustment problems manifest at the time and later. Perhaps the most provocative finding of this research was that temperament measured in the infant, toddler, and pre-school period predicted behavior and emotional problems manifest in childhood and adolescence.

In this tradition there have been a few studies of the relationship of temperament to the adjustment of children as measured in a school context. The studies reviewed here are limited to those in which the measure of adjustment was provided by the teacher. The reviewed research can be conveniently divided into that involving unselected samples of children and those involving handicapped children. Research on unselected samples is reviewed first.

Carey, Fox, and McDevitt (1977) obtained parental temperament ratings on the Behavioral Style Questionnaire (McDevitt and Carey, 1978) and teacher adjustment ratings on the Bommarito Socialization Scale for 51 first-grade children. They found that only Adaptability scores were significantly correlated with school adjustment, and the relationship was a modest one ($r = 0.35$).

Burk (1980) studied 125 gifted children in kindergarten, first, and second grade and obtained similar results. Again, parent temperament ratings were obtained on the Behavioral Style Questionnaire while school adjustment was rated by teachers on the Child's Behavior Trait Scale. A significant correlation was obtained for Adaptability ($r = 0.23$) and for Persistence ($r = 0.35$). The significance of persistence in this study was interpreted as relating to the importance placed on this type of behavior in programs for gifted children.

Matthews-Morgan (1984) also studied gifted children and a group of children in the near gifted range. All 95 children were in pre-school and had been rated by teachers on the Bristol Social Adjustment Guide (Stott, 1974). Significant negative correlations were obtained between mother-rated Adaptability and Approach/Withdrawal and the Under-reactive score (anxiety, withdrawal depression) from the Bristol Social Adjustment Guide. Activity was positively related to the Over-reaction score (aggression, impulsivity, activity, etc.), while Adaptability and Persistence were negatively related to this score. All correlations were in the 0.20 to 0.35 range.

In another study of adjustment in pre-schoolers, Feuerstein and Martin (1981) obtained parental temperament ratings on a revision of the Thomas and Chess Parent Temperament Questionnaire. These children were also rated by their nursery school teachers on the California Preschool Social Competence Scale (CPSCS), and on a one-item continuum designed to be a global measure of social adjustment to school. In addition, sociometric data were obtained. Adaptability was found to be significantly related to both the CPSCS ($r = 0.25$) and the one-item ratings ($r = 0.48$). No relationship was found between temperament and the sociometry measure.

In an older sample of children (eighth-grade students) Lerner (1980) found that self-rated Adaptability was the best predicter of positive peer nominations, and Mood was the best predicter of negative peer nominations. Multiple $R$s were in the 0.38 to 0.49 range when all temperament variables were entered as predicters. The differences in outcome between the Lerner and the Feuerstein and Martin studies with regard to sociometric measures are probably related to the differences in reliability in the sociometric measures obtained from the eighth-grade sample in the Lerner study, and the pre-school sample in the Feuerstein and Martin study.

In one of two predictive studies that could be found (other than studies using NYLS data), Garrison, Earls, and Kindlon (1984) explored the relationship between parent-rated temperament on the Parent Temperament Questionnaire (Thomas and Chess, 1977) obtained at the age of 3, and school adjustment ratings in the first grade. First-grade adjustment was rated by teachers on the Child Behavior Checklist (CBCL) (Achenbach and Edelbrock, 1983). No relationship was found in correlational analysis. However, when children with significant symptoms were isolated, based on parent, teacher, and clinician judgment and compared to children without significant symptoms, persistence rated at 3 years of age was a significant predicter of group membership.

The second predictive study that was found (Kohnstamm, 1986) utilized a Dutch translation of the Bates Infant Characteristics Questionnaire and the Child Characteristics Questionnaire, and other mother and child characteristics, to predict three personality dimensions (timid-bold, sociability, accuracy) rated by kindergarten teachers. Initial temperament assessment took place when some children were as young as a few months of age, while others were approaching 3 years of age. In a multi-regression analysis the temperament dimensions of Adaptability and Persistence as rated by mothers contributed significantly to the rating of the kindergarten teacher on all three dimensions. The prediction of accuracy was better for girls, while the prediction of Sociability was better for boys.

Palermo (1981) and Lerner, Lerner, and Zabski (1985) have utilized self-rated temperament scores to predict teacher-rated adjustment. Palermo (1981) found that self-rated Reactivity (a variable made up of mood and intensity) was a significant predictor of adjustment for fifth graders ($r = -0.22$). When teacher ratings of temperament were used in the same study, again a negative relationship between adjustment and Reactivity was obtained ($r = -0.23$) as well as a positive correlation ($r = 0.20$) for Attention Span/Distractibility. Using similar procedures, Lerner, Lerner, and Zabski found no relationship between self-rated temperament and teacher-rated adjustment.

Two studies were located that focused on the temperament and school adjustment of exceptional children. Lambert and Windmiller (1977) studied three groups of children defined in the educational setting as exhibiting problem behavior (low achievers, children with adjustment problems, and hyperactive children), and a control group. Using a parent interview based on the Thomas and Chess interview, they found that hyperactive children were seen by parents as more extreme than any other group in terms of negative temperament characteristics. However, only parent-rated distractibility differentiated this group from the other groups. Low achievers and adjustment-problem children were not differentiated from other groups by temperament scores.

Studies by Keogh and associates (see Keogh, in press, for a review) of learning in disabled children have shown that they are distinguished on teacher temperament ratings as being low in Task Orientation; that is, they have a low ability to control activity, are not persistent and tend to be distractible.

Two generalizations about this research can be made. First, when significant relationships are obtained between temperament ratings and school adjustment, the relationships most frequently involve adaptability and persistence. Given that learning in traditional classroom takes place in a crowded social environment, it is logical that social adaptability should play a major role in school adjustment. The place of persistence is equally reasonable, in that this variable is heavily loaded with variance related to attention, and attention is a prerequisite for most kinds of learning. General adjustment outside of school has been found by several researchers to be predicted best by ratings of emotional intensity and mood (Terestman, 1980; Thomas and Chess, 1977). The fact that these variables do not relate well to school adjustment seems to demonstrate the effects of environmental press in determining those behaviors that are central to adjustment. At home negative mood and high emotional intensity are expressed more freely than in the relatively public environment of the school. It seems logical that in the intimate relationship of the family, moody, intense behaviors are troublesome. In the school environment where ability to adjust to rules and strangers is an important skill adaptability takes on much greater importance than in the familiar world of the family. Similarly, the central task at school is learning, so attention and related behavior play a much greater role in this environment than in the home (Martin, 1986).

The second generalization that can be made about the temperament–school adjustment research is that the relationships obtained between temperament and adjustment are low. In part, this seems to be attributable to the fact that the raters of temperament are usually mothers who do not see their child in the classroom environment.

Little is gained at this point in the development of temperament research in continuing to show that temperament relates to adjustment in the school setting. The issue in need of clarification concerns the nature of the caretaker and setting factors, as well as student factors, that produce teacher perceptions of maladjustment in children at risk due to negative temperaments. Those factors that affect the perceptual set of the teacher such as job stress would appear to be worthy of consideration. Similarly, factors that stress the coping capabilities of the child could be isolated and studied as they interact with temperament to produce behaviors that are indicative of poor adjustment.

## RELATIONSHIP OF TEMPERAMENT TO TEACHER ATTITUDE

Whether the researcher is interested in academic performance outcomes or social adjustment in the classroom, teacher attitudes and perceptions may play an important role as a moderate variable. Only a few studies of the relationship of temperament to teacher attitude have been published but they have produced some of the most provocative findings of all the studies reviewed in this chapter.

For example, Martin, Nagle, and Paget (1983) studied the relationship between temperament ratings by teachers, and teacher attitudes toward individual students. Teacher attitudes were measured by asking teachers four questions: (a) Name three children in your class you would like to have in class again for the sheer joy of it; (b) Name three children you would be least prepared to talk about at a parent–teacher conference; (c) Name three children you would spend more time with if you could; (d) If you could reduce your class by three children, which three children would it be? These four questions are said to measure the attitudes of attachment, indifference, concern, and rejection, respectively (Silberman, 1969). It was found that the attachment group was distinguished from others by being more adaptable, approaching, and persistent. The indifference group was distinguished from others by being less active, less approaching, and less intense. No temperament variables differentiated between the concern group and others. The rejection group was differentiated from the others by being more active and more distractible.

In an extension and elaboration of this study, Connor (1983) obtained teacher and teacher aide temperament ratings for 80 black kindergarten children. When these children reached first grade, their first-grade teachers nominated children in their class in response to the four Silberman attitude questions. Also, effects of achievement level on nominations were controlled. Children nominated for the attachment and indifference groups in first grade were found to have been rated as less active and more adaptable by teachers and teacher aides (an aggregate measure) in kindergarten. The rejection group was found to have a higher emotional intensity rating than those not nominated for this group. Somewhat different temperament variables differentiated between the attitude groups in this study and in Martin, Nagle, and Paget (1983); this may be attributable to the differences in the samples studied (for the Martin *et al.* study the sample was predominately middle class and in first grade when temperament ratings were obtained; for the Connor study, the sample was exclusively lower class black children who were in kindergarten when temperament was assessed). However, the Connor study shows that when temperament is rated independently of attitude measurement, and even when attitude measurement is taken one year later, significant relationships between teacher attitudes toward children and temperament are obtained.

Lerner, Lerner, and Zabski (1985) obtained measures of the expectations/demands teachers held for children in their class. The measure used was a modification of the Dimensions of Temperament Survey, in which the stem of each item was modified to ask what the teacher would prefer in terms of child behavior. For example, 'The child stays with an activity for a long time,' was changed to 'I want my students to stay with an activity for a long time.' Lerner *et al.* (1985) report that there was little variance among the fourth-grade teachers studied. All expected low activity level, low distractibility, high adaptability and approach, and low emotional reactivity.

The relationship of temperament to teacher ratings of teachability has been studied by Keogh and colleagues (see Keogh, 1982, for a review). Teachability was assessed on the 33-item Teachable Pupil Attribute Scale. In a study of 80 pre-school children for whom teacher temperament ratings were also available, the Task Orientation factor (primarily distractibility and persistence items) of the temperament measure had the highest relationship to overall teachability ($r = 0.47$). Correlations between three teachability dimensions and three temperament factors ranged from 0.14 to 0.69.

The research reviewed demonstrates a remarkable, though not surprising, consistency. Teachers prefer low activity, highly adaptable, high approaching, low distractibility, and low intensity children. This cluster of variables is quite similar to the easy child category delineated by Thomas and Chess based on data obtained from parents. However, activity level and distractibility have not typically been included in the easy/difficult child cluster of variables. The importance of these variables to teachers is undoubtedly related to their caretaking role; that is, they must carry out their profession in a relatively crowded environment in which attention to materials to be learned is the essential behavioral element. Distractibility and activity become very troublesome given these demands.

Children who exhibit the characteristics that are consistent with the demands of the teaching-learning environment should be at an advantage in this environment. One study demonstrating such positive effects was carried out by Holbrook (1982). He obtained teacher estimates of IQ 95 children in first-grade classes, as well as teacher temperament ratings on adaptability and approach/withdrawal. These two temperament variables were chosen because they were similar to those assessed in a previous study of the relationship of temperament to teacher estimates of intelligence (Gordon and Thomas, 1967). A correlation of 0.50 was obtained between the Adaptability rating and estimated IQ with variance due to measured IQ partialled out. A similar partial correlation ($r = 0.43$) was obtained for Approach/Withdrawal. These results show that teachers tend to over-estimate the intellectual capabilities of children they see as adaptable and approaching. The results of this study replicated those of Gordon and Thomas.

Pullis (1979) also studied the relationship between teacher estimates of cognitive capability and temperament. He found that the Task Orientation factor and the Flexibility factor of an abbreviated form of the Teacher Temperament Questionnaire (Thomas and Chess, 1977) significantly related to teacher estimates of pupil ability with variance due to measured IQ controlled. The Flexibility factor is heavily loaded with items that appear in the

Adaptability and Approach/Withdrawal scales of the original scale. Thus, this study supports the findings of Holbrook, and Gordon and Thomas.

## RELATIONSHIP OF TEMPERAMENT TO
## TEACHING DECISION-MAKING

Keogh and his colleagues have carried out a program of research on the effects of temperament on teacher decision-making, with particular emphasis given to decisions involving classroom management and special classroom placement (see Keogh, 1982, for a summary). One approach has been to use vignettes in which the nature of the information provided, characteristics of handicapped students, and characteristics of their teachers, are systematically varied. Findings from several such studies indicate that the Task Orientation factor (primarily distractibility and persistence items) of their brief temperament measure (Keogh, Pullis, and Cadwell, 1982) is significantly related to teacher decisions. One important finding is that if the child described has a more severe handicap (regardless of type), and a negative temperament (particularly a low score on the Task Orientation factor), decisions to refer for special education placement are likely; such a decision is much more likely than if the severe handicapping condition or the negative temperament were present in isolation.

Pullis and Cadwell (1982) investigated the effects of temperament on teacher classroom management decisions for a large sample of unselected elementary school children. The instrument used was the 23-item abbreviation of the Teacher Temperament Questionnaire developed by Keogh and his colleagues (Keogh, Pullis, and Cadwell, 1982). Teachers were asked a series of questions about the classroom management decisions they made with regard to each child. How frequently do you have to monitor this child when the class is working individually at their seats? How frequently do you have to monitor this student when the class is engaged in small-group activities? The Task Orientation factor, again, played the major role in predicting these teacher management decisions. Flexibility also appeared as a significant contributor in some of the regression equations.

## GOODNESS-OF-FIT RESEARCH

Thomas and Chess in their writings on temperament (e.g. Thomas and Chess, 1977) have emphasized their belief that being at one extreme or the other of any temperament variable does not necessarily predispose the child to negative outcomes. What is important is the 'goodness-of-fit' between the child's predispositions and the demand characteristics of the environment in which the child finds him/herself. A few simple examples make this point vividly. The highly active child helping his parents on a farm is experiencing a better fit between his characteristics and the demands of the environment than the same child in a traditional classroom setting. The emotionally intense child whose parents view this as lusty, vigorous behavior is experiencing a better goodness-of-fit than the intense child whose parents value emotional control and do not understand why their child gets so upset about small things.

While much of the research reviewed to this point has implications for the goodness-of-fit between the child's temperament and the demands of the school environment, none of this research has directly addressed this issue. Jacqueline Lerner and colleagues have carried out a program of research on goodness-of-fit in educational settings. One of the earliest studies in this group was Lerner's dissertation research (Lerner, 1980). She assessed the self-reported temperament of 99 eighth-grade children using the Dimensions of Temperament Survey (Lerner, Palermo, Spiro, and Nesselroade, 1982). Situational demands were assessed from the teacher and peer point of view using a 9-item questionnaire, each item tapping one of the 9 Thomas and Chess dimensions. The questions were phrased in terms of the characteristics that the teacher and peer respondents preferred. Peer situational demands were the mean of all peer responses. In addition, each student's perceptions of the teacher's and peers' demands or preferences were assessed. These data made possible the calculation of four discrepancy scores for each subject: (a) the discrepancy between self-rated temperament and teacher-rated preferences or demands; (b) the discrepancy between self-rated temperament and peer-rated preferences; (c) the discrepancy between self-rated temperament and perceptions of teacher preferences; (d) the discrepancy between self-rated temperament and perceptions of peer preferences. These scores were used to predict a variety of academic adjustment measures such as grade point average, teacher ratings of academic and social competence, positive and negative peer nominations, and self-esteem. Regression analysis demonstrated that discrepancy scores between self-ratings and perceived preferences, whether teacher or peer, predicted academic outcome variables better than the discrepancies between self-ratings and actual teacher and peer preference scores.

In another investigation in this series, Palermo (1981) assessed the self- and parent-rated temperament of 91 fifth-grade children, as well as the demands/expectations of their teachers. Both sets of variables served as predicters of various outcome measures such as teacher ratings of academic ability, social adjustment, and degree of conformity to teacher expectations. Peer popularity ratings were also obtained, an index of goodness-of-fit was developed by subtracting self- or parent-rated temperament scores on the Dimensions of Temperament Survey from the teacher demand/expectancy score obtained from a modification of the same measure. The discrepancy score for self-rated Reactivity correlated significantly with peer negative popularity ratings ($r = 0.23$), and with teacher ratings of child conformity with teacher expectation ($r = -0.26$). The Attention Span/Distractibility discrepancy score correlated significantly ($r = 0.23$) with teacher ratings of conformity, and the Adaptability/

Approach discrepancy score correlated significantly with social adjustment ratings made by the teacher ($r = 0.24$). The discrepancy score for parent-rated Attention Span/Distractibility correlated significantly with all teacher ratings and child popularity ratings (correlations ranged from 0.20 to 0.31). The parent-related Adaptability/Approach discrepancy score correlated significantly with teacher ratings of social adjustment ($r = 0.25$) and the Reactivity discrepancy score correlated significantly with conformity ($r = 0.21$) and peer positive popularity ($r = -0.28$).

In a recent follow-up and extension of these investigations, Lerner, Lerner, and Zabski (1985) studied 194 fourth-grade students. Each child completed the Dimensions of Temperament Survey, and their teacher completed the modified version of the same instrument designed to assess teacher expectancy/ demands. Again, the discrepancy score approach was utilized as an index of goodness-of-fit. A significant relationship was obtained between the Reactivity discrepancy score and SAT reading ($r = -0.19$), as well as teacher ratings of the child's ability ($r = -0.26$). (The negative correlation indicates that as the child's self-rating of emotional reactivity increased to levels above the teacher's expectancy/demand score, the achievement and ability ratings decreased.) No significant relationships were obtained for discrepancy scores and teacher-rated adjustment.

The discrepancy score approach was also used by Keogh and his colleagues (see Keogh, 1982, for a review). In one study, 49 teachers each rated 10 to 15 pupils on the Teachable Pupil Attribute Scale. This scale was completed twice, once as a rating of the actual child, and once as a rating of an ideal child. The discrepancy score of interest in this research was the discrepancy between the child's actual teachability rating and the teacher's ideal teachability model. Children with high actual-ideal discrepancy scores had high Reactivity scores, and low Task Orientation and Flexibility scores.

Another approach to the issue of goodness-of-fit in educational settings is exemplified by the work of Barclay (1983). He reviews research which used the Barclay Classroom Assessment System (Barclay, 1982) to classify third- through seventh-grade children. This system is a multi-method procedure consisting of self-ratings, peer ratings, and teacher ratings. Through this system, children can be designated as belonging to one of six personality/ temperament types: (a) Type 1—energetic, active, individualistic, retiring; (b) Type 2—energetic, active, socially outgoing; (c) Type 3—compliant, passive, individualistic, retiring; (d) Type 4—compliant, passive, socially outgoing; (e) Type 5—energetic, blend of retiring-retiring-outgoing; and (f) Type 6— compliant, blend of retiring-outgoing. A meta-analysis of research on the educational outcomes for these types of children is reported for six environmental treatments: a traditional classroom, an open classroom, a behaviorally oriented treatment environment, a consultation environment, a group counseling environment, and a mastery learning situation. The results demonstrate that there are different outcomes for the types of children in the different environments. For example, traditional classroom environments were shown to be effective in improving task–order achievement and sociability in Type 1 children, but somewhat detrimental for other groups. Open classroom environments are effective in a number of ways for Types 1, 2, and 5, particularly in increasing sociability and energy level. However, for Types 3 and 4 (children who have self-control problems and poor achievement), there are marked negative effects. The behavioral approach fosters the development of control, energy, and internality in Types 1, 3, and 6, but has a negative effect for Types 1 and 2 children.

A third approach to the goodness-of-fit issue was demonstrated by Gordon (1981). She used parent ratings on the Thomas and Chess Parent Temperament Questionnaire to select 74 pre-schoolers from 244 who meet criteria as being difficult or easy based on Thomas and Chess definitions. Children were chosen who were at the top and bottom third of the distribution on each constituent variable. Each selected child was placed in a experimental situation in which an adult created a controlling or a permissive environment, and such variables as child-initiated behavior, time on task, and experimenter controlling behavior were observed. Significant interactions between temperament, sex, and condition were found for some of the observed behaviors. For example, child-initiated behaviors were highest for difficult boys in the permissive condition, and were lowest for difficult girls in the permissive condition. However, in the controlling condition, difficult girls took the lead more than difficult boys.

A provocative study utilizing physiological measures of temperament was carried out by Koestler and Farley (1982). They assessed the skin conductance level and mean pulse level of 98 first-grade children, half of whom were in open classrooms, with the remaining half in traditional classrooms. The physiological measures were thought of as indices of arousal level. The research was based on the empirical finding that as arousal level increases, stimulus seeking decreases. It was also based on the assumption that open classrooms provide a greater amount of external stimulation than traditional classrooms. It was hypothesized that low-arousal children would perform better in an open classroom than in a traditional classroom, and that higher-arousal children would perform better in the traditional classroom. Measures of performance were teacher ratings on the Conners Behavior Rating Scale, a visual discrimination task similar to the Matching Familiar Figures Test, and two mazes. All variables were assessed at the beginning and end of the first year of school. Results showed that children at either extreme of the arousal continuum who were in the traditional classroom improved their performance on the visual discrimination task over time, as did low-arousal children in the open classroom. However, the performance of high-arousal children in the open classroom decreased. No other class type by arousal level by time interaction occurred. These results provided limited support for the goodness-of-fit model.

These research efforts indicate that the goodness-of-fit notion is alive and well among temperament researchers studying educational environments and outcomes. Effect sizes have tended to be small in the discrepancy score approach utilized by Lerner and her associates, but the research has a great deal of appeal due to the direct manner in which goodness-of-fit is assessed. It is probable that the measurement problems encountered in assessing teacher expectancies/demands, as well as the small amount of variation in teacher expectancies/demands, account for the low correlations. The research of Barclay and, more clearly, that of Gordon, demonstrates that if environments are very clearly differentiated, stronger effect sizes can result.

The goodness-of-fit model has a number of implications for educational practice, the most obvious one being that classroom placements could be made based on child temperament, in a manner similar to the approach used in assigning children with different abilities to different classes (gifted, normal, mentally handicapped). Placements could be based on teacher tolerance for given characteristics or skill in working with children with exceptional temperament characteristics. Placements might also be based on the general organization of the classroom and the instructional delivery model (e.g. open classroom vs. traditional classroom; self-paced instruction vs. teacher-centered instruction). In all probability temperament and learning ability will be found to interact in important ways in producing effects on achievement and adjustment, so that such placement would take into account both social/emotional and intellectual predispositions of the child. A good deal more research is needed before such placement practices could be appropriately conceptualized and carried out. However, it seems clear that the educational system cannot rely on the individual sensitivity of the classroom teacher to adjust instruction to fit children who are temperamentally very different if the potential of all children is to be maximized.


## CONCLUSION

It is clear from this review that the demand characteristics of traditional classroom-based teaching/learning situations favor children who are highly persistent and adaptable. Such students have been shown to have greater scholastic ability, greater achievement (with scholastic ability controlled), and are rated as better adjusted than their peers. Further, persistence and adaptability play a role in the attitudinal orientation teachers have toward students. For example, while persistent and adaptable students, in fact, are brighter and achieve at higher levels than their peers, their teachers tend to over-estimate their scholastic ability and give them higher grades than standardized achievement performance would suggest is appropriate. Teachers, also, feel more personal attachment toward such students. These results have been found for students from pre-school through junior high school, using a variety of temperament measures.

One implication of this set of findings is that the easy/different child dimension has a somewhat different meaning from one environment to another. Persistence and distractibility do not play a major role in most conceptions of the easy or difficult child as seen in the context of the family. The reasons for this are clear. The demand for sustained attention to difficult learning tasks is not a dominant feature of home life for most families; it is the central demand characteristic of the school. Mood and emotional intensity rarely are seen as major correlates of academic outcomes, but are often the best predicters of adjustment in the home. It seems likely that the range of mood-related behavior and emotional intensity expressed in the home is far wider than in the classroom. In the public atmosphere of the classroom, children probably inhibit manifestations of these behaviors after the age of 5 or so. The intimacy and familiarity of the social relationships in the home probably make the expression more likely, and the negative consequences of negative mood and intense emotion more costly since there is no escape from the relationship.

Educational researchers will not be able easily to address some of the basic questions about the nature of temperament. Behavior geneticists, personologists, and infant researchers seem to be in a better position to deal with these issues. However, the educational environment offers a ready-made, real-life contrast to the home environment, making possible important comparative research on the temperament–environment interaction. In this way educational research on temperament may make a fundamental contribution to the more general understanding of this class of variables.

In the application of temperament to educational concerns, two general avenues of research seem to be promising. First, it is important to understand more completely than is now possible, the meaning of temperament ratings made by teachers. For example, are the items on an adaptability scale that deal with following rules in the classroom most related to educational outcome, or are those items related to adjusting to altered social groups most central? Since item–item correlations are not high for most temperament-rating instruments, it cannot be assumed that all items carry equal weight in specific predictions. Similarly, it may prove fruitful to know what student characteristics serve as biasing factors in teaching ratings. Age, sex, race, physical attractiveness, and socio-economic status of parents might be variables worthy of study. The systematic and thoughtful accumulation of data of this type might help to clarify the constructs being measured and labeled as temperaments.

The second research thrust that would build on current knowledge is one in which factors which interact with student temperament are studied with the potential for improving prediction of educational outcomes. One class of such variables might be environmental stressors which lower teacher tolerances for student behavior. These could include job-related factors, home factors, or factors related to the health and general well-being of the teacher. Teacher expectations have been studied in the goodness-of-fit literature, but the finding that there is little variation in expectation among teachers has reduced the meaningfulness of the results. If teachers were chosen who were under varying levels of stress, behavioral expectations and tolerances could be expected to vary over a wider range, and clearer interactions with temperament could result. The interaction of student stressors and temperament on academic outcomes is another example of research of this type that might prove informative.

## REFERENCES

Achenbach, T.M., and Edelbrock, C.S. (1983). *Manual for the Child Behavior Checklist and Revised Child Behavior Profile.* Burlington, VT: Department of Psychiatry, University of Vermont.

Barclay, J.R. (1982). *Manual of the Barclay Classroom Assessment System.* Los Angeles: Western Psychological Services.

Barclay, J.R. (1983). A meta-analysis of temperament–treatment interactions with alternative learning and counseling treatments. *Developmental Review,* **3**, 410–443.

Billman, J., and McDevitt, S. (1980). Convergence of parent and observer ratings of temperament with observations of peer interactions in nursery school. *Child Development,* **51**, 395–400.

Brophy, J.E., and Good, T.L. (1969). *Analyzing classroom behavior: A more powerful alternative* (Report No. 26). Austin: Research and Development Center for Teacher Education, University of Texas.

Burk, E. (1980). Relationship of temperamental traits to achievement and adjustment in gifted children. Unpublished doctoral dissertation, Fordham University.

Carey, W., Fox, M., and McDevitt, S. (1977). Temperament as a factor in early school adjustment. *Pediatrics,* **60**, 621–624.

Connor, R.E. (1983). The relationship between student temperament and behavioral characteristics and teacher attitudes of attachment, concern, indifference and rejection. Unpublished doctoral dissertation, The University of Georgia.

Feuerstein, P., and Martin, R.P. (1981, March). *The relationship between temperament and school adjustment in four-year-old preschool children.* Paper presented at the annual meeting of the American Educational Research Association, Los Angeles.

Garrison, W., Earls, F., and Kindlon, D. (1984). Temperament characteristics in the third year of life and behavioral adjustment at school entry. *Journal of Clinical Child Psychology,* **13**, 298–303.

Gordon, B.N. (1981). Child temperament and adult behavior: An exploration of goodness-of-fit. *Child Psychiatry and Human Development,* **11**, 167–178.

Gordon, E.M., and Thomas, A. (1967). Children's behavioral style and the teacher's appraisal of their intelligence. *Journal of School Psychology,* **5**, 292–300.

Holbrook, J.W. (1982). Pupil temperament characteristics, the teacher's appraisal of their intelligence and assignment of grades. Unpublished doctoral dissertation, University of Georgia.

Jensen, A.R. (1973). *Educability and group differences.* New York: Harper and Row.

Jensen, A.R. (1979). *Bias in mental testing.* New York: Free Press.

Keogh, B.K. (1982). Children's temperament and teachers' decisions. In R. Porter and G.M. Collins (eds), *Temperamental differences in infants and young children.* London: Pitman.

Keogh, B.K. (in press). The influence of temperament on the educational experiences of at-risk and handicapped children. In J. Burke and M. Rubenstein (eds), *Temperament interaction in the educational process*.

Keogh, B.K., Pullis, M., and Cadwell, J. (1982). A short form of the Teacher Temperament Questionnaire. *Journal of Educational Measurement*, **19**, 323–329.

Koestler, L.S., and Farley, F.H. (1982). Psychophysiological characteristics and school performance of children in open and traditional classrooms. *Journal of Educational Psychology*, **74**, 254–263.

Kohnstamm, G.A. (1986). *Prediction of variance in kindergarten teacher ratings of pupil characteristics*. Paper presented at the second European Conference of Developmental Psychology, Rome.

Lambert, N.M., and Windmiller, M. (1977). An exploratory study of temperament traits in a population of children at risk. *Journal of Special Education*, **11**, 37–47.

Lerner, J.V. (1980). The role of congruence between temperament and school demands in school childrens' academic performance, personal adjustment, and social relations. Unpublished doctoral dissertation, The Pennsylvania State University.

Lerner, J.V., Lerner, R.M., and Zabski, S. (1985). Temperament and elementary school children's actual and rated academic performance: A test of a 'goodness-of-fit' model. *Journal of Child Psychology and Psychiatry*, **26**, 125–136.

Lerner, R.M., Palermo, M., Spiro, A., III, and Nesselroade, J.R. (1982). Assessing the dimensions of temperament individuality across the life-span: the Dimensions of Temperament Survey (DOTS). *Child Development*, **53**, 149–159.

Martin, R.P. (1984). *The Temperament Assessment Battery—Manual*. Athens, GA: Developmental Metrics.

Martin, R.P. (1986). *Context and the difficult child: Illustrations from home and school*. Paper presented at the sixth occasional temperament conference, Pennsylvania State University.

Martin, R.P., Gladdis, L.R., Drew, K.D., and Moseley, M. (1986). *Prediction of elementary school achievement from preschool teacher temperament ratings: Three studies*. Paper presented at the annual meeting of the American Psychological Association, Washington, D.C.

Martin, R.P., and Holbrook, J. (1985). Relationship of temperament characteristics to the academic achievement of first grade children. *Psychoeducational Assessment*, **3**, 131–140.

Martin, R.P., Nagel, R., and Paget, K. (1983). Relationship between temperament and classroom behavior, teacher attitudes, and academic achievement. *Journal of Psychoeducational Assessment*, **1**, 377–386.

Martin, R.P., Hooper, S., and Snow, J. (1986). Behavior rating scale approaches. In H.M. Knoff (ed.), *The assessment of child and adolescent personality*. New York: Guilford Press.

Matthews-Morgan, J. (1984). Relationship of temperament and IQ to school adjustment. Unpublished doctoral dissertation, University of Georgia.

McDevitt, S.C., and Carey, W.B. (1978). The measurement of temperament in 3–7 year-old children. *Journal of Child Psychology and Psychiatry*, **19**, 245–253.

Paget, K., Nagle, R., and Martin, R.P. (1984). Interrelations between temperament characteristics and first-grade teacher–student interactions. *Journal of Abnormal Child Psychology*, **12**, 547–560.

Palermo, M. (1981). Child temperament and contextual demands: A test of the goodness-of-fit model. Unpublished Ph.D. dissertation, The Pennsylvania State University.

Plomin, R. (1986). *Development, genetics, and psychology*. Hillsdale, N.J.: Erlbaum.

Pullis, M. (1979). An investigation of the relationship between children's temperament and school adjustment. Unpublished doctoral dissertation, University of California, Los Angeles.

Pullis, M., and Cadwell, J. (1982). The influence of children's temperament characteristics on teachers' decision strategies. *American Educational Research Journal, 19,* 165–181.

Scarr, S. (1981). *Race, social class, and individual differences in I.Q.* Hillsdale, N.J.: Erlbaum.

Silberman, M. (1969). Behavior expressions of teachers' attitudes toward elementary school students. *Journal of Educational Psychology, 60,* 402–407.

Stott, D.H. (1974). *Manual to the Bristol Social Adjustment Guides.* San Diego, CA: Educational and Industrial Testing.

Terestman, N. (1980). Mood quality and intensity in nursery school children as predictors of behavior disorders. *American Journal of Orthopsychiatry, 50,* 125–138.

Thomas, A., and Chess, S. (1977). *Temperament and development.* New York: Brunner/Mazel.

Psychological Bases for Early Education
Edited by A.D. Pellegrini
© 1988 John Wiley & Sons Ltd.

CHAPTER 8

# Children's Play and its Role in Early Development: A Re-evaluation of the 'Play Ethos'

Peter K. Smith

Play is a well-noticed and well-loved part of the behavioral repertoire of young children. It is well-noticed because it takes up an appreciable part of children's free-time activity. It is well-loved because it is normally enjoyable to take part in (and watch as an adult), normally harmless, and can show the unfettered and creative aspects of a child's interests and personality. Indeed, within the recent 'play ethos' which has characterized Western societies for some decades, play has also been valued and encouraged as a significant educational experience; even as vital for cognitive growth and healthy development. Perhaps as a consequence, play has also been well-researched. At least, certain kinds of play have been well-researched, in certain ways. Yet, in this author's opinion and that of some other play researchers, our knowledge and theories about play are undergoing a re-evaluation at the present time. Without much exaggeration, one could talk about a crisis in play research. This debate undoubtedly has an impact on, and will be affected by, the related debates about the appropriate curricula for early education, and their psychological bases.

Most of this chapter will be devoted to the presentation and examination of this recent debate, which centers on one issue: is play really important for early development? Prior to this, however, it will be useful to consider what we mean by 'play,' and the attempts to classify the types of play observed through the pre-school years.

## WHAT IS 'PLAY'?

As with most 'real-life' concepts, it is not really satisfactory to attempt to give a definition, one definitive statement, of what is or is not 'play.' For too many behaviors, it is uncertain whether they constitute play, or not. We would probably all agree that children running around 'pretending' to be spacemen are playing; but what about a child doing a jigsaw, or painting at an easel? What about listening to a story? We might not all agree on these latter instances.

One alternative approach is to identify 'play criteria.' These are cues, or criteria, which we use in making a judgment as to whether a behavior is playful or not. The more such cues are present, the more likely someone is to decide 'this is play.'

Psychologists have suggested a number of such criteria, either explicitly, or implicitly, in trying to give a single definition. In an exhaustive review, Rubin, Fein, and Vandenberg (1983) claimed that the following 6 features distinguished play:

(1)  It is intrinsically motivated.
(2)  It is characterized by attention to means rather than ends.
(3)  It is distinguished from exploratory behavior. The latter is guided by 'what is the object and what can it do?' while play is guided by 'what can I do with this object?'
(4)  It is characterized by nonliterality or pretense.
(5)  It is free from externally applied rules (in contrast to games).
(6)  The participant is actively engaged (in contrast to day-dreaming or idling).

A similar approach was adopted by Krasnor and Pepler (1980). They hypothesized that four criteria were important in making 'play' judgments:

(1)  Flexibility.
(2)  Positive affect.
(3)  Nonliterality.
(4)  Intrinsic motivation.

The last two of Krasnor and Pepler's criteria are identical to criteria (1) and (4) in Rubin *et al.*'s list. Altogether, these criteria represent the most common and apparently sensible ones culled from the psychological literature. However, it does not mean that they are the criteria actually used by people in making play judgments. They are hypothetical criteria, based on armchair theorizing and speculation and only indirectly on experience.

Some studies have looked at how people (adults or children) actually make play judgments. The most systematic study was by Smith and Vollstedt (1985). They obtained judgments from 70 subjects on behavior episodes of nursery school children, recorded on videotape. They examined five criteria: the four of Krasnor and Pepler (1980) cited above, and the 'means rather than ends' criterion (number (2) from the list of Rubin, Fein, and Vandenberg). An empirical examination was made of whether the presence of these criteria coincided with judgments that 'play' was occurring.

In this study, it was found that nonliterality, positive affect, and flexibility were indeed all used as criteria of play, and in an additive way (the more criteria which were present, the more certainly were play judgments made). The means/ends criterion was also associated with play judgments, but added nothing to the predictive value of the other three criteria. The final criterion examined, intrinsic motivation, was not associated with play judgments to any significant extent. Many episodes—such as walking to another area, fastening paper, or standing and watching other children—were regarded as intrinsically motivated, but not as play. Conversely, playful episodes such as crawling or fleeing from other children were not seen as intrinsically motivated, perhaps because they were responses to external social demands or constraints.

Two other studies, by King (1979) and Chaille (1977) have asked children what they mean by 'play.' Generally, it seems that children distinguish 'play' from 'work,' primarily by such features as whether adults are involved, and whether external constraints are present. Probably, children are developing the concepts of 'play' and 'work' from the way in which parents and teachers use these terms in conversation with them. Adults characteristically oppose 'play' and 'work' in conversation, even though they may argue that 'play is a child's work' in theoretical discussion. Usually, the freedom to engage in play is contrasted with the external sanctions applied to work. This distinction is close to the criterion of intrinsic motivation. Yet how based is it in reality? Some of the 5-year-olds interviewed by Chaille (1977, pp.96, 98) actually defined play as being imposed on them. 'It means if your mom says go play, you go play with your dolls or something' (5-year-old). The older children replied in a more 'adult' way, 'you don't have to do work or anything, you could just go out and play around' (9-year-old), or 'what you do after study' (11-year-old).

It looks as though adults, and older children, say that play is intrinsically motivated, contrasting it with the external motivation necessary for work. Yet intrinsic motivation is not actually used by adults in making play judgments, and young children too do not describe play in this way. Has our ideology of play made too strong a contrast between the freedom of play and the sanctions of work? This would be one explanation. Sutton-Smith and Kelly-Byrne (1984) have developed this, arguing also that criteria such as flexibility, and positive affect, need not apply to play. Their examples regarding the latter, however, relate to older children (where, for instance, a game may become coercive and unenjoyable). For pre-schoolers, the evidence so far is that positive affect and flexibility are useful criteria.

Another approach to the issue of definition is to categorize different types of play. Here, the most influential scheme has been Smilansky's adaptation of Piaget's framework. Piaget (1951) distinguished practice play, symbolic play, and games with rules. Practice play embraced the sensorimotor and exploratory play characteristic of the young infant, symbolic play the pretend, fantasy and socio-dramatic play of the pre-school child, and games with rules the play of school-age children from about 6 years onward. Symbolic play especially was regarded by Piaget as primarily assimilative rather than accommodative, with the child adapting reality to his or her own wishes. Thus, activities with an end-point constrained outside the child's wishes—for example, a jigsaw puzzle or construction toy—would be less playful on Piaget's analysis; the more so, the nearer the accommodative end of the continuum they came at.

Smilansky (1968) changed this scheme in one major respect, by calling those kinds of activity with a more constrained end-point 'constructive play.' This accords with the fact that many adults regard these activities as play, though it departs from Piaget's analysis. Smilansky renamed practice play as 'functional' and symbolic play as 'dramatic,' and thus, retaining 'games with rules,' obtained a four-fold classificatory scheme. Smilansky's scheme has been used by other investigators (e.g. Rubin, Fein, and Vandenberg, 1976; Pellegrini, 1982), and has been found to be a reliable classificatory device, with the definitions simplified to:

> Functional: simple repetitive muscle movements with or without objects.
> Constructive: manipulation of objects to construct or 'create' something.
> Dramatic: the substitution of an imaginary situation to satisfy the child's personal needs and wishes.
> Games with rules: the acceptance of pre-arranged rules and the adjustment to these rules.

In part, Smilansky's scheme can be seen as an alternative to the 'criterion' approach to play definition, and in part the two approaches can be interrelated. For example, it would be possible to examine which criteria are used by people in judging the different play types of Smilansky. The Smith and Vollstedt (1985) study was on 'play' generally, and thus cannot answer this question, although the majority of play episodes in their study appear to have been of the symbolic/dramatic type. A provisional analysis by Rivka Glaubman and Smith on these data has indicated that the play criterion of means/ends does not apply to functional or constructive play, and that the play criterion of nonliterality associates negatively with functional and constructive play (as might be expected from their definitions).

Two main problems have been raised with the Smilansky scheme (Smith, Takhvar, Gore, and Vollstedt, 1986). One is that certain kinds of play are not well accommodated by it. Rough-and-tumble play provides one example. It need not be dramatic and is certainly not constructive, and it need not involve rules. Thus, it often must be functional: yet it does not really fit the definition, and we also know that rough-and-tumble play is the play form that continues furthest into middle childhood and early adolescence (Humphreys and Smith, 1984). Language play is another example that is difficult to accommodate.

A second difficulty arises if Smilansky's scheme is taken not only as descriptive, but (as she recommended) as a hierarchy, from functional to constructive to dramatic to games with rules, in order of increasing maturity. The most contentious issue here is whether dramatic play is more mature than constructive play. Both are characteristic of the pre-school period of 2 to 5 years, and according to Piaget's analysis they represent alternate kinds of activity at a given developmental level, rather than a developmental sequence. The empirical evidence supporting Smilansky's assertion is also equivocal (Smith *et al.*, 1986).

In summary, the breakdown of play into functional, constructive, and dramatic types may be useful, especially when some other specific types of play, such as rough-and-tumble, are treated separately. However, the use of this scheme as a developmental hierarchy remains more contentious. Having discussed what constitutes play, we will now look at the views and the evidence concerning its role in behavioral development.

## CHANGING VIEWS ON THE IMPORTANCE OF PLAY

The prevailing view as to whether play is of significant or vital importance in development seems to have shifted twice in the last hundred years. Up to the turn of the century, and to some extent for the next couple of decades, it is clear that there was a variety of views on this matter, and that what might be termed a 'skeptical' view of play was at least a respectable one, held at least for certain types of play. The 'surplus energy' theory itself suggests a less than vital function of play, and considering play as 'the aimless expenditure of exuberant energy' (Schiller, 1875), or 'superfluous and useless exercise of faculties that have been quiescent' (Spencer, 1878, p. 630) does not ascribe vital developmental functions to it, even though play does have some biological functions in the writings of, for example, Spencer and Hall. Montessori, a pioneer of modern nursery education, valued self-initiated activity on the part of the child, under adult guidance. She valued constructive play materials which helped in sensory discrimination or color and shape matching, but she did not encourage pretend or socio-dramatic play. She saw pretense as an undesirable escape from reality, and preferred to encourage real-life activities, such as preparing food, rather than pretend domestic play. Montessori's philosophy may have had some influence on Piaget, who carried out his early research at a modified Montessori school, and was for many years President of the Swiss Montessori Society. Certainly, Piaget's distinction between assimilation and accommodation, with symbolic (pretend) play being placed at the assimilative pole, makes it difficult to ascribe strong cognitive/learning benefits to this form of play.

Of course, more positive views of the developmental significance of play were present, and especially in the writings of Groos (1901), who advocated the exercise or practice theory of play. Indeed, Groos argued that 'perhaps the very existence of youth is largely for the sake of play.' However, such positive views of play do not seem to have become an orthodoxy until well into the twentieth century.

By the 1960s and 1970s, however, this orthodoxy was definitely present. It had become a commonplace to say that play was essential for development, the child's way of learning. For example, in Britain a Department of the Environment report on play (1973, p. 1) stated that 'the realization that play is essential to development has slowly but surely permeated our educational system and cultural heritage.' The proceedings of an American conference (1979; cited in Martin and Caro, 1985, p.62) state that 'play is vital to the healthy development of all so-called higher animals.' This prevailing view is echoed in textbooks. A typical example from a popular and high-quality text (Hetherington and Parke, 1979, pp. 481–482) states:

> What are the functions that play serves in the development of children? First, play facilitates the cognitive development of children. It permits them to explore their environment, to learn about objects, and to solve problems. Second, play advances the social development of the child. Particularly in fantasy play, through acting out roles, the child learns to understand others and to practice roles she will assume as she grows older. Finally, play permits the child to solve some of her emotional problems, to learn to cope with anxiety and inner conflicts in a nonthreatening situation.

While perhaps more moderate in language than the other quotes, these assertions are made as accepted facts rather than hypotheses, even though little evidence was given to back them up. They are more in the nature of beliefs than well-proven findings.

Most mid-twentieth-century play theorists have advocated strong developmental functions for play. Susan Isaacs, influenced probably both by Groos's writings and by the psychodynamic arguments of the Freudians, argued through the 1930s and 1940s that play was essential to both cognitive and emotional growth in children. 'Play is indeed the child's work, and the means whereby he grows and develops. Active play can be looked upon as a sign of mental health; and its absence, either of some inborn defect, or of mental illness' (Isaacs, 1929, p.9). Isaacs greatly influenced the climate of thinking of early education in Great Britain (counteracting the skeptical view of pretend play coming from Montessori). Later play theorists, such as Jerome and Dorothy Singer, Sara Smilansky, Brian Sutton-Smith in his earlier writings, Jerome Bruner, and Kenneth Rubin, have continued to argue the cognitive and social benefits of play in children's development. In this climate of orthodoxy, even Piaget's views on play tended to be reinterpreted (via the active nature of the child in learning) as emphasizing the importance of early play experience.

Yet, apart from some general evolutionary arguments stemming from Spencer, Groos and others, and some curricular studies by Dorothy Gardner (Susan Isaacs' successor at the Institute of Education, London University), there seems to have been remarkably little empirical evidence to sustain this position, up to the 1970s. An understanding of why this play orthodoxy became prevalent may well be more an exercise in social history and the sociology of science, than of theory modification in response to empirical investigation. Some consideration of the issues has been made by Sutton-Smith and Kelly-Byrne (1984). They discuss, for example, the movement at the turn of the century to provide more sports and play facilities so as to organize young people's leisure and 'keep them off the streets.' This needed a philosophy to back it up. Amongst other factors, the increasing separation of more techno-logical adult work roles from childhood experience would have reduced the opportunity for young children really to help adults, as Montessori envisaged. Pretending at adult life, and also constructive play opportunities, would have been encouraged by the growing toy industry. Obligingly, too, psychologists concentrated on pretend and constructive play in their studies, ignoring the rough-and-tumble forms of play which Spencer and Groos had written about, and for which useful, 'civilized' functions may seem less obvious.

Through the 1970s, however, empirical substantiation for the play ethos began to appear. Both correlational and experimental studies of play suggested that it did have the cognitive and social benefits proposed. The experimental studies were of both short- and medium-term duration, and exploited several paradigms, all based on comparing children who received extra play experience or opportunity with those who did not. These studies will be reviewed shortly.

Over the last few years, these studies have been critically re-evaluated by a number of authors (Brainerd, 1982; Smith and Simon, 1984; Christie and Johnsen, 1985; Martin and Caro, 1985). The main criticisms appear to be threefold:

(1) Selective interpretation of results. This refers to such phenomena as carrying out a large number of analyses in order to find a few that are significant and can be quoted; quoting nonsignificant trends as substan-tive findings; and discounting negative results as being due to inadequate measurement procedures, or other procedural variables which are nonthreatening to the theoretical preconceptions. To some degree these phenomena can be expected in any research programme with a strong theoretical base or which is working out expected results in the tradition of 'normal' science (e.g. Kuhn, 1970). However, it is also open to subsequent workers to point to these phenomena, without any *ad hominem* intent, when an established paradigm comes under attack.

(2) Effects of experimenter bias. Although the possibility of experimenter effects is well-known in psychological research, it is generally true that precautions are taken only when it has been found to be necessary. Perhaps because of this, many early experimental studies of play did not take such precautions. Often, the same experimenter(s) designed the study, administered the different conditions, and tested the subjects. Bias could be possible in administering the conditions (if the experimen-ter was more relaxed or friendly in one condition, for example), in testing the subjects (if the experimenter was more relaxed with certain

subjects, or even unconsciously gave them some help as in the 'clever Hans' effect), or in scoring the results.

(3) The use of inappropriate control groups. The benefits of play opportunity or experience must be compared with something. Too often, this has been a no-treatment control. If superiority over a no-treatment control is shown, this indicates either that the play was beneficial, or that the control children had had less experience of the laboratory context or the experimenters involved, and were thus more inhibited in the testing situation. An alternative-materials control group, which equalizes experimenter exposure but which is not playful (or not in the way hypothesized to be important in the study) is the only satisfactory way to exclude the latter explanation.

These criticisms will be reviewed in the context of a detailed examination of the evidence. It will appear that, when these methodological faults are controlled for, there has often been a failure to replicate significant findings.

## EVIDENCE RELATING PLAY OPPORTUNITIES IN CHILDREN TO DEVELOPMENTAL OUTCOMES

### Correlational studies

A large number of studies have reported correlations between the amount or complexity of types of play shown by individual children, and various measures of developmental (usually cognitive or social) competence. Ostensibly, the evidence from these studies would be weaker than that from experiments; it cannot be ascertained whether the play produced the competence, or vice versa, or whether some third factor (e.g. intelligence, or confidence) was responsible for both. Nevertheless, a consistent pattern of findings would certainly provide some support for the play ethos.

It would be impossible here to review all such studies. Instead, a few recent studies will be reviewed, with the intention of showing that results are varied, and that a consistent pattern of positive correlation between play variables and cognitive development is certainly not obtained.

Johnson, Ershler, and Lawton (1982) examined intellective correlates of spontaneous play in 34 American 4-year-olds. They found that constructive play correlated with intelligence measures, but that dramatic play did not. They conclude that 'the mere quantity of sociodramatic play is unrelated to cognition in middle-class preschool children' (Johnson, Ershler, and Lawton, 1982, p. 121). In a study of 165 English 3- and 4-year-olds at home, Davie, Hutt, Vincent, and Mason (1984) also found no correlation between the time spent in fantasy play or complex fantasy, and IQ scores. In a study of 78 American 2- to 6-year-olds, Cole and LaVoie (1985) found that neither role-taking measures nor the PPVT correlated significantly with ideational or socio-dramatic play. Li (1985) studied 59 Canadian children aged 2 to 5 years. Out of 24 correlations between observed or rated make-believe play and various measures of cognition and affect, only two were significant. Thomas (1984) looked at correlates of reading skill in 56 American 4-year-olds. She found that '4-year-old non-readers enjoyed and valued fantasy play more than readers' (Thomas, 1984, p. 420). Finally, Connolly and Doyle (1984) observed 91 American children aged 3 to 5 years. There was no correlation between the amount or complexity of social fantasy play and IQ, or role-taking skill, though some positive correlations with social competence were obtained.

In summary, there is a mixed pattern of findings, but some consensus among recent studies that fantasy or socio-dramatic play does not correlate with cognitive or role-taking skills. This is not what the play ethos suggests, and it puts the burden on other sources of evidence, perhaps experimental studies, to come up with more positive support.

## Experimental studies

### Associative fluency studies

These studies were pioneered by Dansky and Silverman (1973, 1975) and followed by Li (1978) and Dansky (1980). They were premised on the supposition that free play with objects would foster creative or flexible uses of those objects, as measured by the alternative uses test of associative fluency (e.g. 'how many uses can you think of for a paper clip?'). Subjects were all American pre-schoolers, who were seen individually or in pairs for periods of about 10 minutes. They either had some form of play opportunity, or some form of observation/imitation/training, or experienced an alternative materials control (e.g. crayoning). These studies found that free play enhanced associative fluency for nonstandard uses both of the objects played with, and of other objects. Dansky (1980) produced evidence in support of the assertion that play was only effective in this way when make-believe play was involved, although the results of Li (1978) do not strongly support this.

These studies had good control groups, and in the Dansky and Silverman studies the results are clear and substantial. However, an important weakness is that none of these studies guarded against testing bias; the same experimenter administered the experimental conditions, and the subsequent fluency test. For several reasons, this might be held responsible for the positive findings. First, the associative fluency task has been admitted by Dansky to be subject to 'rather fragile set effects' (Dansky, 1985, p. 282), which might be easily affected by context and experimenter attitude. Second, Pepler and Ross (1981) included the task in a study where tester bias was not possible; the superiority of the play condition was significant only at the $p < 0.06$ level, not significant by conventional criteria. Thirdly, studies by Pellegrini (1984) found that sequenced questioning was a superior facilitator of associative fluency compared with free play, and indeed that free play was not significantly superior to the control condition; Pellegrini's studies also did not protect against testing bias, but, if testing bias were held to be important here, then *ipso facto* the case against the Dansky and Silverman findings is strengthened. Finally, Smith and Whitney (1987) closely followed the Dansky and Silverman design but with full precautions to eliminate any experimenter effects; no significant differences were found between the play, training, or control conditions. This result questions whether the short 10-minute session has any appreciable effect on the fluency task, irrespective of content.

*Lure-retrieval studies*

This paradigm was pioneered by Sylva (1977), acknowledging Kohler's earlier reports on problem-solving in chimpanzees. The aim was to have a more 'real-life' task involving a creative cognitive solution, than the associative fluency test provided. Pre-school children had a short period of either play or training experience with sticks and clamps, and were then given a lure-retrieval task which could only be solved by joining two long sticks with a clamp to rake in the lure. With slight variations, Sylva's study was repeated and elaborated by Smith and Dutton (1979) and Vandenberg (1981). In general, it seemed that children did better at the lure-retrieval task than did children who experienced a training condition, or no-treatment controls.

In fact, on close examination the results of these first studies are less impressive. As Cheyne (1982, p. 83) argued, 'the performances of the two experimental groups were highly similar . . . however, Sylva *et al.* (1976) repeatedly attempted to impute superiority to the play condition.' Really, the superiority of the play condition in Sylva's study is small and what there is, quite probably artifactual (Cheyne, 1982). In Vandenberg's study too, the play experience proved superior only for one of two tasks, for one of three age groups. However, Smith and Dutton did seem to have found a highly significant play superiority in their second task (involving the joining of three sticks together).

But as Cheyne (1982) first pointed out, these studies had not protected against experimenter effects. Attempts to replicate the Smith and Dutton result, taking precautions against experimenter effects, have consistently failed (Simon and Smith, 1983, 1985; Smith, Simon, and Emberton, 1985). Furthermore, a plausible explanation for the Smith and Dutton results, based on the unintentional way the experimenter gave hints, has been suggested (Simon and Smith, 1985).

Another problem with the lure-retrieval studies is that they employed no-treatment control groups. Alternative materials control groups are necessary to show that actual experience with the experimental materials (sticks and joins) has any effect, whether by play or training. The Simon and Smith (1985) study did employ an alternative materials control group, and it performed as well as the play and training groups. Again, the implication is that the short 10-minute periods of experience with sticks and joins are not having any significant impact on the ability to solve the lure-retrieval problem.

## Conservation studies

These studies were initiated by Golomb and her co-workers, and examined the effects of symbolic play training on conservation attainment. It was hypothesized that the transformations occurring in pretend play involve a kind of pseudo-reversibility which might be linked to the concept of reversibility which characterizes the achievement of conservation. Thus, symbolic play sessions were used, which emphasized the transformation of objects from 'real' to 'pretend', and back again. Golomb and Cornelius (1977) found that 4-year-olds who experienced three 15-minute sessions of this play training showed a significant increase in conservation of quantity, compared to children in a 'constructive play' condition (doing puzzles and drawing tasks). Golomb and Bonen (1981) found that both symbolic play training, and additional conservation training of a more traditional kind, were equally effective compared to a no-treatment control. In two further studies, Golomb, Gowing, and Friedman (1982) found that a combination of pretense and conservation training (first study), or a combination of child-initiated and adult-initiated pretense (second study) had most effect compared to no-treatment control.

While some of the treatment effects are not large (e.g. in the first study of Golomb, Gowing, and Friedman, 1982, the pretense play condition did not prove superior to no-treatment control), others are quite appreciable, and seem to demonstrate a surprisingly large effect for such a small investment of training, well before conservation is usually achieved. The methodology of the studies deserves further examination, however. Golomb and Bonen (1981), and the first study of Golomb, Gowing, and Friedman (1982) indicated that pretense play training may help conservation compared to no-treatment control, but is no more effective (in fact slightly less effective) than traditional conservation training. The superiority of both conditions over a no-treatment control group (and of various pretense play conditions over no-treatment control in the second study of Golomb, Gowing, and Friedman, 1982) is less impressive, given that the no-treatment control children were relatively unacquainted with the examiners. Only Golomb and Cornelius (1977) employed a satisfactory alternative-materials control group and established a superiority of the pretense play condition.

The other worrying feature is that in all three reports (all four studies) children experienced the same examiner in the training and testing. Although scoring bias was eliminated, experimenter testing effects are clearly a possibility.

Guthrie and Hudson (1979) controlled for such experimenter effects, and failed to obtain any significant effects in an attempt to replicate the results of Golomb and Cornelius (1977). The two studies did differ in the social-class background of the children, but the later results of Golomb and Bonen (1981) were achieved with children of lower socioeconomic status, so this is unlikely to be the explanation of Guthrie and Hudson's nonreplication. Unfortunately, Guthrie and Hudson (1979) used different experimenters for each of the three training sessions, which, as Golomb, Gowing, and Friedman (1982) point out, could adversely affect rapport with the child. It would be preferable to have one experimenter for all the training sessions, and a different experimenter for testing. If failure to obtain significant results was then obtained, blaming this on lack of rapport would be effectively conceding that any effects of pretense play on conservation are not robust (as has already been conceded by Dansky, 1985, in the case of the associative fluency studies).

## Play-tutoring studies

The many studies on the effects of fantasy or socio-dramatic play tutoring fall into a paradigm pioneered by Smilansky (1968), which can claim to be more ecologically valid than the tightly controlled experimental studies we have just examined. The play-tutoring studies are more in the nature of comparing pre-school educational curricula; the different treatment conditions are sustained for weeks or months, and usually a battery of assessment measures has been used.

Smilansky (1968), working in Israel, was concerned at the low levels of socio-dramatic play shown in kindergarten by children whose families had recently immigrated from Middle Eastern countries. She found that the amount and complexity of such play could be increased by 'play tutoring,' in which adults (e.g. nursery staff) initiate and help to sustain episodes of such play with small groups of children. Smilansky believed that this would have benefits for cognitive, linguistic, and social development. Her work led naturally to a paradigm in which one group, or class, of children received extra play tutoring for some extended period of time, while a control group or class received a nonfantasy experience or were no-treatment controls. It was then possible to see whether the increases in fantasy or socio-dramatic play had beneficial spinoff in other areas of the children's development, as Smilansky predicted.

Through the 1970s a large number of studies were carried out in the USA, generally with pre-school children from poor SES backgrounds, following this design. These studies confirmed that play tutoring did enhance fantasy and socio-dramatic play, and also found, fairly uniformly, positive effects on a wide range of outcome measures, such as: group cooperation, social participation, creativity, conservation, sequential memory, language development, impulse control, and perspective-taking tasks. Ostensibly, this corpus of 12 or more reports provided strong evidence for the 'play ethos.' This first generation of studies has been reviewed by Smith and Syddall (1978), Brainerd (1982), and Christie and Johnsen (1985). It would now appear that there were problems in the nature of control groups and the robustness and interpretation of effects, and that better controlled studies fail to achieve results which the earlier studies would have led us to expect.

The problem of adequate control groups was first raised explicitly by Smith and Syddall (1978). They pointed out that in previous studies, while considerable information was given on how the play tutoring was done, the control group was typically described in a sentence or a short paragraph. Many control groups were little more than 'no-treatment' conditions, with an adult available to provide a warm, facilitative atmosphere. Even when the adult did more, there are insufficient details of what the adult did (in either play-tutored or control conditions) to know whether the amount of adult–child contact or interaction was roughly equivalent in the two conditions. In the absence of such control, any superiority of the play-tutored condition can be ascribed either to the play (the traditional explanation) or to the tutoring contact *per se*, irrespective of play content (a 'tutoring stimulation' or 'verbal stimulation' hypothesis).

The best way to compare these two hypotheses is to match a play-tutoring program against a skills-tutoring program which involves roughly equal tutor contact and verbal stimulation, but which does not involve fantasy. This was done by Smith and Syddall (1978), who found that (with the exception of social participation, and one role-taking test) both conditions were equally effective in promoting competence, notably on cognitive and linguistic measures. They therefore suggested that the verbal stimulation hypothesis would be a parsimonious explanation of previous positive findings. Saltz and Brodie (1982) argued against the verbal stimulation hypothesis. For example, they pointed to the small scale of the Smith and Syddall (1978) study. However, a larger-scale study by Smith, Dalgleish, and Herzmark (1981) found that play tutoring and skills tutoring had very similar impact on measures of cognitive, socio-cognitive and linguistic development (though again, social participation was favored by play tutoring). This provided a substantial replication of Smith and Syddall (1978), and strongly supported the verbal stimulation explanation in the cognitive and linguistic domains.

Saltz and Brodie also argued that 'for vocabulary development, the pattern of results in the Saltz et al. (1977) study is simply not consistent with the contention that high verbal stimulation alone, led to the obtained differences . . .' (Saltz and Brodie, 1982, p. 112). However, some of the earlier studies, including that of Saltz, Dixon, and Johnson (1977) have been criticized for being selective in their presentation of results. As Galda (1984, p. 111) put it:

Saltz *et al.* (1977) attempted to replicate results obtained in an earlier study (Saltz and Johnson, 1974), which indicated that thematic fantasy play improved story recall and story-telling abilities in young children . . . . In an effort to support their contention that it is the fantasy element in thematic fantasy play which contributes to cognitive growth, the authors seemed to ignore their results.

Brainerd (1982) has also noted that the results of the earlier play-tutoring studies are sometimes inconsistent (for example in the details of findings) and small in size of effect. Brainerd summarized two of his own studies which did not produce strong positive outcomes favouring play tutoring. Burns and Brainerd (1979) compared the effects of dramatic play tutoring, and constructive (nonfantasy) play tutoring, on perspective-taking tasks. Compared to no-treatment control, both tutoring groups improved equally. The authors acknowledge that it may have been simply adult-guided group activity (the verbal or tutoring stimulation hypothesis) that produced these effects (indeed, they state that the only data to argue against such an interpretation would be positive correlations between spontaneous dramatic play and perspective taking; we saw earlier that the evidence is not strong here, e.g. Cole and LaVoie, 1985). In a related study, Scheffman (1981, cited in Brainerd, 1982) compared both individual and group dramatic or constructive play tutoring with no-treatment control, on a wider range of role-taking tasks. No significant effects of any of the tutoring conditions, compared to control, were found. This was a nonreplication even of the positive findings of Burns and Brainerd (1979), with the proviso that the children were one year younger (4 instead of 5 years). Brainerd argues that this latter is 'the only plausible explanation of the discrepancy' (1982, p. 126). However, the Burns and Brainerd (1979) experiment, at least, seems to have used the same experimenter for testing and training, so experimenter effects are another possible explanation.

Two recent studies compared dramatic or make-believe play tutoring with a more vaguely specified control condition which provided the opportunity to do construction-type play, or puzzles and mastery tasks. Udwin (1983) found positive effects of play tutoring on associative fluency, and on some measures from the CAT (Children's Apperception Test) and the Draw-a-Man test. Li (1985) also found positive effects on associative fluency, but no effects on productive language, self-concept, empathy, field-dependence, or impulsivity. Neither study controlled adequately for tutor interaction, and neither study apparently controlled for experimenter effects in training and testing.

One other recent study has controlled for tutor interaction, comparing play and skills tutoring as did Smith and Syddall (1978). This report, by Christie (1983), also indicates that different experimenters did the training, and the testing. They examined measures of play quality, verbal intelligence, and creativity. As Christie remarks (1983, pp. 329–330):

there were no significant differences between the play tutoring and skills tutoring groups' scores on any of the dependent variables . . . . Because both groups received a similar amount and quality of adult tuition, this finding suggests that the play tutoring gains were caused primarily by the adult contact factor rather than by play.

This conclusion is similar to that of Smith, Dalgleish, and Herzmark (1981), who also controlled for both amount and quality of tuition, and experimenter effects (for test variables, though not for some observational measures). Thus, so far as many measures of cognitive, socio-cognitive, creative or linguistic ability are concerned, substantial results from dramatic play tutoring seem either suspect, small or nonexistent in comparison to adequate controls. One interpretation, as Brainerd (1982, p. 127) remarked about conceptual development, is that 'the data of play-learning experiments are signalling us that dramatic play is a poor way to do the job.' However, a more positive interpretation can be made if we assume that the usually poorer performance of no-treatment controls in the play-tutoring studies is not artifactual. In that case, as Smith, Dalgleish, and Herzmark (1981) and Christie (1983) comment, the data do suggest the usefulness of adult–child tutorial interactions for certain domains, whether the interactions are in a fantasy play context, or not. The conclusion then would be that dramatic play tutoring is an effective way to certain educational ends, but no more so than many other forms of tutorial experience.

## DISCUSSION

It was earlier argued that the 'play ethos' has seen play as important, if not essential, for development. So far as education is concerned, the interest and evidence has related mainly to the domains of cognitive development, language skills, creativity, and perspective- or role-taking abilities. Also, fantasy, dramatic or symbolic play has been the kind of play (in Smilansky's terminology) which has been most often linked to these competence domains by theory, and investigated empirically. This form of play is the most characteristic and definitive kind of play at the pre-school age, and the kind which observers most readily seem to agree on.

However, the results linking dramatic play opportunities to gains in these competence domains are not so forceful as they appeared to be, between five to ten years ago. When alternative interpretations are excluded by using adequate control groups and taking precautions against experimenter effects, the general picture is one of failure of replication.

If this re-evaluation of results remains a consistent picture, then what does this mean? Three possibilities are that: (a) the wrong procedures have been used to demonstrate the importance of dramatic play; (b) the wrong outcome measures have been assessed; and/or (c) that the theoretical framework behind the 'play ethos' is, in part at least, incorrect.

It could be that play has important benefits but that the wrong procedures have been used so far, to verify this. Certainly, the charge could be levelled that the short-term experimental studies, involving a few sessions of some 10 minutes, fall into this category. From what we know of naturally occurring play, similar bouts are repeated many times over successive days or weeks, and often in a social context with peers or adults. In the short-term experimental studies (whether involving associative fluency, lure retrieval or conservation paradigms) one or both of these aspects is violated. Thus, the so-called 'play' conditions may not approximate to the kinds of play which occur in more natural contexts. In short, these experiments may lack ecological validity. The lack of any effects relative to alternative-materials control groups, found in some of these studies, supports this interpretation.

However, this charge seems less applicable to the larger-scale studies on dramatic play tutoring. Here, the spontaneous play of the play-tutored children has usually been raised, and the nursery or pre-school–center environment is not radically changed by the experimental interventions. It is difficult to see how one could design any other procedures to test the play ethos, which would have superior ecological validity without losing so much control of relevant variables that interpretation would become highly problematical. Even if the play-tutoring studies were dismissed, it should also be noted that the correlational evidence does not strongly support the 'wrong procedures' explanation.

A second possibility is that play opportunities are having effects, but primarily in ways not detected by the assessment or measuring instruments used. Given the range of tests and instruments used in the dramatic play-tutoring studies, this would be tantamount to admitting that the relevant variables may not be cognitive or linguistic ones, at least as conventionally conceived. A case could well be made that the benefits of socio-dramatic play, for example, are more in the social domain. Although this has received somewhat less attention in many studies, positive effects of play tutoring on social participation does seem a more secure finding than many other results. The benefits of rough-and-tumble play, if any, may also well be social ones (Humphreys and Smith, 1984). Also, the possible effects of play on aspects of emotional development, such as self-confidence (suggested by Piaget), or independence of judgment, or resolution of emotional problems (suggested by play therapists) has received very little close evaluation.

Finally, it may be that play does not have the important or essential role in development that many theorists, and the play ethos, have suggested. This would be a radical conclusion, and one that would require careful qualification and evaluation. One important issue would be the type of play referred to, and what it is compared with. The correlational and experimental evidence seems to indicate that, for cognitive development, dramatic play is no more beneficial than constructive play, or perhaps many other kinds of active experience the child may have with other adults, or with the environment. Clearly, however, all of these would be more beneficial than inactivity, or performing some very passive forms of behavior. It would be perverse to argue that nothing was learnt in play, since inevitably play brings the child into experience with objects, and peers, the main sources of developmental experience. However, play is not the only way of getting experience with objects and peers, unless we define play so broadly that the concept becomes meaningless.

Also, the context of play may be very important. Some degree of structuring of play experiences may, for some children, be very beneficial; the issue would be what degree of structuring, what degree of more 'work-like' or accommodative or constraining factors might be optimal, for certain goals. Similarly, an important issue may be how much time spent in play of a certain type is educationally useful. It might be that the educational benefits of a particular form of play (such as piling blocks, or sand-play) are relatively quickly exhausted, but that many children may choose to do much more of this play, perhaps in quite a repetitive format.

Possibilities such as these do not amount to a reversal of the 'play ethos,' but they do amount to a substantial re-evaluation. First, they would suggest that the word 'essential' be removed from hypotheses linking play and cognitive development. Second, they would suggest that we qualify hypothesized links in terms of what kinds of play, in what context, and for what periods of time. A next generation of play research might move to consider some of these questions, in so far as educational goals of play are sought.

The critical emphasis presented here on the educational value of play is in line with the theme of this book, on 'psychological bases of early education.' Yet it would be wrong, and harmful, to conclude on this note. Whatever its educational value, play, and especially fantasy and socio-dramatic play, will remain enjoyable to children, fascinating to adults, fun to watch and to take part in. At the very least, it is a pleasurable and harmless recreational activity. Many adult recreational activities (some more harmful) have more resources devoted to them, than children's play. Thus, whatever the outcome of the re-evaluation of the educational significance of play, this should not be used to justify giving less resources to playgrounds or play facilities. The arguments for play in terms of enjoyment and life-enhancement should be decoupled from the more puritanical emphasis on its cognitive or educational benefits. The consideration of the latter is, however, relevant to issues such as: should we urgently foster socio-dramatic play in children who show little of it? or, should we allow large amounts of free play in order to get some educational benefits in pre-school curricula? It is in these domains that the present ferment in play research should be most actively considered, and future research designed accordingly.

## REFERENCES

Brainerd, C.J. (1982). Effects of group and individualized dramatic play training on cognitive development. In D.J. Pepler and K.H. Rubin (eds), *The play of children: current theory and research* (pp. 114–129). Basel: S. Karger.

Burns, S.M., and Brainerd, C.J. (1979). Effects of constructive and dramatic play on perspective taking in very young children. *Developmental Psychology*, **15**, 512–521.

Chaille, C. (1977). The child's conceptions of play, pretending, and toys: A developmental study of the concepts of symbolic play of 5 to 11-year old children. Unpublished Ph.D. thesis, University of California, Los Angeles.

Cheyne, J.A. (1982). Object play and problem solving: methodological problems and conceptual promise. In D.J. Pepler and K.H. Rubin (eds), *The play of children: current theory and research* (pp. 79–96). Basel: S. Karger.

Christie, J.F. (1983) The effects of play tutoring on young children's cognitive performance. *Journal of Educational Research*, **76**, 326–330.

Christie, J.F., and Johnsen, E.P. (1985). Questioning the results of play training research. *Educational Psychologist*, **20**, 7–11.

Cole, D., and LaVoie, J.C. (1985). Fantasy play and related cognitive development in 2- to 6-year olds. *Developmental Psychology*, **21**, 233–240.

Connolly, J.A., and Doyle, A.-B. (1984). Relation of social fantasy play to social competence in preschoolers. *Developmental Psychology*, **20**, 797–806.

Dansky, J.L. (1980). Make-believe: a mediator of the relationship between play and associative fluency. *Child Development*, **51**, 576–579.

Dansky, J.L. (1985). Questioning 'A paradigm questioned': a commentary on Simon and Smith. *Merrill–Palmer Quarterly*, **31**, 279–284.

Dansky, J.L., and Silverman, I.D. (1973). Effects of play on associative fluency in preschool-aged children. *Developmental Psychology*, **9**, 38–43.

Dansky, J.L., and Silverman, I.D. (1975), Play: a general facilitator of associative fluency. *Developmental Psychology*, **11**, 104.

Davie, C.E., Hutt, S.J., Vincent, E., and Mason, M. (1984). *The young child at home*. Windsor: NFER-Nelson.

Department of the Environment (1973). *Children at play: Design Bulletin 27*. London: HMSO.

Galda, L. (1984). Narrative competence: play, story telling, and story comprehension. In A. Pellegrini and T. Yawkey (eds), *The development of oral and written language in social contexts* (pp. 105–117). Norwood, N.J.: Ablex.

Golomb, C., and Bonen, S. (1981). Playing games of make-believe: the effectiveness of symbolic play training with children who failed to benefit from early conservation training. *Genetic Psychology Monographs*, **104**, 137–159.

Golomb, C., and Cornelius, C.B. (1977). Symbolic play and its cognitive significance. *Developmental Psychology*, **13**, 246–252.

Golomb, C., Gowing, E.D., and Friedman, L. (1982). Play and cognition: studies of pretense play and conservation of quantity. *Journal of Experimental Child Psychology*, **33**, 257–279.

Groos, K. (1901). *The play of man*. London: Heinemann.

Guthrie, K., and Hudson, L.M. (1979). Training conservation through symbolic play: a second look. *Child Development*, **50**, 1269–1271.

Hetherington, E.M., and Parke, R.D. (1979). *Child psychology: A contemporary viewpoint*, 2nd edition. New York: McGraw-Hill.

Humphreys, A.P., and Smith, P.K. (1984). Rough-and-tumble in preschool and playground. In P.K. Smith (ed.), *Play in animals and humans* (pp. 241–266). Oxford: Basil Blackwell.

Isaacs, S. (1929). *The nursery years*. London: Routledge & Kegan Paul.

Johnson, J.E., Ershler, J., and Lawton, J.T. (1982). Intellective correlates of pre-schoolers' spontaneous play. *Journal of Genetic Psychology*, **106**, 115–122.

King, N.R. (1979). Play: The kindergartener's perspective. *The Elementary School Journal*, **80**, 81–87.

Krasnor, L.R., and Pepler, D.J. (1980). The study of children's play: Some suggested future directions. In K. Rubin (ed.), *Children's play* (pp. 85–95). San Francisco: Jossey-Bass.

Kuhn, T. (1970). *The structure of scientific revolutions* (2nd edn). Chicago: University of Chicago Press.

Li, A.K.F. (1978). Effects of play on novel responses in kindergarten children. *Alberta Journal of Educational Research*, **24**, 31–36.

Li, A.K.F. (1985). Correlates and effects of training in make-believe play in preschool children. *Alberta Journal of Educational Research*, **31**, 70–79.

Martin, P., and Caro, T.M. (1985). On the functions of play and its role in behavioral development. *Advances in the Study of Behavior*, **15**, 59–103.

Pellegrini, A.D. (1982). Social participation among preschool children. *Perceptual and Motor Skills*, **55**, 1109–1110.

Pellegrini, A.D. (1984). The effects of exploration and play on young children's associative fluency: a review and extension of training studies. In T.D. Yawkey and A.D. Pellegrini (eds), *Child's play: developmental and applied*. Hillsdale, N.J.: Lawrence Erlbaum.

Pepler, D.J., and Ross, H.S. (1981). The effects of play on convergent and divergent problem solving. *Child Development*, **52**, 1202–1210.

Piaget, J. (1951). *Play, dreams and imitation in childhood*. London: Routledge & Kegan Paul.

Rubin, K.H., Fein, G.G., and Vandenberg, B. (1983). Play. In P.H. Mussen and E.M. Hetherington (eds), *Handbook of child psychology* (4th edn), Vol. 4. Basel: S. Karger.

Rubin, K.H., Maioni, T.L., and Hornung, M. (1976). Free play behaviors in middle- and lower-class preschoolers: Parten and Piaget revisited. *Child Development*, **47**, 414–419.

Saltz, E., and Brodie, J. (1982). Pretend-play training in childhood: a review and critique. In D.J. Pepler and K.H. Rubin (eds), *The play of children: current theory and research* (pp. 97–113). Basel: S. Karger.

Saltz, E., Dixon, D., and Johnson, J. (1977). Training disadvantaged preschoolers on various fantasy activities: Effects on cognitive functioning and impulse control. *Child Development*, **48**, 367–380.

Schiller, F. (1875). *Essays, aesthetical and philosophical*. London: George Bell.

Simon, T., and Smith, P.K. (1983). The study of play and problem solving in preschool children: Have experimenter effects been responsible for previous results? *British Journal of Developmental Psychology*, **1**, 289–297.

Simon, T., and Smith, P.K. (1985). Play and problem solving: A paradigm questioned. *Merrill–Palmer Quarterly*, **31**, 265–277.

Smilansky, S. (1968). *The effects of sociodramatic play on disadvantaged preschool children*. New York: Wiley.

Smith, P.K., Dalgleish, M., and Herzmark, G. (1981). A comparison of the effects of fantasy play tutoring and skills tutoring in nursery classes. *International Journal of Behavioral Development*, **4**, 421–441.

Smith, P.K., and Dutton, S. (1979). Play and training in direct and innovative problem solving. *Child Development*, **50**, 830–836.

Smith, P.K., and Simon, T. (1984). Object play, problem-solving and creativity in children. In P.K. Smith (ed.), *Play in animals and humans* (pp. 199–216). Oxford: Basil Blackwell.

Smith, P.K., Simon, T., and Emberton, R. (1985). Play, problem solving and experimenter effects: a replication of Simon and Smith (1983). *British Journal of Developmental Psychology*, **3**, 105–107.

Smith, P.K., and Syddall, S. (1978). Play and nonplay tutoring in preschool children: is it play or tutoring which matters? *British Journal of Educational Psychology*, **48**, 315–325.

Smith, P.K., Takhvar, M., Gore, N., and Vollstedt, R. (1986). Play in young children: Problems of definition, categorisation and measurement. In P.K. Smith (ed.) *Children's play: research developments and practical applications* (pp. 39–55). London and New York: Gordon & Breach.

Smith, P.K., and Vollstedt, R. (1985). On defining play: An empirical study of the relationship between play, and various play criteria. *Child Development*, **56**, 1042–1050.

Smith, P.K., and Whitney, S. (1987). Play and associative fluency: Experimenter effects may be responsible for previous positive findings. *Developmental Psychology*, **23**, 49–53.

Spencer, H. (1878). *The principles of psychology*, Vol. 2. New York: Spencer, Appleton.

Sutton-Smith, B., and Kelly-Byrne, D. (1984). The idealization of play. In P.K. Smith (ed.), *Play in animals and humans* (pp. 305–321). Oxford: Basil Blackwell.

Sylva, K. (1977). Play and learning. In B. Tizard and D. Harvey (eds), *Biology of play* (pp. 59–73). London: SIMP/Heinemann.

Thomas, B. (1984). Early toy preferences of four-year-old readers and nonreaders. *Child Development*, **55**, 424–430.

Udwin, O. (1983). Imaginative play training as an intervention method with institutionalised preschool children. *British Journal of Educational Psychology*, **53**, 32–39.

Vandenberg, B. (1981). The role of play in the development of insightful tool-using strategies. *Merrill–Palmer Quarterly*, **27**, 97–109.

# Educational and Psychological Processes In Context

In this final section we examine the ways in which children interact in two contexts, school and home. The reasoning behind the choice of these contexts is straightforward. First, this volume is about early educational processes so the choice of the school context was obvious. Second, schools are embedded in a wider community context and in order to understand children in schools we must understand the values of both their communities and the values of the school. The importance of understanding this community–school interface is documented by recent early education intervention programs in America. Those educational programs with parent involvement components tended to be most effective.

The two chapters in this section examine both micro- and macro-aspects of context. On the micro-level, Pellegrini and Perlmutter examine the extent to which aspects of the pre-school classroom (i.e. play contexts and age and gender group composition characteristics) affect socio-cognitive aspects of children's behavior. In keeping with other chapters in this volume this chapter examines both social and cognitive aspects of behavior and illustrates the ways in which they can vary as a function of context. This chapter is important for psychologists in that it illustrates the ways in which specific contextual variables affected behavior. Further, it illustrates the ways in which sex-role appropriate behavior develops in different play contexts. Educators should find the chapter useful in designing classroom play context.

The final chapter, by Ogbu, examines the interface between two macro-contexts and the ways in which they affect children. He discusses the impact both of socio-political and of economic processes on school decision-making. He further suggests that the value placed on education by a particular community is directly related to the social and economic benefits which they have experienced as a result of education. In short, this important chapter tries to explain why certain segments of the population consistently succeed in school while others do not.

In summary, these chapters examine children's behavior in particular contexts. They both convey a similar message: context affects behavior. As psychologists and educators we must be aware of the ways in which certain kinds of children (e.g. from different ethnic groups) interact in certain contexts. If we do not understand these complex relations we will, in all likelihood, not really understand children. Based on such misinformation, our efforts at designing educational environments will surely fail.

Psychological Bases for Early Education
Edited by A.D. Pellegrini
© 1988 John Wiley & Sons Ltd.

CHAPTER 9

# The Role of Verbal Conflicts in Pre-school Children's Socio-cognitive Development

A.D. PELLEGRINI AND JANE C. PERLMUTTER

The role of verbal conflicts among peers in early childhood is a topic of theoretical importance. Verbal conceptual conflict is defined in this paper, following Berlyne (1960) and Johnson and Johnson (1979), as the state resulting from informational incompatability between interlocutors. Such conflict typically results from information being introduced which does not 'match' (Hunt, 1961) with existent information. Though the source of such conflict can be external or internal (Sigel, 1979), we are only concerned with informational conflict which is external, that which is discussed between children.

In the two studies presented here we will examine factors affecting the occurrence of children's verbal conflicts and the adaptive value of their conflicts. The positive role of peer conflict has a basis in Piagetian (1970) theory. The theory posits that children's socio-cognitive development is stimulated by peer conflict to the extent that by engaging in resolvable conflicts participants accommodate to the perspective of their peer(s). More specifically, when children interact with peers, their perspectives of people, events and/or ideas are likely to clash. Such conflict results in the conceptual disequilibration. As a result of this initial conflict, children come to realize that others have a different view of the world. Because most children value the sustenance of peer interaction, they try to resolve these conflicts (Pellegrini, 1985a; Piaget, 1970; Rubin and Pepler, 1980). In the process of attempting to resolve conflicts children re-examine their positions in the conflict vis-à-vis the conflicting information (Eisenberg and Garvey, 1981; Smith, Johnson, and Johnson, 1981). Equilibration is restored when the conflict is resolved. Piagetian-oriented research suggests that such conflict-resolution is adaptive to the extent that children have had to represent and re-examine existent concepts in light of new information (Pellegrini, 1984; Sigel, 1979). Conflict resolution typically results in children accommodating, at least partially, to their peers' perspective. Thus, in order for conflicts to be adaptive they should be taking place in a cooperative context wherein children want to resolve the conflict (Johnson and Johnson, 1979; Pellegrini, 1985a).

While the role of conceptual conflict in early childhood has an extensive theoretical foundation, there is a paucity of empirical studies of the phenomenon. The empirical work on the topic has generally been limited to elementary school children (e.g. Johnson and Johnson, 1979). This work has been typified by experimental interventions wherein competent peers try to induce conceptual conflict in less competent children as a treatment to facilitate logical thinking (e.g. Murray, 1980; Zimmerman and Bloom, 1983). Further, socio-linguistic work (e.g. Brenners and Lein, 1977) has described the interaction processes of elementary-school-aged children's conflicts.

The studies presented in this paper follow the experimental tradition of the elicitation of children's verbal conflicts. In the experiments presented below, however, we attempted to elicit conflicts in a more indirect fashion, by exposing children to different peer and play contexts. The assumption behind this design was that different peer and physical contexts elicit very different behaviors in children (Johnson and Johnson, 1979; Lewin, 1954). Previous experimental work has shown that group composition has a powerful effect on the elicitation of children's conflicts, generally (Hartup, 1983), and conceptual conflict, specifically (Johnson and Johnson, 1979). Further, the socio-cognitive level of children's play and oral language productivity can be reliably manipulated by having them play in different play contexts (Pellegrini, 1983, 1985b, 1986).

## EXPERIMENT 1

Our first experiment was designed such that the social composition of play group and props that children played with were similar to those with which they played in their regular pre-school classrooms (see Pellegrini and Perlmutter, in press). In Experiment 1, we had same-age, same-sex dyads playing, on separate occasions, with blocks and dramatic props. Research suggests that pre-school children tend to play in same-age, same-sex dyads and that boys tend to play with blocks and girls with dramatic props (Hartup, 1983; Pellegrini and Perlmutter, in press). As such, our experimental design, according to Parke (1979), has a moderate degree of ecological validity. Further, previous research suggests that the socio-cognitive aspects of children's play in this experimental context do not differ significantly from their play in a classroom containing similar context (Pellegrini and Perlmutter, in press). This finding meets Bronfenbrenner's (1979) criterion for an ecologically valid experiment.

An experimental, rather than a naturalistic, paradigm allowed us to control possible confounds, such as self-selection into play environments, on factors affecting children's verbal conflicts. Control of children's self-selections into environments is important in light of the potent effect that this variable has on children's behavior. It has been suggested that self-selection into specific activities has a more potent effect on children's peer interaction than children's personality characteristics (Carpenter, 1983).

Our categorization of children's verbal conflicts is based on the work of Eisenberg and Garvey (1981). Further, the adaptive value of specific forms of conflict has been suggested (Eisenberg and Garvey, 1981). The components of the model represent a continuum of directiveness in conflict initiation and resolution. The more indirect measures are more adaptive to the extent that their use indicates that speakers take their listeners into consideration when posing or responding to a conflict.

The model categorizes conflicts into two superordinate categories, initial oppositions and reactions to opposition. Initial oppositions are verbal acts by which children first express their opposition to preceding act(s) or utterance(s). Reactions to oppositions are those verbal acts which follow initial oppositions. The work of Eisenberg and Garvey (1981) and Pellegrini (1985a) suggests that these superordinate categories account for most of the pre-schoolers' verbal conflicts.

Previous research on pre-schoolers' conflicts, however, has not documented the effects of age, group composition or play props. Hypotheses for the effects of these variables on children's verbal conflicts can be generated, however, based on the peer-interaction literature. Regarding the effects of age, socio-linguistic research suggests that children's ability to sustain socially adaptive conversation, such as the ability to initiate and resolve verbal conflicts, increases with age (e.g. Garvey and Hogan, 1973; Mueller, 1972; Pellegrini, 1981). Further, children's perspective-taking should increase with age. As a result, we hypothesize that both the number and the level of verbal conflicts will increase with age.

Regarding sex effects, we predict boys will engage in more conflicts than girls. Research suggests, generally, that boys are more aggressive (Hartup, 1983), and more willing to disagree with and dominate their peers (Carpenter, 1983), than are girls. Girls, on the other hand, tend to be more easily influenced (Eagly and Carli, 1981) and less likely to disagree with peers.

Sex effects, however, should be mediated by the setting in which children are interacting. Indeed, it has been recently claimed that differences in the sex-stereotypicality of children's play are a result of the activities into which boys and girls consistently self-select themselves (Carpenter, 1983; Hartup, 1983). Support for this argument is based on data suggesting the sex differences in activity selection are observed earlier and with more consistency than are gender-related personality differences. Further, boys and girls discourage each other from engaging in nonstereotyped activities. For these reasons, we predict a gender-play context interaction. Boys should engage in more conflict in the female-preferred dramatic context than in the male-preferred block context. Girls, on the other hand, should engage in more conflict in the block than in the dramatic context.

## Methods

### Subjects

The 80 children, 32 boys and 48 girls, who were involved in this experiment were part of a larger ongoing project (Pellegrini, 1985b). The sample was drawn from pre-schools in a small southeastern city. The schools served predominantly middle-class families. Dyads of same-age and same-sex children were constructed from lists of students in age-graded classrooms. The children in the younger age group had an average age of 50.31 months ($SD = 3.21$) and the children in the older age groups had an average age of 62.04 months ($SD = 4.05$).

The children were observed in experimental playrooms, of equal spatial density, in their pre-schools. Children's behavior was recorded with an unobtrusive videocamera. For the dramatic context, the following props were set out on a 2.5 ft × 3 ft table: two doctors' kits, two dolls, two smocks, blankets, and pill bottles. For the constructive context the following props were set out on the same table: wooden and colorful plastic blocks of various sizes, numerous styrofoam shapes, and pipe cleaners.

### Procedure

An experimenter escorted each of the dyads to the experimental playroom for the four separate observations. Children were told to play with the toys and each other as they would in their classrooms. The experimenter left the play area and entered an adjacent observation area to record their behavior with a videocamera. Each dyad was observed for four separate sessions, each lasting approximately 20 minutes: twice in the constructive context and twice in the dramatic context. The order of observations was counterbalanced. In the 12 cases in which dyads were unwilling to play for the full 20 minute period, they were taken back to their rooms before the period was over. Children typically wanted to leave playrooms to go to the restroom.

### Scoring

Transcripts were prepared from the videotapes. Utterances were transcribed verbatim and corresponding contextual cues were noted. From these transcripts children's verbal conflicts were noted, following the procedure of Eisenberg and Garvey (1981) and Pellegrini (1985a). More specifically, conflicts were noted according to the following categories:

### Initial oppositions

(1) Simple negation (e.g. No).
(2) Reason: justification for opposition.
(3) Countering move: substitute for desired object.
(4) Temporize: postpone compliance.
(5) Evade: hedge by addressing the propositional content of the utterance rather than acknowledging its illocutionary force.

### Reactions to opposition

(1) Insistence: supports the same speaker's utterance and adds no new information.
(2) Aggravation: increased directives (e.g. No).
(3) Mitigation: increased indirection (e.g. please).
(4) Reasons: explanation or justification given.
(5) Counter: speaker suggests an alternate proposal.
(6) Conditional directive: a commissive and a directive linked together (e.g. 'I'll be your friend, if you come').
(7) Compromise: some form of sharing involved.
(8) Request for explanation: used to elicit reason or explanation.

In addition, we measured the total number of initial oppositions, total reactions, and the variety of each of these subcategories. Eisenberg and Garvey (1981) suggest that this system represents a hierarchy of directiveness. That is, the subcategories within both initial oppositions and reactions to opposition are graded from most to least directive forms of opposition.

Interrater agreement was established by having the second author identify and code all instances of conflicts. The first author then recorded 10 percent of the transcripts. The rate of agreement was 87 percent.

The unit of analysis was the dyad because of the interdependence of social behavior in dyadic contexts (Applebaum and McCall, 1983; Jacklin and Maccoby, 1978).

### Results/discussion

The intent of Experiment 1 was to determine the effects of age (2:4 and 5 years), sex (2), and play content (4:2 blocks and 2 dramatic) on children's generation of verbal conflicts. This objective was measured initially with a $2 \times 2 \times 4$) MANOVA. A significant main effect for *sex*, $F(19, 14) = 2.37 \, p < 0.05$, was observed. No other main effects or interactions were significant. The MANOVA analysis used, SAS, also generated $2 \times 2 \times 4$ univariate analyses on each of the measures of verbal conflict. We examined only the sex effect in these univariate analyses because it alone had an effect in the MANOVA.

Significant sex effects were observed for simple negatives, $F$ (1,39) = 4.96, $p$ <0.03, and aggravations, $F$(1,39) = 7.53, $p$ <0.009. Boys generated more of these measures than girls (simple negations: $M^B$ = 6.30, $M^G$ = 4.30; Aggravations: $M^B$ = 5.05, $M^G$ = 7.30).

Our sex-related hypothesis was supported. Boys, more than girls, tended to initiate conflicts, in the formed simple negations, and to react to conflict, through aggravations. Both of these strategies used by boys are rather bold-faced forms of verbal conflict. Simple negations state initial opposition in its simplest form, *No*. Neither reasons nor indirect speech acts (Searle, 1975) were used to soften their oppositions. Boys' responses to initial oppositions were equally direct, through the use of aggravations. Aggravations also deny initial oppositions in simple and direct terms, No. The use of both of these forms of verbal conflicts by boys supports the sex-stereotypic view of boys as being more dominant and insistent than girls.

The lack of age, context and interactive effects, however, was not predicted. The lack of an age effect was probably due to the difference of only one year between the two groups. Previous research on children's discourse production suggests that pre-schoolers are fairly sophisticated in their use and comprehension of different speech acts (Pellegrini, 1981; Shatz, 1983). For example, pre-schoolers are adept at comprehending (e.g. Shatz, 1983) and following (e.g. Pellegrini, Brody, and Stoneman, 1987) rules governing their participation in conversations.

The lack of a significant context – sex interaction can be explained in at least two ways. First, the props in each of the contexts may have been responsible for the lack of effects. In the dramatic context boys engaged in sex-sterotypic male behavior by enacting doctor roles. In the block context, girls may have engaged in socio-dramatic play, a female-preferred form of play, rather than engaging in the more male-preferred constructive play. This hypothesis is plausible in light of the extant literature suggesting that girls, more than boys, do use low-structured props, such as blocks, to enact make-believe play (i.e. ideational transformations) themes (McLoyd, 1982). Indeed when the present data set was coded for children's play it was found that girls did engage in socio-dramatic playing in both contexts and that boys enacted doctor roles (Pellegrini, 1985b). As a result, neither of the contexts elicited nonsterotypic behavior that could have, in turn, led to verbal conflicts.

The second explanation for the absence of a context–sex interaction may have been due to the gender composition of the dyads themselves. That is, children in same-sex groups seem to engage in less conflict than children in mixed-sex groups (Johnson and Johnson, 1979). Mixed-sex groupings, like other forms of group heterogeneity, (e.g. SES, personality variables, and reasoning skills) should facilitate conceptual conflict. As noted above, boys and girls interact with peers and toys in very different ways. This is particularly true of the ways in which boys and girls interact in same and mixed-sex groups with sex-sterotypic props.

## EXPERIMENT 2

In Experiment 2 we constructed mixed-sex dyads in order to elicit a context–sex interaction. As in Experiment 1, we hypothesized that boys would initiate more conflicts than girls. Further, boys' reactions to girls' initial conflicts should be more direct, particularly in the male-preferred block context. Boys, however, should not respond as directly in the female-preferred dramatic context. Girls' conflicts, on the other hand, should be less direct, particularly in the male-preferred block context. In short, children in the presence of an opposite-sex peer should respond less directly in the context with which they are less familiar.

The second objective of this experiment was to examine the relation between types of verbal conflict and children's level of perspective-taking. The literature suggests that conceptual conflict and perspective-taking should be highly related. Indeed, Piagetian research suggests a casual relation between conceptual conflict and perspective-taking. In the present study we will identify those aspects of verbal conflict which are the most closely related to perspective-taking. Previous research with pre-schoolers does suggest that the variety of verbal conflict strategies used by children is related to their use of audience-sensitive language (Pellegrini, 1985a). It should follow, then, that the variety of conflicts used by children should also be related to perspective-taking status. Use of a variety of strategies indicates that children have a large behavioral repertoire of strategies from which to draw and, in turn, to apply to different people in different situations.

Further, the less direct conflict strategies should be positively related to perspective-taking. The use of indirect strategies indicates that speakers are sensitive to the socio-contextual demands of speech acts (Ervin-Tripp, 1977). For example, children use less direct forms when interacting with strangers and social superiors than with familiar and social subordinates, respectively. Because the use of indirect strategies indicates that speakers have taken the perspective of their audience into consideration, they should be significantly and positively related to perspective-taking. Conversely, the more direct forms of conflict should be negatively related to perspective-taking.

To summarize, in Experiment 2 we were, first, interested in the effects of age, sex, and play context on children's verbal conflicts. Second, we were interested in the relationship between these measures of verbal conflict and children's perspective-taking status.

### Method

*Subjects*

Eighty-six children (43 boys and 43 girls) were observed in Experiment 2. Within each age-graded classroom, mixed-sex dyads were formed, based on random assignment. There were 21 and 22 same-age, mixed-gender dyads at the 3- and 5-year-old level, respectively. The 3-year-old had a mean age of 41 months and the 4-year-old had a mean age of 56 months.

### Procedure

The procedure for Experiment 2 was identical to that for Experiment 1. Dyads were observed playing in an experimental playroom for four sessions: twice in a constructive context and twice in a dramatic context. Similar props to those used in Experiment 1 were used in this experiment.

### Scoring

Children's verbal conflicts were scored according to measures outlined in the previous experiment. In this study, unlike Experiment 1, the individual, not the dyad, was the unit of analysis. This was done in order to test for sex differences in the mixed-sex dyads. The individual scores, however, were deviation scores (Cronbach, 1976). That is, an individual's score for a particular measure (e.g. Reason) was derived by subtracting it from the mean score on that measure for that dyad. This procedure minimizes scores' interdependence and thus makes them appropriate to use with parametric statistics (Cronbach, 1976). Further, proportion scores, not frequencies, were analyzed because not all dyads played for the full 20 minutes. Interrater agreement was established following procedures outlined in Study 2. The mean agreement was 89 percent.

Children's cognitive (Flavell, Botkin, Fry, Wright, and Jarvis, 1968; Burns and Brainerd, 1979) and affective (Borke, 1973; Light, 1979) perspective-taking status was also assessed. Cognitive perspective-taking tasks assess the extent to which children realize that people have different perspectives of an event, depending on presence or absence of knowledge (Enright and Lapsley, 1980). Affective perspective-taking assesses the extent to which children can infer the feeling states of others (Enright and Lapsley, 1980).

For both perspective-taking tasks individual children were tested in the halls adjacent to their classrooms and given both measures, in counterbalanced order. Responses were entered on to data collection forms. The cognitive perspective-taking task was based on the Burns and Brainerd (1979) adaptation of the Flavell et al. (1968) task. In this task children sat at a table with the experimenter. The following items were haphazardly arranged on the table: a plastic flower, a purse, a necklace, a pair of men's socks, a tie, a Barbie-type doll, and a truck.

The child was asked to choose an item from the array in response to each of the following:

(1)  A birthday gift for mother (purse, necklace, or flower).
(2)  A birthday gift for father (tie or socks).

(3)  A birthday gift for a boy in class (truck).
(4)  A birthday gift for a girl in class (doll).
(5)  A gift for their teacher (purse, jewelry or flower).

Each response was scored 1 for an appropriate response and 0 for an inappropriate response; thus, scores ranged from 0–5. The affective perspective-taking task was based on Light's (1979) adaptation of Borke's (1973) procedure. Each child was given four faces representing the following affective states: happy, sad, angry, and scared. Each child was then read eight stories. At the end of each story the child was told to point to the fact that best described the main character in the story. Children were scored for their responses to all nine stories. The scores ranged from 1–5. The scoring procedure was as follows: 5: got correct response for all nine stories; 4: not more than one scared, sad, and angry and used wrong; 3: more than one scared, sad, and angry used wrong; 2: uses happy wrong, 1: mismatches all faces.

*Design*

To analyze the variation in verbal conflicts, age (2:3- and 4-year-olds) and sex (2) were used as between-subjects variables and play context (4: blocks and 2 dramatic) was the within-subjects variable. Verbal conflicts were analyzed in two stages. First, an age (2) × sex, (2) × play context (4) MANOVA was used to analyze the total number of conflicts. Second, univariate analyses were used on each of the measures of conflict (Hummell and Sligo, 1971). *Post hoc* comparisons on significant and interactive effects utilized Student's Newman–Keuls procedure, at the 0.05 level.

In order to determine the extent to which verbal conflicts were related to children's perspective-taking, measures of verbal conflict were regressed, through a forward step-wise procedure, onto an aggregate score of perspective-taking. The two measures of perspective-taking were aggregated because they were significantly intercorrelated ($r = 0.45$, $p < 0.003$). When intercorrelated measures are aggregated they provide more stable measures of the construct than do individual measures (Rushton, Brainerd, and Pressely, 1983).

**Results/discussion**

The MANOVA to determine the effects of age (2), gender (2), and play contexts (4) on verbal conflicts revealed a significant main effect for sex, $F(24, 43) = 3.20$, $p < 0.004$, and significant between age–sex interactions $F(24, 43) = 3.33$, $p < 0.0001$, and sex–context, $F(24, 43) = 3.33$, $p < 0.0001$.

The subsequent 2 × 2 × 4 ANOVAS on individual measures of verbal conflicts revealed significant main effects for sex on one measure of initial opposition, temporize, where girls ($M = 0.07$) used more than boys ($M =$

$-0.07$), and on two measures of reactions to opposition, aggravate and require explanation of which boys used more of both: aggravation: ($M^B = 0.121$ $M^G = -0.1210$); require explanation ($M^B = 0.134$ $M^G = -0.134$). Age–sex interactions were also detected on those last two measures: 5-year-old boys used more aggravations than 5-year-old girls ($M^B = 0.20$ $M^G = -0.20$), and therefore require explanation, 4-year-old boys used more than 4-year-old girls ($M^B = 0.35$ $M^G = -0.38$). Significant sex–context interactions were observed on one measure of initial opposition (temporized) and four reaction measures (aggravate, reason, require explanation, and agree). For temporize, girls in the second block observation ($M = 0.05$) used significantly more than boys in both the first ($M = 0.00$) and the second ($M = -0.50$) block observations.

Regarding aggravation, boys in both the first block ($M = 0.36$) and the second dramatic ($M = 0.36$) observations used more than girls in the first block observation ($M = -0.36$). For reasons and agree, differences were observed only in the second dramatic observation. Girls used more reasons ($M = 0.75$) and more agreements ($M = 0.25$) than did boys ($M = 0.75$) and $M = -0.25$, respectively). The findings for require explanations were the reverse; in the second dramatic observations boys ($M = 0.30$) used significantly more than girls ($M = -0.30$). The results of these univariate analyses are summarized in Table 9.1.

In order to determine the relationship between children's verbal conflict strategies and their perspective-taking status a forward stepwise multiple regression model was constructed wherein the measures of conflict were the predictors and the aggregate of two measures of perspective-taking was the criterian measure. This analysis is summarized in Table 9.2.

The variables were entered into the equation in unspecified order. The best predictors of children's perspective-taking were: variety of conflicts, compromise, total initial oppositions, and insistence; the model accounted for 42 percent of the variance in our measures of perspective-taking. It should be pointed out that total oppositions and insistence were negative predictors.

These results, first, support our initial hypothesis that mixed-sex dyads would elicit sex–context interactions. Boys, more than girls, used bald-faced conflict strategies (i.e. aggravate) in the male-preferred block context. When boys were in the female-preferred context, however, they tended to act more indirectly and were unsure of themselves in their use of conflict strategies (i.e. require explanation). Girls' conflict strategies, which generally were indirect, tended to be elicited in the female-preferred dramatic context. These gender–context interactions are consistent with previous findings suggesting that sex-sterotypic behavior is elicited by specific activities (Hartup, 1983) and that conceptual conflicts are elicited by heterogeneity. The heterogeneity of the dyads probably raised conceptual conflict in each child when they were in opposite-sex preferred contexts because they saw their opposite-sex peer playing with props in an unfamiliar, at least unstereotypic, way.

Table 9.1 ANOVA summaries for the effects of age, gender and play context on verbal conflicts in mixed gender dyads

| Conflict measure | Gender 1 | | | Age gender 2 | | | Gender context 3 | |
| --- | --- | --- | --- | --- | --- | --- | --- | --- |
| | $MS$ | $F$ | Contrast | $F$ | Contrast | $F$ | | Contrast |
| Temporize | $6.22^a$ | 0.077 | G>B | 0.65 | 175 | 3.87 | | $GD_1>BD_2+BC_1$ |
| Aggravate | $4.99^b$ | 0.156 | B>G | $5.98^a$ | 4:B G | $3.91^a$ | | $BD_2+BB_1>GB_1$ |
| Reason | 0.24 | 1.58 | NS | 0.62 | 175 | $2.73^b$ | | $GD_2>BD_2$ |
| Require explanation | $2.46^b$ | 0.493 | B>G | $6.93^a$ | 3:B G | $2.89^b$ | | $D_2$:B>G |
| Agree | 1.78 | 0.185 | NS | 0.22 | 175 | $3.51^b$ | | $D_2$:B>G |

[a] $p<0.01$   [b] $p<0.05$

1. B = Boy; G = Girl.   2. 3 = 3-year-olds; 4 = 4-year-olds.   D = Dramatic; $B_1$ = Blocks; 1 = 1st observation; 2 = 2nd observation.

Table 9.2  Stepwise multiple regression for verbal conflict predictors of perspective-taking

| Variables entered | Step | F | p | $R^2$ | B-value |
|---|---|---|---|---|---|
| Variety of reactions to conflicts | 1 | 38.27 | 0.0001 | 0.32 | 6.89 |
| Compromise | 2 | 24.06 | 0.0001 | 0.37 | 1.75 |
| Total of initial oppositions | 3 | 17.94 | 0.0001 | 0.40 | −6.31 |
| Insistence | 4 | 14.38 | 0.0001 | 0.42 | −0.127 |

The lack of a sex–context effect for total initial oppositions suggests that children did not initially disagree differentially. They did, however, respond differentially to initial oppositions. The data for boys in both contexts is particularly illustrative. In the male-preferred context boys took control by responding to conflicts in a very direct way (i.e. aggravations). Boys made it clear that they knew how to play in this context and girls should not question their leads. When boys were in the female-preferred dramatic context, however, they changed their response strategies by asking for explanations. In short, boys are the behavioral models and high-status participants in the male-preferred context and girls are the models and high-status participants in the female-preferred context.

These results are consistent with expectation states theory (e.g. Burger, Conner, and Fisek, 1974; Lockhead, Harris and Nemceff, 1983) which posits that sex is viewed as a status characteristic affecting social interaction. The theory predicts that participants will exert influence in an interaction (e.g. serving as models) as a function of their expertise in a task involving mutual interdependence. In such tasks, participants typically defer to those with the expertise. This seems to be what happened to boys and girls in the dramatic and blocks contexts, respectively.

The regression analyses supported our hypothesized relations for verbal conflict and perspective-taking. The results indicated that a variety of reactions to conflicts and compromises were positively related to perspective-taking, while insistence and total initial oppositives were negatively related. Variety of responses to initial conflicts indicates a varied repertoire of interaction strategies. It may be that children with such a repertoire use different strategies according to the situational demands of interaction. In short, they may be using their perspective-taking skills to determine the most appropriate way of responding to an initial conflict.

Compromise was also positively related to perspective-taking status. As was argued above, the use of indirect speech acts, like compromise strategies, indicates that speakers are taking others' points of view into consideration and thus 'soften' their response to an initial conflict. Listeners are typically not offended by indirect speech acts, e.g. *Please open the door.* They may be offended, however, by a more direct form, e.g. *Open the door.*

Compromise is also accommodative, in a Piagetian sense. That is, when compromises are used, by definition, the speaker is recommending a solution in which both parties have input. Speakers take others' points of view into consideration and accommodate them to theirs. Compromise strategies may be the paradigm case for the role of conceptual conflict in socio-cognitive development. For these reasons, it is not surprising that the ability to use indirect speech acts is positively related to perspective-taking.

The negative relations of number of initial oppositions and insistence to perspective-taking are probably a result of their being mirror images of the positive strategies discussed above. Where compromise was an indirect conflict-resolution strategy, insistence was direct. As such, it reflects speakers' insensibility to interlocutors. Further, these negative relations suggest that frequent conflict initiation is not a positive component of the conflict-resolution cycle. As was noted above, in order for conceptual conflicts to be adaptive children must attempt to accommodate to diverse views by resolving the conflict. The frequent occurrence of conflict indicates that this accommodative process is not taking place.

## SUMMARY

In the two experiments reported here we examined the contexts in which children's conflicts appear. It was found that the occurrence of conceptual conflict between peers was mediated by the sex of their playmate and by the toys with which they were playing. When children are in same-sex dyads their play seems to follow sex-role sterotypic patterns, despite the play props. When children play in mixed-sex dyads, however, this changes. When boys play with girls in female-preferred contexts they are less directive and insistent about the way in which to play than when they are in the male-preferred context. These findings are consistent with expectation states theory.

The relation between conceptual conflict and perspective-taking skills was established. The correlational nature of the data limits our discussion of the directionality of this relation, however. It may be that conflict predicts perspective-taking or vice versa. For this reason we recommend experimental studies to test the causality of this relation. Training pre-school children to use less directive and more varied conflict strategies should predict improved perspective-taking.

## REFERENCES

Applebaum, M., and McCall, R. (1983). Design and analysis in developmental psychology. In W. Kessan (ed.), *Handbook of child psychology.* Vol. 1 (pp. 415–476). New York: Wiley.

Berlyne, D. (1960). *Conflict, arousal, and curiosity.* New York: McGraw-Hill.

Borke, H. (1973). The development of empathy in Chinese and American children between three- and six-years-of-age. *Developmental Psychology,* **9,** 102–108.

Brennis, D., and Lein, L. (1977). 'You fruithead': a sociolinguistic approach to children's dispute settlement. In S. Ervin-Trip and C. Mitchell-Kernan (eds), *Child discourse* (pp. 49–66). New York: Academic.

Bronfenbrenner, U. (1979). *The ecology of human development.* Cambridge: Harvard.

Burger, J., Conner, T., and Fisek, M. (1974). *Expectation states theory.* Cambridge: Wintrop.

Burns, S., and Brainerd, D. (1979). Effects of constructive and dramatic play on perspective-taking in very young children. *Developmental Psychology,* **15,** 512–21.

Canton, G. (1983). Conflict, learning, and Piaget. *Developmental Review,* **3,** 39–53.

Carpenter, C. (1983). Activity structure and play: implications for socialization. In M. Liss (ed.), *Sex roles and children's play* (pp. 117–145). New York: Academic.

Cronbach, L. (1976). Research on classrooms and schools: formulation of questions, design, and analysis. *Occasional Papers of the Stanford Evaluation Consortium.*

Dewey, J. (1938). *Experience and education.* New York: Collier.

Eagly, A., and Carli, L. (1981). Sex of researcher and sex-typed communications as determinants of sex differences in influenceability: a meta-analysis of social influence studies. *Psychological Bulletin,* **90,** 1–20.

Eisenberg, A., Garvey, C. (1981). Children's use of verbal strategies in resolving conflicts. *Discourse Processes,* **4,** 149–170.

Eisenberg, N. (1983). Sex-typed toy choices: what do they signify? In M. Liss (ed.) *Social and cognitive skills* (pp. 45–70). New York: Academic.

Enright, R., and Lapsley, D. (1980). Social role-taking: a review of the constructs, measures, and measurement properties. *Review of Educational Research,* **50,** 647–674.

Epstein, S., and O'Brien, E. (1986). The person-situation debate in historical and current perspective. *Psychological Bulletin,* **98,** 513–537.

Ervin-Tripp, S. (1977). Wait for me, Roller skate: In S. Ervin-Tripp and C. Mitchell-Kernam (eds), *Child discourse* (pp. 165–188). New York: Academic.

Fagot, B., and Leinbach, M. (1983). Play styles in early childhood: social consequences for boys and girls. In M. Liss (ed.), *Sex roles and children's play* (pp. 93–116). New York: Academic.

Flavell, J., Botkin, P., Fry, C., Wright, J., and Jarvis, P. (1968). *The development of role-talking and communication skills in children.* New York: Wiley.

Garvey, C., and Hogan, R. (1973). Social speech and social interaction: egocentrism revised. *Child Development,* **74,** 562–568.

Hartup, W. (1983). Peer relations. In E.M. Hetherington (ed.), *Handbook of child psychology,* Vol. IV (pp. 103–196). New York: Wiley.

Hummell, T., and Sligo, J. (1971). Empirical comparison of univariate and multivariate analysis of variance procedures. *Psychological Bulletin,* **76,** 49–57.

Hunt, J. (1961). *Intelligence and experience.* New York: Ronald Press.

Huston, A. (1983). Sex typing. In E. Hetherington (ed.) *Handbook of child psychology: socialization, personality, and social development,* Vol. V (pp. 387–468). New York: Wiley.

Jacklin, C., and Maccoby, E. (1978). Social behavior at thirty-three months in same-sex and mixed-sex dyads. *Child Development,* **49,** 557–569.

Johnson, D., and Johnson, R. (1979). Conflict in the classroom. *Review of Educational Research,* **49,** 51–70.

Lewin, K. (1954). Behavior and development as a function of the total situation. In L. Carmichael (ed.), *Manual of child psychology* (pp. 918–970). New York: Wiley.

Light, P. (1979). *The development of social sensitivity.* Cambridge: Cambridge University Press.

Lockhead, M., Harris, A., and Nemceff, W. (1983). Sex and social influence: does sex function as a status characteristic in mixed-sex groups of children? *Journal of Educational Psychology,* **75,** 877–888.

McLoyd, V. (1983). The effects of the structure of play objects on the pretend play of low-income preschool children. *Child Development,* **54,** 626–634.

Mueller, E. (1972). The maintenance of verbal exchanges between young children. *Child Development,* **43,** 930–938.

Murray, F. (1980). Teaching through social conflict. *Contemporary Educational Psychology,* **7,** 257–271.

Parke, R. (1979). Interactional designs. In R. Cairns (ed.), *The analysis of social interaction* (pp. 15–35). Hillsdale, N.J.: Erlbaum.

Pellegrini, A. (1980). Explorations in preschoolers' construction of cohesive text in two play contexts. *Discourse Processes,* **5,** 101–108.

Pellegrini, A. (1981). One aspect of the development of preschoolers' communicative competence: specific answers to specific answers. *Psychological Reports,* **49,** 581–582.

Pellegrini, A. (1983). The sociolinguistic context of the preschool. *Journal of Applied Developmental Psychology,* **4,** 397–405.

Pellegrini, A. (1984). Identifying causal elements in the thematic fantasy play paradigm. *American Educational Research Journal,* **21,** 691–703.

Pellegrini, A. (1985a). Relations between symbolic play and literate behavior. In. L. Galda and A. Pellegrini (eds), *Play, language and story: the development of children's literate behavior* (pp. 79–97). Norwood, N.J.: Ablex.

Pellegrini, A. (1985b). Social-cognitive aspects of children's play. The effects of age, gender, and play context. *Journal of Applied Development Psychology,* **6,** 129–140.

Pellegrini, A. (1986). Play centers and the production of imaginative language. *Discourse Processes,* **9,** 115–125.

Pellegrini, A., Brody, G., and Stoneman, Z. (1987). Children's conversational competence with their parents. *Discourse Processes,* **10,** 93–106.

Pellegrini, A., and Perlmutter, J. (in press). The effects of classroom ecological variables on the social-cognitive aspects of children's play. In M. Bloch and A. Pellegrini (eds), *The ecological context of children's play.* Norwood, N.J.: Ablex.

Piaget, J. (1970). Piaget's theory. In P. Mussen (ed.), *Carmichael's manual of child psychology,* Vol. 1 (pp. 703–732). New York: Wiley.

Rubin, K., and Pepler, D. (1980). The relationship of child's play to social-cognitive growth and development. In H. Foot and A. Chapman (eds), *Friendship and social relations in children* (pp. 209–234). Chichester: Wiley.

Rushton, J., Brainerd, C., and Pressley, M. (1983). Behavioral development and construct validity: The principle of aggregation. *Psychological Bulletin,* **94,** 18–38.

Searle, J. (1975). Indirect speech acts. In. P. Cole and J. Morgan (eds), *Syntax and semantics,* Vol. 3 (pp. 59–83). New York: Academic.

Serbin, L., Connor, J., Burchardt, C., and Citron, C. (1979). Effects of peer presence on sex-typing of children's play behavior. *Journal of Experimental Child Psychology,* **27,** 303–309.

Shatz, M. (1983). Communication. In J. Flavell and E. Markman (3ds), *Handbook of child psychology: Cognitive development,* Vol. III (pp. 841–890). New York: Wiley.

Sigel, I. (1979). On becoming a thinker: a psycho-educational model. *Educational Psychologist,* **14,** 70–78.

Smith, K., Johnson, D., and Johnson, R. (1981). Can conflicts be constructive?

Controversy versus concurrence seeking in learning groups. *Journal of Educational Psychology,* **73,** 651–663.

Zimmerman, B., and Bloom, D. (1983). Toward an empirical test of the role of conflict in learning. *Developmental Review,* **3,** 18–38.

Psychological Bases for Early Education
Edited by A.D. Pellegrini
© 1988 John Wiley & Sons Ltd.

CHAPTER 10

# Culture, Development and Education

JOHN U. OGBU

## INTRODUCTION

This chapter is about the influence of culture on human development and subsequent intellectual functioning and social behavior in school. Studies of cultural influence on development in school context have been conducted mainly in connection with intervention efforts on behalf of 'disadvantaged children' *and* in reaction to the interventionist assumptions about culture and development. These two orientations determine the data available for our purpose. Basically, there are two contrasting views on linkages between culture, development, and schooling: the universalist perspective and the relativist perspective. We will review the two perspectives in the first part of the chapter; and in the second part we will suggest another way to look at the linkages, especially as they affect the education of certain minorities.

## COMPETING VIEWS ON CULTURE, DEVELOPMENT, AND EDUCATION

### The universalist view and deficit model

The universalists are developmentalists who seem to expect the same outcomes of development for all people, produced by the same processes of development, under normal circumstances. Their assumptions pertinent to the subject of this chapter can be summarized as follows. One, there are more or less direct and causal linkages between early experience, certain types of competencies or skills and later social adjustment and academic performance in school (Hunt, 1969; Ramey and Suarez, 1985; B. White *et al.*, 1979). Two, the outcomes of human development (i.e. cognitive, linguistic, and socio-behavioral competencies) are determined primarily by early childhood experience. In other words, the origins of human competencies lie in intrafamilial relationships, especially in interaction between a child and its parents or between a child and its surrogate parents in the early years of life (Connolly and Bruner, 1974; Kaye, 1982; Ogbu, 1981a; B. White *et al.*, 1979). Three, the skills directly and causally linked to social adjustment and academic success, on the one hand, and on the other hand the early experience which produces them, are found among contemporary white middle class. Four, poor children and ethnic minority children do not adjust well socially or perform well academically in school because they lack the competencies for adjustment and academic success *and* they lack these competencies because of inadequate parenting and early experience (Ramey and Gallagher, 1975; Ramey and Suarez, 1985; Williams, 1970). Poor children and minority children are therefore developmentally retarded because they are lacking 'in intellectual functioning and adaptive behaviors in the course of ontogeney' (Ramey, MacPhee, and Yeates, 1982, p. 345). Five, poor children and ethnic minority children are at birth 'at risk' of becoming retarded, but they can avoid retardation, that is, they can develop appropriate skills for school adjustment and academic performance, if they are given specially designed early childhood education before the age of 5 or if their parents are trained to bring them up as white middle-class parents bring up their own children. Six, methodologically, the development of cognitive, linguistic, and socio-behavioral skills can be adequately studied by observing and analyzing the child's early experience in the family and similar settings, particularly by analyzing its interaction with its mother and/or surrogate mother(s).

*The role of culture*

On the surface the universalists appear to assign a prominent place to culture in human development. They say, for instance, that poor children and ethnic minority children do not develop the type of cognitive, linguistic, and social skills possessed by middle-class children because the former come from culturally deprived backgrounds or because they are culturally disadvantaged. That is, poor children and minority children do not develop appropriate cognitive, linguistic, and social competencies because they do not come from middle-class culture which, apparently, determines the type of early experience that produces the middle-class type of comptencies (Bloom, Davis, and Hess, 1965). But what do the universalists mean when they say that the poor and ethnic minorities are 'culturally deprived'? Do they mean that the children have no culture (which would be nonsense), or do they mean that the children lack white middle-class type of culture? In saying that the children are culturally disadvantaged (Miller, 1967), do the universalists mean that the children possess a 'wrong' culture for proper development? Whatever the universalists mean by these terms, their consensus seems to be that poor children and ethnic minority children need 'cultural enrichment' and early childhood education during the first five years of life to provide them with the early experience of white middle-class children and thus prevent retardation. Alternately, the parents of poor children and ethnic minority children should be trained to provide them with similar early experience.

What do the universalists mean by culture? Here again this is unclear. But upon close inspection they apparently do not mean the same thing that anthropologists mean by culture. The universalists often depict the culture of the poor and ethnic minorities:

> as a list of indicators of poverty, such as lack of education, unemployment, poor housing; aspects of social organization of these groups which differ from those of the middle class, such as high incidence of single-parent families and female-headed households; some behaviors of the poor and ethnic minorities which differ from those of the middle class, such as the fact that the entire family may not eat at the table together, that children are given responsibility in the family at an early age, or that parents supposedly do not read to their children or talk to them the way middle-class parents do. (Ogbu, 1978, p. 46)

In the work cited above we pointed out that 'the mere fact of listing these as traits or characteristics of the culturally deprived (or the culturally disadvantaged, culturally different, etc.) does not indicate an understanding of the culture of the poor and ethnic minorities; [nor] does it provide a sufficient guide to the source of their problem at school; [nor does it indicate] what can be done to help their children achieve white middle-class type of school success' (Ogbu, 1978, p. 46).

Nevertheless, the universalists, especially those involved in intervention studies and remediation, more or less continue to equate family traits of poor children and ethnic minority children with cultures influencing their development. They assume that these cultures or family environments of the poor and ethnic minorities are not as effective as middle-class culture or middle-class family environment, in promoting desirable instrumental competencies for later school adjustment and academic performance. Thus, when they compare the test scores of poor and minority children on cognitive, linguistic, and socio-behavioral tasks with those of middle-class children or when they observe and compare social behaviors among the former with similar observations among the latter, they attribute the differences to differences in early experience due to cultural deprivation or cultural disadvantage. Let us take a closer look at the universalist view of the role of culture in development of cognitive, linguistic, and socio-behavioral competencies.

## Cognitive competencies or intellectual functioning

Because universalists assume that white middle-class cognitive competencies are ideal for social adjustment and academic performance in school and because they assume that middle-class childrearing practices that produce them are the right ones, universalists usually design studies to determine the extent to which the early experience of poor children and minority children approximates that of middle-class children and the extent to which the former manifest middle-class children's type of competencies. In most cases researchers find that poor children and minority children are lagging behind (Bloom, Davis, and Hess, 1965; Deutsch, 1963; Powledge, 1967; Stanley, 1973; S. White *et al.*, 1973). In this kind of research design, inquiry into the role of culture is limited to studying events in the family, daycare centers, and similar micro-settings. The universalists do not usually study the indigenous or ethno-cognitive competencies, that is, the skills that poor children and minority children develop because they are needed by the realities of life in their communities or cultures. Studies of cognitive development by the universalists thus tell us almost nothing about the role of culture, in the broader anthropological sense, in developing cognitive skills.

*Language competencies*

According to the universalists, the standard English language of the middle class is the functional language of the school and the process of developing it lies in the early experience of the middle class. Poor children and minority children who do not have this early experience come to school lacking adequate development of and language functioning in the standard English. Their inadequate language arises from the fact that their parents do not provide them with the same amount and quality of verbal stimulation as white middle-class parents provide for their own children. Consequently, poor children and ethnic minority children are 'retarded' in language development and are verbally deprived: they cannot speak complete sentences, do not know names of objects, cannot form concepts, or convey logical thoughts. Their language is said to be primarily concrete, not abstract; it has little capacity for conceptual learning, and is context-bound (Bereiter, 1965; Bereiter and Engelman, 1966; Deutsch, 1963; Deutsch *et al.*, 1967; Jensen, 1968; Labov, 1972; Whiteman and Deutsch, 1968).

It is difficult, however, to support the thesis of verbal deprivation or inadequate language for minorities like black Americans when one moves away from the limited 'process-product' research design in a circumscribed setting to actual observation or study of language form and functioning in the minority community. Inner-city black Americans cannot be labeled 'verbally deprived' because verbal skills are one of the most highly prized among both adults and children (Abrahams, 1972; Foster, 1974; Kochman, 1972, 1982; Perkins, 1975). The importance of verbal skills among low-income inner-city blacks can be seen in the following description of residents of a neighborhood in Washington, D.C. by one European anthropologist:

> The skill of talking well and easily is widely appreciated among ghetto men;

although it is hardly itself a sign of masculinity, it can be very helpful in realizing one's wishes. 'Rapping', persuasive speech, can be used to manipulate others to one's own advantage. Besides talking well is useful in cutting losses as well as in making gains. However, all prestige accrued from being a good talker does not have to do with the strictly utilitarian aspect. A man with good stories well told and with quick repartee in arguments is certain to be appreciated for his entertainment value, and those men who can talk about the high and mighty, people and places, and the state of the world may stake claims to a reputation of being 'heavy upstairs'. (Hannerz, 1969, pp. 84–85)

Some universalists have modified their views about language development of poor children and minority children partly because of criticism by historical dialectologists and anthropological linguists and partly because intervention programs based on the early experience paradigm have not produced expected results in the development of the standard English. In some recent studies emphasis seems to shift from deficiency in acquisition of *language per se* to deficiency in acquisition of *language use*. For example, Feagans (1981) argues that poor and minority children lack narrative and discourse skills, rather than that they lack adequate language. She points out that teacher–pupil interaction and the instructional materials in the public schools require children to hold and demonstrate discourse and narrative skills. She says that inner-city black children do not appear to possess these skills when they come to school because they grow up in communities where they have no opportunity for sustained adult–child conversations on the same topic. She suggests that the remedy lies in teaching the children the conversational and narrative skills of the middle class. As she puts it (1981, p. 113): 'Much emphasis should be placed in preschool and school-age programs in developing a one-to-one interaction that fosters the sequence of moves needed to understand and express narrative information.' Feagans assumes that there is one correct form of discourse and narrative strategies, that of the middle class and the public schools. On the contrary, discourse rules and narrative skills and strategies vary cross-culturally (Hymes, 1971; Gumperz and Heramsichuk, 1972).

*Social competencies*

Universalists find poor children and minority children lacking in middle-class social competencies or adaptive social behaviors at school and they attribute this to inadequate early experience of the children. Minority children's lag in development of middle-class social competencies can be illustrated with re-search findings concerning children's approaches to resolution of interpersonal conflicts. In a series of studies conducted by Shure and associates the resear-chers claimed that middle-class children behave well in school (i.e. they do not fight or disrupt classes) because their early experience enables them to develop certain thinking skills and abilities for resolving interpersonal conflicts (Shure and Spivack, 1972, 1979, 1980; Shure, Spivack, and Jaeger, 1971; Shure *et al.*, 1972). For example, middle-class children are able to think up alternative solutions to a conflict situation, such as may arise when one child wants a toy belonging to another or when one child breaks something owned by another child. The alternative solutions would include using the teacher as a mediator, negotiating with the other child, fighting over the item and so on. The thinking skills involved include conceptualizing the alternative solutions, recognizing potential outcomes or consequences of each solution, and thinking in terms of cause-and-effect.

The researchers administered a battery of tests to poor black children and to white middle-class children to assess their development of thinking skills in solving interpersonal conflicts. They also observed how the children actually go about resolving interpersonal conflicts. They found that poor black children do not think like white middle-class children about resolving interpersonal conflicts and that they do not go about resolving the conflicts in the same manner. The researchers concluded from these findings that poor black children are deficient in development of competencies for resolving interpersonal conflicts. Their conclusions and recommendations imply that the supposed developmental deficiencies are a major contributor to classroom disruptive behaviors of lower-class black children.

In summary, the universalist view is that of a deficit model of development in poor and minority children. The central idea is that these children do not develop appropriate competencies for social adjustment and academic success because of inadequate early experience or inadequate parenting. The latter is caused by cultural deprivation or cultural disadvantage. The situation can, however, be remedied by replacing the children's indigenous but inappropriate competencies with more appropriate competencies or by preventing the former from developing in the first place through specially designed programs to provide the children with the kind of early experience that will stimulate them to develop the right competencies for school adjustment and academic success.

There are both theoretical and methodological problems with the universalist view of human development and education, especially when the perspective is applied to different populations or cross-culturally. The difficulties arise from the universalists' assumptions summarized earlier. For example, the assumption that white middle-class cognitive and social competencies and how they develop ontogenetically are more or less the natural ideals is based on a lack of understanding of the evolutionary history of the present mode of cognitive functioning of the middle class. Contemporary Western middle-class cognitive competencies, 'intelligence' or 'IQ', as measured by 'IQ tests', evolved from particular events and situations in Western cultural history (Baumrind, 1976; Ogbu, 1978; Vernon, 1969). The competencies and behaviours evolved as an adaptation to particular needs of Western middle-class culture and thus may not be present in other cultures to the same extent or even be very useful to other cultures, which may need or emphasize other cognitive competencies because of different histories and different cultural-ecological tasks or requirements.

White middle-class children acquire middle-class cognitive competencies and behaviors as well as the standard English language because these are adaptive features of their culture or community. Other children who grow up in other cultures or subcultures (e.g. poor children, ethnic minority children) acquire the cognitive competencies and behaviors characteristic of their own communities since they will need these skills to be competent in the cognitive tasks of their culture; they do not simply acquire some abstract, universal ideal cognitive skills. The same is true of the language and socio-behavioral skills that children develop. The language and socio-behavioral skills children develop are those of their community which their early experience usually adequately prepares them to develop.

There are some methodological problems inherent in universal research design. Because the universalists divorce skills or competencies from cultural requirements their research design is too simplistic to capture the influence of culture or real-life situations. By this we mean that their research design forces them to focus primarily on the process of transmission and acquisition of skills in a limited and circumscribed context. This process-product research design can provide a partial explanation of how a set of skills which already exists in a culture (e.g. strategies for solving interpersonal conflicts in middle-class culture) is acquired or transmitted; but it cannot tell us why a particular form of competency is acquired by children from one culture and not by children from another culture.

For decades the universalist perspective and the early experience paradigm provided the basis for professional intervention effort that sought to prevent intellectual, linguistic, and socio-behavioral 'retardation' among poor children and minority children (Ramey and Suarez, 1985). But now, even the universalists themselves are increasingly recognizing that the paradigm and the perspective are indequate because the intervention programs they generated have not been very effective; because it is now known that development continues beyond early childhood; because plasticity has been discovered throughout life and this means that intervention can take place after early childhood (Lerner, 1984; Ogbu, in press, a); and because, as will be seen below, relativists have criticized the universalist perspective on culture and development as white middle-class centric.

## The relativist perspective and difference model

The universalist thesis has been challenged both by ethnic minorities and by scholars from several disciplines. We shall designate the latter as relativists. The minorities' challenge to the universalist thesis was begun in the 1960s when the minorities began to question it as an adequate explanation of their children's development and academic difficulties, as well as an adequate explanation of their own adult unemployment and poverty. The minorities argued instead, that their children's academic problems and their own adult economic problems were caused by the policies and practices of the members of the dominant group. They rejected the suggestion that they were culturally deprived or culturally disadvantaged, asserting that they had their own cultures that were just as viable as the white middle-class culture. And they began to demand equal recognition for their cultures. As for their children's education, the minorities protested that the schools disregarded their cultures and forced their children to learn in the white middle-class culture. This, they said, resulted in two problems for their children: a loss of ethnic identity and academic failure. As a solution the minorities proposed multicultural education, bicultural education, bilingual education and the like (Boykin, 1978; Gibson, 1976a; Ramirez and Castenada, 1974; Wright, 1970).

The challenge of scholars came from several disciplines, including anthropology, historical dialectology, linguistics, and psychology. Anthropologists, for instance, pointed out that the universalists who explained minority children's school failure in terms of the deficit model did not understand the meaning of the concept of culture and had misused it. From an anthropological point of view there are no populations—poor, ethnic minorities, tribal people, peasants, and the like—who are culturally deprived; neither does a list of traits constitute a culture. For anthropologists the role of culture in human development and education was different from that suggested by the universalists. Unlike the latter, anthropoligists do not believe that minority children fail in school because of developmental deficiencies due to cultural deprivation or inadequate parenting; rather, anthropologists claim that minority children fail because they are being educated in a culturally different or alien learning environment which causes discontinuities and conflicts. As Philips (1976) put it; 'Because they come from a different cultural environment, minority children do not acquire the content and style of learning which are presumed by the curriculum and teaching methods of the [public] schools.' To strengthen their case, anthropologists and other critics have conducted studies to establish that the ethnic minorities have different cultures, and languages, which cause the minorities to develop different cognitive, communicative, and socio-behavioral skills, and, further, that the conflicts between the cultures and competencies the children bring to school and those demanded by the school are the principal causes of the school adjustment and learning problems of these minority children.

*Minority cultures*

For some minorities, such as American Indians, there can be no question that they have their own cultures. Anthropologists have been studying and describing the tribal cultures of American Indians for generations. For other minority groups, like black Americans, the relativists have had to do more research to establish the existence of their separate cultures. A good deal of progress has been achieved in this regard since the 1960s. In the case of black Americans, it is now well established that they, too, have a distinct culture, with roots in African cultures and black American experience in the United States (Hannerz, 1969; Keil, 1977; Levine, 1977; Lewis, 1976; Valentine, 1979; Williams, 1981; Young, 1970). Other scholars have gone further to describe the distinct cognitive styles (Shade, 1982), language form and communicative styles (Kochman, 1972, 1982; Labov, 1972; Mitchell-Kernan, 1972), and social interactional styles (Hannerz 1969; Rainwater, 1974; Young, 1970, 1974; Stack, 1974) required and promoted by black culture.

## Cognitive competencies

While many strongly object to the deficit model of cognitive development and intellectual functioning, few have made a serious effort to show that the different ethnic minority cultures require and promote different cognitive competencies. Instead many relativists are content to design research that would enable them to manipulate test contents and situations to obtain minority scores that are comparable to those of the whites. We can, however, begin to understand how cultural differences affect development of cognitive competencies and cognitive functioning if we turn to examine studies among non-Western people outside Western societies.

Ciborowski (1979) notes quite appropriately that to study adequately the cognitive competencies required and promoted in a culture a researcher must acquire a thorough knowledge of that culture, including knowledge of the cognitive competencies that are important to members of the culture in their daily activities. It is not enough to search among the members of a culture for the presence or absence of cognitive skills that the researcher considers important (Ciborowski, 1979). The few cross-cultural psychologists who have succeeded in doing good cross-cultural studies of cognitive competencies are those who have followed Ciboroski's observation, that is, those who gained a good knowledge of the indigenous activities, the people's folk knowledge and conceptual systems of what they do, and then proceeded to study the skills used by the people in their activities ((Ciborowski, 1979). This approach is exemplified by the following cases described by Ciborowski.

A pioneer in this kind of research is Price-Williams (1961, 1962) who studied classification among the Tivs of Nigeria in the late 1950s. In that research he first studied Tivs' knowledge of what they classified and the skills they needed to classify it. He also learned the Tiv language before starting the research on the classification. As Ciborowski summarized Price-Williams' approach: 'Armed with important cultural knowledge as well as Tiv verbal skills Price-Williams was able to demonstrate that even young Tiv children could engage in complex conceptual and classificatory behavioral skills' (Ciborowski, 1979,

p. 112; see also Price-Williams, 1961, 1962). Later, in collaboration with Gordon and Ramirez (1969), Price-Williams used the same approach to study conservation in Jalisco, Mexico. The researchers began by studying what the sons of potters know about estimating quantities of clay from their experience in helping their fathers with pottery-making. They also gained familiarity with the language. When they studied conservation among children of potters and children of nonpotters they found that: 'The experiential knowledge of [potters] children [was] very helpful as they were strikingly more competent in a typical Piagetian conservation task of continuous quantity [i.e. clay] than the children of non-potters' (Ciborowski, 1979, p. 112).

Another example is Lave's study (1976) of tailoring activity, measuring skills, and arithmetic skills among traditional tailors in Liberia. She began by collecting extensive data 'about the everyday working skills' (waist and fly, measurements, etc.) of the tailors. Using her data from the study of tailors' activities and knowledge, Lave constructed some arithmetic tests; she also constructed some other arithmetic tests based on nontailoring activities data. In this way she was able to study 'transfer of knowledge gained in daily activities to a different domain.'

A fourth example is about the influence of culture on mathematical skills. Posner and Saxe (Posner, 1982; Saxe and Posner, 1983) report a study of two contrasting West African cultures whose economic activities required different degrees of numerical skills. Members of the Dioula culture are merchants whose principal economic activities require extensive use of numerals. In this culture mathematical skills are valued and children are provided with many opportunities to acquire and practice the skills. In contrast, the Baoule people, the second culture, are subsistence farmers whose economic activities do not make use of numerical skills. Baoule people do not particularly value mathematical skills and do not stress them for their children as much as the Dioula do. When children from both groups who had not been to Western-type school were tested, Dioula children proved to be superior in mathematical skills. Saxe and Posner (1983, pp. 302–303) summarize the difference between the two groups of children by saying that the unschooled Dioula children 'adopt more economic strategies than their unschooled Baoule, the agricultural group, counterpart. In particular, they use a greater number of memorized addition facts and regrouping by tens ($7 + 5 = 10 + 2$), as compared to the Baoule.'

Scribner's (1975) study among the Kpelle and the Vai of Liberia is our final example of cultural influences on cognitive competencies. She studied the influence of culture on modes of thought as manifested in folk logic. She conducted several small studies on the interrelationship between knowledge and culture as demonstrated by the people's ability to solve logical syllogisms that were culturally relevant. She began the study by first acquiring an extensive knowledge of the people's cultures, their cultural knowledge, their knowledge of their system of logic and the skills required by that system. Then she designed a study showing that the Kpelle and the Vai were capable of arriving at 'logically airtight conclusions, even though in many cases, one (or even two) of the premises of the syllogism was either outright denied or changed' (Ciborowski, 1979; see Scribner, 1975, 1976).

## Language and communicative competencies

The relativists have also studied language and communicative competencies among the poor and ethnic minorities. Their research shows that minorities like black Americans have distinct dialects and that their children acquire their dialects in the normal course of development just as white middle-class children acquire the standard English or their own 'dialect' as they grow up in their community. Thus, the relativists argue that black English dialect and the standard English are structurally equal, 'since any verbal system used by a speech community is a well-ordered system with predictable sound patterns, grammatical structure, and vocabulary' (Williams, 1970).

The relativists established that there is a distinct black English dialect as a complete language system through a combination of historical research (Dillard, 1972; Stewart, 1970) and ethnographic research (Labov, 1972). Historical dialectologists traced the origins of black English dialect to the eighteenth-century West African pidgin English dialect, through the evolution of the latter into the Creole English dialect of the Plantation South and through the process of decreolization following emancipation, leading up to the present-day form of inner-city black English. Ethnographers examined the fusion of southern and northern black English dialect of the inner city.

Inner-city black children learn the black English dialect because it is the language of their community, not because their parents are incapable of teaching them the standard English of the white middle class, and not because they have no father in the home. As Williams (1970) has observed, languages are learned in the social contexts of their environment. In the author's Ibo culture in Nigeria, for instance, children learn to speak Ibo language not because their fathers are in the home or because their mothers read books to them or because adults engage them in sustained conversations, but because Ibo is the language they hear continually from whatever source and it is the language to which individuals in their environment respond. By the time Ibo children are 5-years-old they have developed Ibo language (i.e. have learned the rules of speaking Ibo according to their speech community).

The discovery of black English dialect as a separate language system initially led some to suggest that black children encounter difficulty when learning to read because of structural interference between their dialect and the standard English. Baratz explains this problem as follows:

> When the middle-class child starts the process of learning to read, his problem is primarily one of decoding the graphic representations of a language he already

speaks. The disadvantaged black child must also 'translate' them into his own language. This presents him with an almost insurmountable obstacle since the written words frequently do not go together in any pattern that is familiar or meaningful to him. (Baratz, 1970, p. 20)

The intervention programs based on the hypothesis of structural interference and, later, on grammatical interference and the like, did not work. As a result, anthropologists and linguists began to examine other aspects of the language issue, eventually moving from language differences *per se* to differences in language use, that is, to the socio-linguistic basis of communication.

Socio-linguistic research revealed that ethnic minorities are not lacking in communicative competencies but that the language use among them is different. And the researchers argued that communicative competence can only be judged in the context of a speech community. Hymes (1971) defines a speech community as a population which shares both *a common language* (e.g. black English dialect, the standard English, etc.) and *a common theory of speaking* or theory of communicative competence. A speech community is distinguished by the following features: (a) speech situations, that is, situations which are considered appropriate for certain types of speeches, such as speeches in connection with parties, election campaigns, love-making, etc. (b) Speech events, which are culturally defined, such as a conversation, a lecture, a confession or a prayer. Hymes states that speech events are 'governed by rules which are learned and known to members of a speech community. Although the same speech event can occur in different situations or contexts, the occurrence is still governed by culturally determined rules' (e.g. the speech event such as a private conversation can take place at a party, a memorial service, a campaign rally, a grocery shop, etc. But in each case it is governed by cultural rules). (c) Other communicative codes besides verbal ones, that is, other means by which members of a speech community can communicate with one another. They include gestures, facial expressions, postures, paralinguistic sounds like intonation, voice loudness, meaningful (but nonlinguistic) sighs, grunts, laughter, cries, and so forth; the distance we maintain from others and the tactics we use to bridge or sustain the distance; clothing, accoutrements we carry with us; and deodorants and scents with which we modify our body odors. (d) Channels of communication. These include verbal channel, kinestic and body movements, such as smiling, etc., and proxemics or culturally patterned use of space.

Socio-linguists have also proposed a theory of speech acts which distinguishes between literary meaning of what is said and the effect it has on the hearer. For example, when a teacher says to students, *We don't sit on the tables,* the literary meaning refers to the fact that people do not sit on the tables; however, it can also be a request or a command not to sit on tables. Whether the students interpret the statements correctly on incorrectly depends partly upon shared background information and partly on their ability to make inferences (Simons, 1979).

Gumperz (1981) refined the theory of speech act by adding the notion of situated meaning or the intent of a speaker in a particular context. Context includes 'the speaker's perceptions of a social situation and social relations, the type of speech activity, and the relation of the utterance surrounding it and the discourse as a whole' (Simons, 1979; see also Gumperz and Heramsichuk, 1972). In order to understand the situated meaning of an utterance, the hearer must know both the literary meaning and the appropriate metacommunication cues or contextualization cues that suggest the meaning of the utterance in a particular social situation. Among the commonly identified contextualization cues are intonation, code switching, stress, choice of lexical items and syntactic structure, rhythms, voice loudness and softness, and utterance sequencing strategies. Both communication strategies and contextualization cues are culturally determined. That is, people from different cultural backgrounds or different speech communities (e.g. inner-city blacks and suburban middle-class whites) will not share the same communication background and will, therefore, differ in their communicative strategies and interpretation of the situated meaning of a given passage or utterance.

Communicative competence in a speech community therefore is the ability of a person to know when it is appropriate to speak and when to remain silent, which communicative code (e.g. gestures, facial expression, paralinguistic sounds, etc.) to use, where, when, and to whom, as well as the ability to interpret correctly situated meanings of utterances. Communicative competence requires not only that an individual be able to convey information in one or more available channels, but also that he or she be able to match channel, form, context, and style to specific context and situation—to use communication skills and strategies appropriately and to interpret situated meanings correctly (Hymes, 1971; Gumperz and Heramsichuk, 1972).

In order to become a competent member of a speech community an individual must be socialized into the community's pattern of speaking. That is, he or she must acquire both the language and the native, community's folk theory of speaking, including its communicative strategies and contextualization cues. 'From a socio-linguistic point of view,' according to Hymes (1971), 'it is not enough for a child or any other individual to acquire a good knowledge of the grammar and vocabulary of a language, if he or she does not know which speech to use, when to talk, . . . when not to talk [and situated meanings]. Therefore in the course of its socialization *a child acquires both the language* used in its speech community *and the habits and sets of attitudes and rules associated with the value and utilization of [the] language. .*' (Emphasis added.) Every normal child growing up in a speech community successfully learns the language of its community and the folk theory of speaking of that community. This is as true for the inner-city black child as it is for the suburban white middle-class child.

From a socio-linguistic point of view, the problems encountered by ethnic minority children in learning to read in school do not come from the fact that the children have not developed the discourse and narrative skills of standard English. Rather, the problems are due to miscommunication between teachers and students who may come from different speech communities and therefore do not share the same discourse rules and narrative skills and rules. An example of how differences in communicative background cause problems for minority children learning to read in school is found in the history of the Kamehameha Early Education Program (KEEP) for native Hawaiian children, described later.

*Social competencies*

Relativists see the behavior problems of minority children in school as caused by conflicts between the adaptive behaviors children learned in their communities and the behaviors expected at school. They support this interpretation with several case studies done by ethnographers who examined the behaviors expected of the children both at school and in the community and who found instances where teachers and minority students held different beliefs about appropriate social interaction styles and language use. These differences resulted in mismatch in interaction and communication which contributed to the children's difficulties in learning to read. We will illustrate the mismatch problem with two case studies.

One is Philips's (1972, 1983) study of Indian students in Warm Spring Reservation in Oregon. She found that Indian students in elementary school classrooms held a different view from their white teachers about how students should interact with teachers and among themselves, as well as about how students should participate in classroom activities. Although the teachers' views generally prevailed, they were not particularly effective in aiding classroom management.

Philips also studied the behaviors of children and adults in the Indian community, that is on the Reservation. When she compared her observations in the community with her classroom observations she concluded that the classroom required one kind of adaptive behavior while the Indian community required and encouraged another. She proposed participant structure as a conceptual framework to describe the differences in the adaptive behaviors of the two settings. Participant structure is, according to Gumperz (1981, p. 5), 'a constellation of norms, mutual rights and obligations that shape social relations, determine participant's perceptions about what goes on and influence learning.' The classroom participant structure required one kind of adaptive or social behavior while the Indian community had another participant structure requiring a different kind of adaptive/social behavior. The participant structure of the classroom required teachers, for instance, to interact with students as a whole group, in small groups or on a one-to-one basis, to control the topic of discussion, to control the floor or setting of activities like reading and to control turn-taking. It also required mandatory participation and individual responses for students, the individual responses being used by the teacher to assess individual knowledge.

The participant structure of the Indian community, in contrast, demanded nothing like those; it did not designate any one person to direct activities verbally. Activities were carried out by the group and the group action served as a guide for individuals to choose how far they wished to participate. Indian children growing up under this participant structure became 'accustomed to self-determination of action accompanied by very little disciplinary control from older relatives at much younger age than middle-class white students do' (Philips, 1972, p. 385). Thus, one of the views the Indian children brought to school about social interaction or social behavior was that one's activities should not be controlled or directed by adults or by peers.

Having been socialized into this kind of thinking and behaving, Indian students arrived at school to confront a different type of thinking and behaving. More specifically, the classroom participant structure required them to assume leadership roles which the Indians were reluctant to do. The teacher called upon them individually to answer questions which the Indians regarded as wrong because it placed the individual student in a position contrary to the norms of their community's participant structure. On the whole the Indian students were more reluctant than the non-Indians to adopt teachers' ideas and rules of appropriate social interaction and language use; and they assumed a kind of 'non-learning' orientation (DeVos, 1984): they often did not remember to raise their hands, they wandered to other parts of the room, and talked to their friends while the teachers were talking.

The other example comes from the Kamehameha Early Education Program (KEEP) mentioned earlier. When the program began in the early 1970s several suggestions were made and discounted as to why the children were not doing well in school, especially why they were not successful in learning to read. Among the suggestions were lack of motivation and cognitive/linguistic deficiencies. Finally, it was thought that the problem might perhaps be due to 'differences in the ways the children learned at home or among their peers and the ways in which they were expected to learn in school' (Au and Jordan, 1981, p. 143). Anthropologists then studied the participant structure of the children's community and discovered that it was different from the participant structure of the classroom. This led to a reorganization of the classroom social and communicative interaction to reflect those of the children's homes and community. Reading lessons, for instance, were reorganized to resemble a 'talk story,' which is a major speech event in Hawaiian culture. A talk story is a local term for 'a rambling personal experience narrative mixed with folk materials' involving adults and children (Au, 1981). This change resulted in improvements in the children's reading.

Philips's study and the research associated with the KEEP program clearly show that differences in cultural beliefs about social interaction and the actual adaptive behaviors affect children's classroom behaviors. Teachers' views of appropriate classroom behaviors reflect dominant-group's participant structure. Minority children's beliefs reflect a different participant structure, the participant structure of their own community. The classroom behavior problems of ethnic minorities may, therefore, be due to conflicts between the teachers' beliefs and behavior expectations on the one hand and on the other the students' beliefs and behavior expectations, rather than due to the fact that the children have not developed adequate social competencies as a result of faulty socialization by their parents.

Whereas the universalists say that poor children and ethnic minority children do not adapt socially and do not perform well academically in school because of deficiencies in early experience resulting in retardation in the development of appropriate competencies or skills, relativists argue that the social adaptation and academic performance problems are caused by discontinuities and conflicts between the competencies required and promoted by the children's culture and those expected at school. A number of studies now support the relativists' position by showing that different cultures do, indeed, require and promote different cognitive, linguistic/communicative and socio-behavioral skills.

However, like the universalists, the relativists have not explained the variability we find in the school adaptation and academic performance of minority-group children. That is, they have not explained why some ethnic minority children who come to school with distinct ethnic competencies (e.g. Punjabi Indians in California, West Indians in the USA, Central American refugees and immigrants on the West Coast of the USA, etc.) adapt well socially and perform well academically in the public schools (Gibson, 1976a, 1983; Fordham, 1984; Suarez-Orozco, 1986), and why other minority-groups children such as blacks and Indians do not adapt socially well or perform academically well (Ogbu, 1986, in press b; Philips, 1972, 1983). It is this aspect of the relationship between culture, development, and education that we will explore in the next section.

## CULTURE, IDENTITY AND EDUCATION:
## A CULTURAL-ECOLOGICAL PERSPECTIVE

There is another way to look at the influence of culture on human development and subsequent intellectual functioning and social behavior in school that more or less supports the relativists' viewpoint but goes further to explain the variability in adaptation and academic performance. This is the cultural-ecological approach (Ogbu, 1981a) which looks at development and education in the context of historical, structural, and cultural forces.

From the point of view of the cultural-ecological approach, culture is broader than one finds in either the universalist or the relativist approach. Culture is more than what is in a person's immediate environment or in the family. Culture is a way of life, a total way of life shared by members of a population and it includes institutionalized public behaviors or customs, the private modes of thoughts and emotions that accompany and support the public behaviors (LeVine, 1974), as well as the things people make or have made that have symbolic meanings for them. Particularly important for the subject of this chapter is that culture includes economic, political, religious, and social institutions—the 'imperatives of culture' (Cohen, 1971)—which form a recognizable pattern influencing behaviors in a fairly predictable manner. When we say that different populations have different cultures we mean that their culture patterns make their predictable behaviors different. That is, they have different institutional arrangements which have evolved over time and which now influence the shared modes of thought and emotions that support and accompany their public behaviors.

## Culture, development, and competencies

Culture influences development by determining the functional skills or competencies used by members of a population to perform their cultural tasks competently as defined by their society. By possessing appropriate competencies a person is then able to perform his or her cultural task (e.g. pottery-making, farming, tailoring, etc.) and by performing the cultural tasks he or she improves his or her skills.

Different cultures present different tasks or problems for people to solve. The cultural tasks vary because even though people face certain common problems in life, such as how to make a living, how to reproduce, how to maintain order within their border and defend it against outsiders, the solutions they have worked out to these problems differ. The differences in solutions arise from the fact that different people live in different physical and social environments which vary in resources; furthermore, historical events which influence people's perceptions of and their relationships with their environments and with one another are different. Therefore there are cultural differences in how to make a living (economy and technology), how to govern themselves (politics), how to organize domestic life for reproduction (family and childrearing) and how to manage relationship with the supernatural (religion). Each of these domains of cultural task both requires and promotes a repertoire of skills. Because the cultural tasks in a given domain (e.g. subsistence task, tasks connected with domestic organization) differ cross-culturally, the repertoire of skills they require and promote also differ cross-culturally.

There are two ways in which culture influences how people develop the skills required to perform their cultural tasks and skills prevalent in their society. One is that by performing the cultural tasks people enhance their skills for those tasks.

The other is that people value skills that make them successful in their cultural tasks and that they tend deliberately to teach their children those skills. Then as the children themselves get older they may actively seek to acquire the skills. For example, potters will teach their children pottery-making and the skills needed for pottery-making; and potters' children will seek to learn how to make pottery as they get old enough to do so. Likewise subsistence farmers will teach their children subsistence farming (Ruddell and Chesterfield, 1977); they do not teach them about urban industrial wage labor and the skills for such wage labor. And children of subsistence farmers will, undoubtedly, seek to learn how to be successful subsistence farmers as they get older.

### Formulae for developing functional competencies or cultural outcomes

Whatever may be the desired cultural outcomes for competencies or skills— cognitive, linguistic, and social—members of a culture usually have *culturally approved formulae* for developing these skills in children through early experience and beyond. The formulae consist of teaching children directly and indirectly, consciously and unconsciously, the instrumental skills already existing in the populations, which parents and other socialization agents know that the children will need as adults to perform their cultural tasks. Parents do not invent the knowledge, beliefs, skills, and behaviors they teach their children. These already pre-exist. Except in a period of social change, the skills parents and other agents of socialization teach children are more or less pre-ordained. This is not a matter of what we would like to think ought to be; it is what happens in every society, including the United States. Thus the skills that contemporary middle-class Americans teach their children, such as self-direction, initiative, independence, competitiveness, and certain cognitive and communicative skills (Connolly and Bruner, 1974; Kohn, 1969; Leacock, 1969; Ogbu, in press a; Vernon, 1969) are not the inventions of individual middle-class parents; rather, they are skills that are adaptive to the high-level, high-paying middle-class occupations and other social positions (see also Seeley, Sim, and Loosley, 1956). Parents in a hunting and gathering society and parents in a peasant community will value and teach other types of competencies to their children which are more adaptive to their particular cultural tasks.

The formulae 'work' because parents and other socialization agents in a population or society use culturally standardized techniques of childrearing that time and experience have shown to be effective. Thus, to some degree, contemporary white middle-class Americans share some standardized knowledge, skills, and practices about raising children which time and experience have shown to be effective in producing the instrumental cognitive and other skills adaptive to middle-class occupations and other cultural tasks. Some middle-class parents rely on 'experts' for advice (e.g. Dr Spock and contemporary child developmental psychologists). These 'experts' are cultural functionaries in a constantly changing culture whose culturally sanctioned task is to study changes in middle-class cultural tasks, especially tasks in the techno-economic sector, to devise and disseminate appropriate changes in childrearing techniques or formulae to enable children to 'develop' new competencies required by the changing cultural tasks (Ogbu, 1981). Thus, not only do competencies or skills vary from culture to culture, but they can also vary from one historical period to the next within the same culture.

## Psychobiological/maturational outcomes vs. cultural outcomes of development

It is obvious then, that the skills that characterize members of a given population or culture are cultural outcomes of development. It is important to distinguish these cultural outcomes from psychobiological or maturational outcomes of development, a distinction which the universalists apparently fail to make. An example of maturational outcome is Piaget's idea of stages of cognitive development. The psychobiological or maturational outcome here is the individual's attainment of the final stage postulated by Piaget, namely, the stage of formal operational thinking. In order to reach this final stage the individual's physical systems—the brain and central nervous systems—must be fully developed or matured for the kind of thought and language characteristic of the formal operational stage (Ginsburg and Opper, 1981).

Although there is no evidence of any human population that has failed to reach this physical system maturity for operational thinking, there are reports in cross-cultural studies of cultural differences in formal operational thinking (Dasen, 1977). The reason seems to be that in some populations cultural tasks require formal operational thinking to a larger extent, so that formal operational thinking is valued and promoted as a developmental cultural outcome. In some other populations or cultures, where the cultural tasks do not call for much formal operational thinking, the development of formal operational thinking is apparently not valued as much or promoted as a cultural outcome in development. The distinction between psychobiological or maturational outcomes from cultural outcomes is also important in language and social development.

## Culture change, development, and education

On the other hand, even though people growing up in different cultures tend to develop different skills, when their cultures change or when they emigrate to other cultures they experience changes in their skills or competencies. Such changes are evident among immigrants, refugees and colonial subjects. In a generation or two some of these people often acquire new cognitive, linguistic, and socio-behavioral competencies that more or less differentiate them from their parents and other members of their original cultures. Such changes in skills or competencies seem also to occur among Western middle-class people. Both Baumrind (1976) and Vernon (1982) suggest that the development of bureaucratic urban industrial economy in the West, for example, gave rise to the modern Western pattern of thinking skills. Industrialization, urbanization, bureaucratization and increased formal education produced new cultural tasks which required and promoted new skills for absorbing complex information, manipulating abstract concepts, and grasping relations. These skills were probably initially used to solve specific problems at school and in the work-place, but they eventually came to permeate almost every daily activity of the middle class.

Today further changes in the cognitive skills of the middle class seem to be occurring because of computer technology with its emphasis on 'precise definition, linear thinking, precise rules and algorithms for thinking and acting' (Committee of Correspondence on the Future of Public Education, 1984). In the United States middle-class people are acquiring the new cognitive skills by 'learning computer' at home, school, and work; they are modifying their childrearing practices and their children's education to enable their children to acquire the new cognitive skills. American schools, too, are deliberately promoting the new skills by rewriting their curricula and teaching methods under public pressures to emphasize the new skills compatible with computer thinking and compatible with other emerging cultural tasks relying on compu-ter and new technological know-hows.

We also find evidence of changes in competencies as a result of culture change among Third World peoples. As people in the Third World come under the influence of Western technology, participate in the new cash economy, bureaucratic organization, urbanization and Western-type schooling, they appear to be undergoing a kind of 'cognitive acculturation.' They are in-creasingly developing cognitive skills similar to those of Western middle-class people, including skills for absorbing complex information, for manipulating abstract concepts and for grasping relations. They are also acquiring new language and communicative competencies (see Cole Gay, Glick, and Sharp, 1971; Cole and Scribner, 1974; Greenfield, 1966; Lancy, 1983; Scribner and Cole, 1973; Seagrim and Lendon, 1980; Sharp, Cole, and Lave, 1978; Stevenson, 1982).

### Minority status, culture change and development

If skills or competencies as cultural products are not fixed the major question becomes: Why do some people adopt new competencies and others do not? For example, why do some ethnic minorities like Punjabi immigrants in Yuba City, California, Chinese, Japanese, West Indian and other immigrant minor-ities to the United States adopt new cognitive, linguistic and socio-behavioral competencies that apparently enhance their chances for school success? Why do other minorities like Warm Spring Indians and inner-city black Americans not adopt school-required competencies, at least to the same degree, to enhance their chances for school success? In other words, why are some minority-group children academically successful even though they may have all the characteristics that early experience hypothesis would label 'disadvantage' and which researchers tend to correlate with school failure, *and* even though these successful minorities do not raise their children as white middle-class parents raise their own children? Why are these minorities academically successful even though they come to school with ethnic competencies and behavior expectations which, according to relativists, would cause conflicts and academic failure? (see Gibson, 1983; Ogbu, 1984; Ogbu and Matute-Bianchi, 1986).

These are some of the questions that neither the universalists nor the relativists addressed, that is, questions regarding the variability in minority school adjustment and academic performance. It is, however, important to explain the variability phenomenon because of the light it may shed on the role of culture in the development and education of ethnic minority children.

Comparative study suggests that to answer the above questions, to explain the variability in minority school performance we have to recognize that there are different kinds of minorities who have different types of relationship with the dominant group and that the types of relationship affect the barriers to minority school learning differently. One kind of minority is that of *autonomous minorities* who are minorities primarily in a numerical sense. Although they are not totally free from prejudice and discrimination, autonomous minorities are not politically, socially or economically subordinated. Autonomous minorities like Jews and Mormons in the contemporary United States have cultural frames of reference that encourage school success.

*Immigrant minorities* constitute the second type. The immigrants (Punjabis in California, Chinese Americans, Japanese Americans, West Indians in the US etc.) are people who have moved to the United States or to some other societies *voluntarily* because they believe that this would lead to greater economic, political or social well-being or opportunities for advancement. These expectations continue to influence their perceptions and behaviors in school and in the society of their host country. There is at least a symbolic feeling among the immigrants that they could return to their 'homeland' or emigrate elsewhere if they had a reason to leave their host country. Refugees and migrant workers (i.e. 'guest workers') are not immigrant minorities in the true sense and their problems of adjustment in school and society are not necessarily the same.

*Subordinate* or *castelike minorities,* the third type, are people who initially were brought into American society (or any other society) *involuntarily* through slavery (as in the case of black Americans) or conquest (as in the case of American Indians and Mexican Americans of the Southwestern United

States), relegated to a menial position in society and denied true assimilation into the mainstream society. These minorities do not usually interpret their presence in the United States as a longed-for opportunity to improve their status. Rather, they resent their enforced incorporation and their lost 'golden age' and feel that the latter will not be matched in the future without continuing 'collective struggle.' These perceptions and interpretations influence their perceptions of and responses to schooling.

Both immigrant minorities and subordinate (i.e. the non immigrant) minorities differ culturally from the dominant group but the cultural differences are not the same and do not create the same educational problems. The immigrants are characterized by *primary cultural differences* while the subordinate minorities are characterized by *secondary cultural differences*. Primary cultural differences are differences the immigrants brought with them to America. For example, Punjabi Indian immigrants in Yuba City, California, came from a culture where they spoke Punjabi, practiced Sikh, Hindu, or Moslem religion, had arranged marriages, and wore turbans *before* they came to America. To some extent the Punjabis still do these things in America and this has at times caused some conflict for them in school and in the community. The immigrant Punjabis try to keep some aspects of their native culture, but they also try to learn features of American culture and language both in the community and at school which they perceive that they need in order to achieve the goals of their emigrating to America (Gibson, 1983).

Secondary cultural differences are differences which a minority group like black Americans or American Indians developed *after* the group became subordinated in order to help members of the group cope with social, economic, political and psychological problems arising from their domination and treatment at the hands of the dominant group and its institutions. Sometimes the coping mechanisms take the form of overt or covert opposition to the dominant-group members' ways of feeling, thinking, speaking, or behaving. Indeed, the coping responses may produce a cultural frame of reference that is in opposition to the cultural frame of reference of the dominant group.

The relationship between the immigrants and the dominant group also differs in one other important respect from the relationship between subordinate minorities and the dominant group, namely, in social or collective identity domain. The immigrants usually bring with them *a sense of different social identity* which they had before coming to America. They appear to keep this sense of different identity at least during the first generation. They know who they are. Subordinate minorities, on the other hand, develop *a new sense of social* or *collective identity* which is not merely different from but *in opposition* to the perceived social identity of the dominant group and they develop this oppositional identity *after* they have become subordinated by the dominant group. Partly in reaction to the ways white Americans treat them (e.g. economic and political discrimination, exclusion from true assimilation into the mainstream society, etc.), subordinate minorities like blacks and Indians develop a new sense of peoplehood based on collective awareness that they are not white, cannot be white, and cannot be allowed to 'join the white race' or even be admitted into the social ranks of white people.

These three elements—type of minority status, type of cultural/language differences, and type of social identity—have important implications for the types of cognitive, linguistic, and socio-behavioral skills that minority children develop and bring to school; they also have implications for the ability or willingness of the minorities to adopt the competencies associated with the dominant group or the institutions the latter controls, such as the schools. In addition to possessing distinct competencies or skills, immigrant minorities and subordinate minorities often appear to face similar problems in school: poverty, parents with little or no formal education, parents with low-status jobs, lack of proficiency in standard English, lack of white middle-class early experience, and job discrimination and other barriers in adult opportunity. But the immigrants are the ones who are more able to overcome these barriers in society and school and to overcome the barriers raised by cultural and language differences and thereby achieve academic success. The immigrants are usually able to overcome these barriers for two reasons. One is that the immigrants more or less expect the cultural/language differences as well as differences in the skills required at school and they interpret these differences as barriers to overcome through some conscious effort on their part in order to achieve the goals of their emigration to America. The other reason is that due to their primary cultural/language differences the immigrants do not interpret their acceptance of school rules of behavior (i.e. school expectations) and standard practices or adopting requirements of school participant structure, as a threat to their own culture, language and identity, or as incompatible with their community's participant structure. Rather, the immigrants perceive the school rules and standard practices instrumentally, as important for their quest to get good educational credentials for future employment and progress in America. Therefore in school the immigrants practice what Gibson (1983) has termed 'accommodation without assimilation'; that is, they try to learn the standard English, adopt other standard practices of the school that enhance academic success, and obey school rules without thinking that they are giving up their own culture, ethnic competencies or identity.

In contrast, subordinate minorities characterized by oppositional cultural frames of reference and oppositional identity cannot easily practice accommodation without assimilation. They tend, instead, to perceive school learning, the acceptance of school rules of behavior, and the adoption of standard English and other standard practices of the school as a threat to their culture, language and identity. Because these minorities may define speaking standard English and adopting other practices that enhance academic success as 'white', to speak standard English and to adopt the academic enhancing behaviors is often construed as 'acting white' and is censored by peers and by self. Indeed, DeVos (1984) has suggested that in a situation involving oppositional process subordinate minority individuals may automatically or unconsciously perceive learning things identified with those considered 'oppressors' as harmful to identity. Learning in such a situation tends to arouse a sense of impending conflict over one's future identity. Of course, not everyone among the subordinate minorities feels this way (Fordham and Ogbu, in press).

In summary, the relativists are probably correct in that minority children develop different skills and that they experience school learning problems because of cultural discontinuities and conflicts. However, they do not address the question of why these discontinuities and conflicts persist among some minorities, thereby resulting in persistent and disproportionate school failure. A comparative study of the minorities themselves would suggest the need to examine the role of oppositional process in cultural frames of reference and identities. The oppositional process may not only affect early experience but also may affect the potential for change when the minorities encounter new situations requiring and enhancing new competencies.

## CONCLUSION

Culture plays a crucial role in human development and education but its role is complex and not yet well understood. In human development studies there is a need to distinguish cultural outcomes from psychobiological or maturational outcomes. The universalists who apparently do not make this kind of distinction imply that white middle-class developmental outcomes are to be expected of other people. The relativists challenge this and their studies show that different developmental outcomes in different cultures may be due to differences in cultural requirements. However, neither the universalists nor the relativists deal sufficiently with the issue of variability when it comes to the school performance of minority-group children. A comparative analysis of minority school experiences suggests that the differences among the minorities in school experience and in academic performance in particular are not merely due to cultural differences or differences in developmental outcomes. The relationship between culture, development and school performance seems to be more complex among the minorities, in that it involves historical, structural and psychological or expressive factors not ordinarily considered by those with a universalist or relativist view of development; nor by early childhood interventionists and school personnel.

## REFERENCES

Abrahams, R.D. (1972). Joking: the training of the man of words in talking broad. In T. Kochman (ed.), *Rappin' and stylin' out: communication in urban black America* (pp. 215–240). Urbana: University of Illinois Press.

Au, K.H. (1981). Participant structures in a reading lesson with Hawaiian children: analysis of a culturally appropriate instructional event. *Anthropology and Education Quarterly*, **11**, 91–115.

Au, K.H., and Jordan, C. (1981). Teaching reading to Hawaiian children: finding a culturally appropriate solution. In H. Trueba, G.P. Guthrie, and K.H. Au (eds), *Culture and the bilingual classroom: studies in classroom ethnography*. Rowley, MA.: Newbury House.

Baratz, J. (1970). Teaching reading in an urban negro school system. In F. Williams (ed.), *Language and poverty: perspective on a theme* (pp. 11–24). Chicago: Markham Press.

Baumrind, D. (1976). Subcultural variations in values defining social competence: an outsider's perspective on the black subculture. Unpublished MS Institute of Human Development, University of California, Berkeley.

Bereiter, C. (1965). *Language programs for the disadvantaged*. Champaign Ill.: National Council of Teachers of English.

Bereiter, C., and Engelman, S. (1966). *Teaching disadvantaged children in the pre-school*. Eaglewood-Cliffs, N.J.: Prentice-Hall.

Bloom, B.S., Davis, A., and Hess, R.D. (eds), (1965). *Compensatory education for cultural deprivation*. New York: Holt.

Boykin, A.W. (1978). Psychological/behavioral verve in academic/task performance: a theoretical consideration. *Journal of Negro Education*, **47**, 343–354.

Ciborowski, T.J. (1979). Cross-cultural aspects of cognitive functioning: culture and knowledge. In A.J. Marsella, R.G. Tharp, and T.J. Ciborowski (eds), *Perspectives on cross-cultural psychology* (pp. 101–116). New York: Academic Press.

Cohen, Y.A. (1971). The shaping of men's minds: adaptations to the imperatives of culture. In M.L. Wax, S. Diamond, and F.O. Gearing (eds). *Anthropological perspectives on education* (pp. 19–50). New York: Basic Books.

Cole, M., Gay, J., Glick, J.A., and Sharp, D.W. (1971). *The cultural context of learning and thinking: an exploration in experimental anthropology*. New York: Basic Books.

Cole, M., and Scribner, S. (1974). *Culture and thought: a psychological introduction*. New York: Wiley.

Committee of Correspondence on the Future of Public Education (1984). *Education for a democratic future: a manifesto*. New York.

Connolly, K.J., and Bruner, J.S. (1974). Introduction. In K.J. Connolly and J.S. Bruner (eds). *The growth of competence* (pp. 3–7). London: Academic Press.

Dasen, P. (ed.) (1977). *Piagetian psychology: cross-cultural contributions*. New York: Gardner Press.

Deutsch, M. (1963). The disadvantaged child and the learning process: some social and developmental considerations. In A.H. Passow (ed.), *Education in depressed area* (pp. 163–179). New York: Teachers College Press.

Deutsch, M., and Associates (1967). *The Disadvantaged Child*. New York: Basic Books.

DeVos, G.A. (1984). *Ethnic persistence and role degradation: an illustration from Japan*. Prepared for the American-Soviet Symposium on Contemporary Ethnic Processes in the USA and the USSR. New Orleans, 14–16 April. Unpublished Ms.

Dillard, J.L. (1972). *Black English: its history and usage in the United States*. New York: Random House.

Feagans, L. (1981). The development and importance of intraconversational narrative in school-age children: implications for research and programs. In L. Feagans and D.C. Farran (eds), *The language of children reared in poverty*. New York: Academic Press.

Fordham, S. (1984). Afro-Caribbean and native black American school performance in Washington, D.C.: learning to be or not to be a native. Unpublished Ms, Department of Educational and Psychological Foundations, University of the District of Columbia, Washington, D.C.

Fordham, S., and Ogbu, J.U. (in press). Black students' school success: coping with the 'burden of "acting white'. *Urban Review.*

Foster, H.L. (1974). *Ribbin', jivin', and playin' the dozens: the unrecognized dilemma of inner city schools.* Cambridge, MA.: Ballinger.

Gibson, M.A. (1976a). Approaches to multicultural education in the United States: some concepts and assumptions. *Anthropology And Education Quarterly,* **7,** 7–18.

Gibson, M.A. (1976b). Ethnicity and schooling: a Caribbean case study. Unpublished Ph.D. dissertation, University of Pittsburgh (ERIC Document ED 46 294).

Gibson, M.A. (1983). Home-school-community linkages: a study of educational opportunity for Punjabi youth. Final -Report, The National Institute of Education, Washington, D.C.

Ginsburg, H., and Opper, S. (1981). *Piaget's theory of intellectual development: an introduction.* Englewood Cliffs, N.J.: Prentice-Hall.

Greenfield, P.M. (1966). On culture and conservation. In J.S. Bruner, R.R. Oliver, and P.M. Greenfield (eds), *Studies in cognitive growth* (pp. 225–256). New York: Wiley.

Gumperz, J.J. (1981). Conversational inferences and classroom learning. In J. Green and C. Wallatt (eds), *Ethnographic approaches to face-to-face interaction* (pp. 3–33). Norwood, N.J.: Ablex P.

Gumperz, J.J., and Herasimchuk, E. (1972). Conversational analysis of social meaning. In R. Shuy (ed.), *Sociolinguistics: current trends and prospects* (p. 99–134). Washington, D.C.: Georgetown University Press.

Hannerz, U. (1969). *Soulside.* New York: Columbia University Press.

Hunt J. McV. (1969). *The challenge of incompetence and poverty: papers on the role of early education.* Urbana: University of Illinois Press.

Hymes, D. (1971). On linguistic theory, communicative competence, and the education of disadvantaged children. In M.L. Wax, F.O. Gearing, and S. Diamond (eds), *Anthropological perspectives on education* (pp. 51–66). New York: Basic Books.

Jensen, A.R. (1968). Social class and verbal learning. In M. Deutsch, I. Katz, and A.R. Jensen (eds), *Social class, race, and psychological development.* New York: Holt.

Kaye, K. (1982). *The mental and social life of babies: how parents create persons.* Chicago: The University of Chicago Press.

Keil, C. (1977). The expressive black male role: the bluesman. In D.Y. Wilkinson and R.L. Taylor (eds), The black male in America today: perspectives on his status in contemporary society (pp. 60–84). Chicago: Nelson-Hall.

Kochman, T. (1972). *Rappin' and stylin' out: communication in urban black America.* Chicago: University of Illinois Press.

Kochman, T. (1982). *Black and white styles in conflict.* Chicago: University of Chicago press.

Kohn, M.L. (1969). Social class and parent-child relationships: an interpretation. In R.L. Coser (ed.), *Life cycle and achievement in America* (pp. 21–48). New York: Harper and Row.

Labov, W. (1972). *Language in the inner city: studies in the black English vernacular.* Philadelphia: University of Pennsylvania Press.

Lancy, D.F. (1983). *Cross-cultural studies in cognition and mathematics.* New York: Academic Press.

Lave, J. (1976). Cognitive consequences of traditional apprenticeship in West Africa. Unpublished MS, University of California at Irvine.

Leacock, E.B. (1969). *Teaching and learning in city schools.* New York: Basic Books.

Lerner, R.M. (1984). *On the nature of human plasticity.* Cambridge: Cambridge University Press.

Levine, L. (1977). *Black culture and black consciousness.* New York: Oxford University Press.

LeVine, R.A. (1974). Child rearing as cultural adaptation. In P.H. Leiderman, S.R. Tulkin, and Rosenfeld, A. (eds), *Culture and infancy: variations in the human experience* (pp. 15–28). New York: Academic Press.

Lewis, D.K. (1976). The black family: socialization and sex roles. *Phylon,* **36,** 221–237.

Miller, H.L. (ed.) (1967). *Education for the disadvantaged.* New York: The Free Press.

Mitchell-Kernan, C. (1972). Signifying, loud-talking, and marking. In T. Kochman (ed.), *Rappin' and stylin' out: communication in urban black America* (pp. 315–335). Chicago: University of Illinois Press.

Ogbu, J.U. (1978). *Minority Education and Caste: The American System in Cross-Cultural Perspective.* New York: Academic Press.

Ogbu, J.U. (1981a). Origins of human competence: a cultural-ecological perspective. *Child Development,* **52,** 413–429.

Ogbu, J.U. (1981b). School ethnography: a multi-level approach. *Anthropology And Education Quarterly* 12(1), 1–20.

Ogbu, J.U. (1984). Understanding community forces affecting minority students' academic effort. The Achievement Council, Oakland, CA. Unpublished MS.

Ogbu, J.U. (1985). A cultural ecology of competence among inner-city blacks. In M.B. Spencer, G.K. Brookins, and W.R. Allen (eds), *Beginnings: social and affective development of black children* (pp. 45–73). Hillsdale, N.J.: Lawrence Erlbaum.

Ogbu, J.U. (1986). Cross-cultural study of minority education: contributions from stockton research. 23rd Annual J. William Harris Lecture, School of Education, University of the Pacific, Stockton, California.

Ogbu, J.U. (in press, a). Cultural influences on plasticity in human development. In J.J. Gallagher (ed.), *The malleability of children.* Baltimore, MD: Paul H. Brookes.

Ogbu, J.U. (in press, b). Variability in minority school responses: non-immigrants vs. immigrants. In G.D. Spindler (ed.), *Education and cultural process.* Hillsdale, N.J.: Lawrence Erlbaum.

Ogbu, J.U., and Matute-Bianchi, M.E. (1986). Understanding sociocultural factors in education: knowledge, identity, and adjustment. In California Dept of Education, Sacramento, CA. Beyond language: social and cultural factors in schooling of language minorities.

Perkins, E. (1975). Home is a dirty street. Chicago: Third World Press.

Philips, S.U. (1972). Participant structure and communicative competence: Warm Springs children in community and classrooms. In C.B. Cazden, V.P. John, and D. Hymes (eds), *Functions of language in the classroom* (pp. 370–394). New York: Teachers College Press.

Philips, S.U. (1976). Commentary: access to power and maintenance of ethnic identity as goals of multi-cultural education. In M.A. Gibson (ed.), Anthropological perspectives on multicultural education. *Anthropology And Education Quarterly,* **7,**(4), 30–32.

Philips, S.U. (1983). *The invisible culture: communication in classroom and community on the Warm Springs Indian Reservation.* New York: Longmans.

Posner, J. (1982). The development of mathematical knowledge in two West African societies. *Child Development,* **53,** 200–208.

Powledge, F. (1967). *To change a child: a Report on the institute for Developmental Studies.* Chicago: Quadrangle Books.

Price-Williams, D.R. (1961). A study concerning concepts of conservation of quantities among primitive children. *Acta Psychologica,* **18,** 293–305.

Price-Williams, D.R. (1962). Abstract and concrete modes of classification in a primitive society. *British Journal of Educational Psychology,* **32,** 50–61.

Price-Williams, D.R., Gordon, W., and Ramirez, M. (1969). Skill and conservation: a study of potter-making children. *Developmental Psychology*, **1**, 769.

Rainwater, L. (1974). *Behind ghetto walls: black families in federal slum.* Chicago: Aldine.

Ramey, C.T., and Gallagher, J.J. (1975). The nature of cultural deprivation: theoretical issues and suggested research strategies. *North Carolina Journal of Mental Health*, **VII**, 41–47.

Ramey, C.T., MacPhee, D., and Yeates, K.O. (1982). Preventing developmental retardation: a general system model. In L.A. Bond and J.M. Joffe (eds), *Facilitating infant and early childhood development*, (pp. 343–401). Hanover and London: University Press of New England.

Ramey, C.T., and Suarez, T.M. (1985). Early intervention and the early experience paradigm: toward a better framework for social policy. *Journal of Children in Contemporary Society*, **7**(1), 3–13.

Ramirez, M., and Castenada, A. (1974). *Cultural democracy, bicognitive development and education.* New York: Academic Press.

Ruddle, K., and Chesterfield, R. (1977). *Education for traditional food procurement in the Orinoco Delta.* Berkeley: University of California Press.

Saxe, G.B., and Posner, J. (1983). The development of numerical cognition: cross-cultural perspectives. In H.P. Ginsburg (ed.), *The development of mathematical thinking* (pp. 291–317). New York: Academic Press.

Scribner, S. (1975). Recall of classical syllogisms: a cross-cultural investigation of error on logical problems. In R.J. Falmagne (ed.), *Reasoning: representation and process.* Hillsdale, N.J.: Lawrence Erlbaum.

Scribner, S. (1976). Modes of thinking and ways of speaking: culture and logic reconsidered. Unpublished MS, Rockefeller University.

Scribner, S., and Cole, M. (1973). Cognitive consequences of formal and informal education. *Science*, **182**, 553–559.

Seagrim, G.N., and Lendon, R.J. (1980). *Furnishing the mind: a comparative study of cognitive development in Central Australian aborigines.* New York: Academic Press.

Seeley, J.R., Sim, H.A., and Loosley, E.W. (1956). *Crestwood Heights: a study of the culture of suburban life.* New York: Basic Books.

Shade, B.J. (1982). Afro-American pattern of cognition. Madison: Wisconsin Center for Educational Research, University of Wisinconsin at Madison. Unpublished MS

Sharp, D., Cole, M., and Lave, C. (1979). Education and cognitive development: the evidence from experimental research. *Monographs Of The Society For Research In Child Development*, Ser. #178, vol. 44, #1–2.

Shure, M.B., Spivack, G., and Jaeger, M.A. (1971). Problem-solving thinking and adjustment among disadvantaged preschool children. *Child Development*, **42**, 1791–1803.

Shure, M.B. *et al.* (1972). Problem-solving thinking: a preventive mental health program for preschool children. *Reading World*, **11**, 259–273.

Shure, M.B., and Spivack, G. (1972). Means-ends thinking, adjustment and social class among elementary school-age children. *Journal of Consulting and Clinical Psychology*, **38**, 348–353.

Shure, M.B., and Spivack, G. (1979). Interpersonal cognitive problem solving and primary prevention: programming for preschool and kindergarten children. *Journal of Clinical Child Psychology*, **2**, 89–94.

Shure, M.B., and Spivack, G. (1980). Interpersonal problem solving as a mediator of behavioral adjustment in preschool and kindergarten children. *Journal of Applied Developmental Psychology*, **1**, 29–44.

Simons, H. (1979). Black dialect, reading interference, and classroom interaction. In L.B. Resnick and P.A. Weaver (eds), *Theory and practice of early reading,* Vol. 3 (pp. 111–129). Hillsdale, N.J.: Lawrence Erlbaum.

Stack, C.B. (1974). *All our kin: strategies for survival in a black community.* New York: Harper.

Stanley, J.C. (ed.) (1973). *Compensatory education for children, ages 2 to 8: recent studies of educational intervention.* Baltimore, MD.: Johns Hopkins University Press.

Stevenson, H. (1982). Influences of schooling on cognitive development. In D.A. Wagner and H.W. Stevenson (eds), *Cultural perspectives on child development,* (pp. 208–224). San Francisco: W.H. Freeman and Company.

Stewart, W.A. (1970). Toward a history of American negro dialect. In F. Williams (ed.), *Language and poverty: perspectives on a theme* (pp. 351–379). Chicago: Markham.

Suarez-Orozco, M. M. (1986). In pursuit of a dream: new hispanic immigrants in American schools. Unpublished Ph.D. dissertation, Department of Anthropology, University of California, Berkeley.

Valentine, B. (1979). *Hustling and other hard work: lifestyles in the ghetto.* New York: Free Press.

Vernon, P.E. (1969). *Intelligence and cultural environment.* London: Methuen.

Vernon, P.E. (1982). *The abilities and achievements of Orientals in North America.* New York: Academic Press.

White, B.L., Kaban, B.T., and Attanucci, J. (1979). *Origins of human competence: the final report of the Harvard Preschool Project.* Lexington, MA.: D.C. Heath.

White, B.L. *et al.* (1979). *Origins of human competence: the final report of the Harvard Preschool Project.* Lexington, MA.: D.C. Heath.

White, S.H. *et al.* (1973). *Federal programs for young children. Review and recommendations: Vol. 1: Goals and standards of public programs for children.* Washington, D.C.: US Government Printing Office.

Whiteman, M., and Deutsch, M. (1968). Social disadvantage as related to intellectual and language development. In M. Deutsch, I. Katz, and A.R. Jensen (eds), *Social class, race and psychological development.* New York: Holt.

Williams, F. (ed.) (1970). *Language and poverty: perspectives on a theme.* Chicago: Markham.

Williams, M.D. (1981). *On the street where I lived.* New York: Holt.

Wright, N., Jr (ed.) (1970). *What black educators are saying.* New York: Hawthorn Books.

Young, V.H. (1970). Family and childhood in a Southern negro community. *American Anthropologist,* **72,** 269–288.

Young, V.H. (1974). A black American socialization pattern. *American Ethnologist,* **1**(2), 415–431.

# Author Index

# Subject Index